DATE DUE

STUDIES IN SOCIAL CHANGE

Other books by Amitai Etzioni

Political Unification: A Comparative Study of Leaders and Forces (1965); The Moon-Doggle: Domestic and International Implications of the Space-Race (1964); Modern Organizations (1964); Winning without War (1964); The Hard Way to Peace: A New Strategy (1962); A Comparative Analysis of Complex Organizations (1961).

STUDIES IN SOCIAL CHANGE

———— ◆◆◆ ————

AMITAI ETZIONI
Columbia University

HOLT, RINEHART AND WINSTON, INC.
New York, Chicago, San Francisco, Toronto, London

ACKNOWLEDGMENTS

The author wishes to thank the following publications for permission to reprint his articles in this volume. Listed with the name of the publication is the original title of the article and the chapter number under which it appears in this volume.

Chapter 1   *American Journal of Sociology*, Vol. 64, No. 5 (March 1959). Published under the title, "The Functional Differentiation of Elites in the Kibbutz." (Copyright 1959 by the University of Chicago.)

Chapter 2   *The American Journal of Sociology*, Vol. 68, No. 5 (January 1963). Published under the title, "The Epigenesis of Political Communities at the International Level." (Copyright 1963 by the University of Chicago.)

Chapter 3   *World Politics*, Vol. 16, No. 1 (October 1963). Published under the title, "European Unification: A Strategy of Change."

Chapter 4   First published here.

Chapter 5   *The Journal of Conflict Resolution*, Vol. 8, No. 3 (September 1964). Published under the title, "On Self-Encapsulating Conflicts."

Chapter 6   *The American Political Science Review*, Vol. 56, No. 4 (December 1962). Published under the title, "The Dialectics of Supranational Unification."

Chapter 7   *Political Science Quarterly*, Vol. 74, No. 2 (June 1959), pp. 196–214. Published under the title, "Alternative Ways to Democracy: The Example of Israel."

Chapter 8   Ferrel Heady and Sybil L. Stokes, (eds.), *Papers in Comparative Public Administration*. Published under the title, "The Decline of Neo-Feudalism: The Case of Israel." (Copyright 1962 by the University of Michigan Press, Ann Arbor, Michigan.)

Chapter 9   *Judaism*, Vol. 11, No. 2 (Spring 1962). Published under the title, "The National Religious Institutions of American Jewry."

PREFACE

Theories of social change have received much increased attention in recent years. Even more than general theories of behavior, however, modern theories of change are, by and large, gradually assembled and pieced together from many theoretical contributions and numerous research papers. One approach is to move "downward," to attempt to derive the basis for a theory of change from general theoretical considerations. Talcott Parsons, who has been criticized for providing sociology with a theory that stressed equilibrium over process and left little room for change of the system, has made a major contribution to a functional analysis of change. The concept of differentiation is central to his formulation.* The first part of the present discussion builds on this functional approach to the study of change.

We augment the functional approach in two ways: by extension and by opposition. Extension involves the introduction of an analysis of control structures on top of the more common sociological models of action. To use a medical metaphor, sociological anatomy studies the relations between various segments of the social structure, such as classes, communities, ethnic groups, or ranks in an organization. Sociological neurology explores communication channels and their pathologies. But there are relatively few studies which focus on the "physiology" of units that control social processes. Few studies explore the relations of elites to the social units they lead, and the role elites play in changing the relationships among such units. We focus on the growth and differentiation of elites as related to differentiation on

* Talcott Parsons, "Some Considerations on the Theory of Social Change," *Rural Sociology*, vol. 26 (1961), pp. 219–239. Reprinted in Eve and Amitai Etzioni (eds.), *Social Change: Sources, Patterns, and Consequences* (New York: Basic Books, Inc., 1964).

the "anatomical" level, that of status-structures. We explore the proposition that as a system evolves a new "arm," its control center, or "brain," also develops a new subdivision, specializing in guidance of that "arm."

The second way we augment earlier work on differentiation is by setting up, in opposition, an alternative model for the study of the evolution of new social systems. Differentiation seems not to exhaust the ways in which fully differentiated systems emerge. Differentiation assumes a primitive unit in which all the basic functions are already fulfilled even though there are not as yet specifically designated structures devoted primarily to their respective services. In the process of differentiation, these structures emerge. We found, however, some systems of considerable importance that initially fulfill *autonomously* only *one* of the basic functions. These systems grow gradually in scope, adding new structures, and serve functions they did not serve before, broadening their control structure. The model for the study of this process is referred to as *epigenesis*. It is of particular relevance to the study of the evolution of new communities—whether nations out of tribes, regional communities out of nations, or metropolitan communities out of cities, suburbs, and townships.

Structural-functional analysis is the conceptual approach which underlies our theoretical discussion. It has often been stated that functional approach is unable to deal with change. While this is not the case, we found it useful to introduce the concept of a *future-system*. Once the functional prerequisites of a future-system are spelled out, one might ask under what conditions, as the result of which processes, advanced to what degree, will these prerequisites be met. When these questions are answered, the conditions under which a system will change to a different one are known. This seems to us to provide a framework for a functional analysis of change.

One major line of development of sociological theory is, as Merton put it, from the "middle range." This has been interpreted as implying that, first, theories will be developed for specific areas such as for stratification, or religious or educational institutions, and when enough theoretical and empirical knowledge has been amassed, these middle-range theories will be interwoven and "roofed" to form a general theory. A second avenue along which the growth of general theory might proceed, the present work suggests, is for the "middle range" level to include not only sub-fields, but also universal components of which none will constitute a general theory in itself, but when combined with each other and with subtheories oriented toward a subfield, might lead toward general sociological theory.*

Our study of elites and control structures (in Chapters 1 and 2) is one such study of a universal though limited component. A closely related one is that of strategies of change, to which the second part of this volume is devoted. Change almost invariably involves an element of conscious, deliberate effort by one or more elites, though these might not be of the "establishment" but rather "revolutionary." The scope of deliberate change as against change that is unplanned grows with modernization and is greater in the more politicized societies. Whatever the scope of guided change, the strategy followed by the elites that do the guiding significantly affects its extent and depth and therefore ought to be an integral part of the study of change. Chapter 3 explores one strategy that was particularly successful and the conditions that accounted for its success. Chapter 4 explores a different, though not unrelated, strategy which relied considerably more on symbols than on manipulation of power; it proved to be less successful, for reasons explored below.

The third part of this volume follows a different tract toward the construction of a theory of social change; models developed in other areas of study are applied to the analysis of change, in particular to the evolution of communities. The relationship is plain: unlimited conflict becomes contained when the parties to a conflict become involved in one and the same community. Less clearly known are the conditions under which such community ties grow out of unlimited conflict. Some tentative propositions dealing with this problem are the subject of Chapter 5. Chapter 6 pushes this analysis a few steps further; it applies theorems derived from the study of the ways consensus is reached in an existing community to a study of the conditions under which a new

---

* Cf. Robert K. Merton, "Introduction" to Allen H. Barton, *Social Organization under Stress: A Sociological Review of Disaster Studies,* Disaster Study No. 17, National Academy of Sciences—National Research Council, Publication 1032.

structure for the formation of such consensus might evolve. In that sense, a future-system is here explored.

The last part of this volume contains three case studies of change which attempt to induce "upward" some general insights from data, rather than using data to illustrate and explore some general conceptions, the procedure followed in earlier chapters. Three kinds of change are illustrated. The first kind are changes in the system, that is, changes which are themselves institutionalized. The system needs some of these changes in order to remain stable, the way a bicycle rider must continue to pedal to maintain his stability. The changes explored here are of the party in office in close relationship to changes in policy preferences of the population; that is, change of government in a democracy. (In this way this study also turns to the problems of consensus formation, explored in the preceding chapter.)

While changes in the system take place, the system itself changes too. We shall point out the hazards that exist in studying changes in the system without studying changes of the system, for the investigator is likely to perceive more stability than is actually present. While it is possible to study one kind of change at a time, the effect of changes *of* the system, it seems, are at least to be charted as background to the study of changes *in* the system. (The opposite might be less essential.)

Both kinds of changes, but in particular those of a system, are affected by and significantly affect the nature of societal values. The last chapter of this volume is devoted to a study of changes of a set of institutions as they are affected by and effect changes in values. As the systems under review are relatively small, a comparative approach is possible; three systems are compared from the same perspective—the dynamic relations between changing values and changing structure.

Data are used illustratively to varying degrees in each of the chapters of this volume. For some chapters, these data are incidental, qualitative, and exploratory. In others, they are somewhat more extensive, occasionally quantitative, and, to a degree, they support the propositions advanced. The data are, however, largely secondary to the theoretical points suggested. The same points could have been illustrated by different data; those included here represent the substantive fields in which the author has worked more than any particular research strategy, so far as theory of change is concerned.

The work presented in this collection of essays benefited from discussion with students of Columbia University who have taken my classes in social change, both graduate and undergraduate, over a period of six years. Their stimulating questions and alert criticisms are much appreciated. In particular, I am indebted to the research assistance of Sarajane Heidt. In doing the work on which these studies are based, I benefited from the support of the Institute of War and Peace Studies and the Council for Research in the Social Sciences, both at Columbia University. The editing of the manuscript was completed during my fellowship at the Center for Advanced Study in the Behavioral Sciences. Miriam Gallaher composed the index.

While all the chapters but one were published previously as articles, all the articles have been somewhat revised for the purposes of this volume. Revision includes omissions to avoid minor repetitions, some updating of references and data, and a few elaborations of the argument. Also, the titles have been modified to enhance the integration of the volume. A brief general introduction and short section introductions have been provided to indicate some themes that run through the various materials.

A. E.

Los Altos, California
June 1966

CONTENTS

STUDIES IN SOCIAL CHANGE

Part One

DIFFERENTIATION VERSUS EPIGENESIS

Most studies of social change presuppose the existence of a unit, and ask: How does it change, why, and in what direction? The analytical framework frequently used for this analysis of social dynamics is the differentiation model,[1] which assumes that the "primitive" social unit contains, in embryonic form, fused together, all the basic modes of social relations that later become structurally differentiated. While relations originally fused gain their own subunits, no new functions are served. According to this viewpoint, every social unit, if it is to exist, must fulfill a given set of functions, those of adaptation, allocation, social and normative integration. On the individual level, the evolution from infancy to maturity can be analyzed in terms of the differentiation of the personality.[2] On the societal level, the evolution of a primitive society, from a traditional into a modern one, is also seen as a differentiation process. All societal functions are fulfilled by the primitive tribe; they merely become structurally differentiated; that is, they gain personnel, social units, and organizational structures of their own. Religious institutions gain churches, educational institutions gain schools, economic institutions gain corporations, and so forth.

[1] This model is applied to the study of small groups by Robert F. Bales and Philip E. Slater, "Role Differentiation in Small Decision-making Groups," in Talcott Parsons, Robert F. Bales, and Edward A. Shils, *Working Papers in the Theory of Action* (New York: The Free Press of Glencoe, 1953); to socialization process by Parsons, Bales, *et al., Family, Socialization and Interaction Process* (New York: The Free Press of Glencoe, 1955), chap. 4; to industrialization by Neil Smelser, *Social Change in the Industrial Revolution* (Chicago: University of Chicago Press, 1959); to the study of the family by Morris Zelditch, Jr., "Role Differentiation in the Nuclear Family: A Comparative Study," in *Family, Socialization* . . . , pp. 307–351, and by Smelser, *Social Change*, chaps. 8 to 10; to the study of elites by the author in Chapter 1; and to the study of underdeveloped countries by Neil Smelser, "Toward a Theory of Modernization," in Amitai and Eva Etzioni (eds.), *Social Change: Sources, Patterns and Consequences* (New York: Basic Books, Inc., 1964).

[2] Parsons, Bales, *et al., Family, Socialization* . . . , chap. 4.

Philosophers and biologists have long pointed out that there is an alternative model for the study of change. While Bonnet, Haller, and Malpighi represented the differentiation (or preformism) approach, according to which the first unit or seed possesses in miniature all the patterns of the mature plant, Harvey, Wolff, and Goethe advanced the epigenesis (or accumulation) approach, according to which "adult" units emerge through a process in which parts that carry out *new* functions are added to existing ones, until the entire unit is assembled. Earlier parts do not include the "representation" of later ones.

The two processes, differentiation and epigenesis, are mutually exclusive in the sense that new units are either institutional "embodiments" of old functions or serve new ones. They may occur at different times in the same social unit: for example, a unit may first follow a differentiation model, then shift to an epigenetic model (or the other way around); or it may simultaneously develop some subunits following one model and some following the other. But unlike the particle and wave theories, which are used to explain the same light phenomena, the change pattern of all sociological units of which we are aware follows at any given period either a differentiation *or* an epigenesis model.

Until now sociology has focused almost exclusively on differentiation models. There are, however, several social units whose development cannot be adequately accounted for by such a model.

Apart from this general consideration, the two studies that follow—one dealing with the internal structure of the kibbutz and the other with relations among states—share three major theoretical themes: the dynamic relations between action and power; the respective roles of parent-systems and dependent ones; and the relevance of the concept of future-systems for functional analysis of social change.

The principle of inertia, in terms of Parsons' theory of action, states: "A given process of action will continue unchanged in rate and direction unless impeded or deflected by opposing motivational forces."[3] The student of social change might apply this

[3] Parsons, Bales, and Shils, *Working Papers in the Theory of Action*, p. 102.

3

proposition in a structural context. Thus translated, it maintains that a given process will continue unchanged in rate and direction unless affected by the exercise of power by one or more units. The change might be brought about by either opposing or supporting units (the former impeding or deflecting the process which Parsons speaks of, the latter contributing to its acceleration). The changes are also likely to vary according to whether they are largely motivational in nature or are rather the result of a new conversion of assets (funds, for example) into power. (By assets we mean possessions that a unit or system has, regardless of those that other units may have. They might be economic, military, cultural, and so forth. By power we mean the actor's ability to induce another actor to carry out his directive or any other norms he supports.)[4]

Often, we suggest, a change in the course of action of a social unit will be primarily determined by the amount of assets or power the actors command and will involve motivational elements only marginally. Both the owners of the corner grocery and those of General Motors might decide (that is, be motivated) to raise their prices because of their irritation with a report of a falling income, but the consequences of these actions for Detroit's economy would be very different. A study of social change, therefore, invariably requires delineation of the action-units, the elite-units that initiated and guided the change, and the power employed by these units.

The exercise of power is invariably involved in overcoming resistance in the initiation of change, and the units that exercise this power are defined as elites. This definition would be correct but uninteresting if all units employed the same amount of power. As this is the case only in "limit" situations, however, the term "elite" reminds us to look for the *differentiation of power* among the units participating in any process of change. The use of the concept in this way does not introduce an "elitist" conception, for such a conception would tend to assume that there is one elite, and a relatively closed one. Since competition or conflict among a number of elites is common, and elites might remain both open

---

[4] For a discussion of these concepts and the rules of conversion of assets into power, see Amitai Etzioni, *Political Unification* (New York: Holt, Rinehart and Winston, Inc., 1965), pp. 38ff.

and responsive to the needs and demands of other units, no such assumption is made in the following analysis of the articulation of action and the power dimensions of social units.

A second set of concepts in both studies is that of "parent" and "dependent" collectivities. It should be remembered that this distinction cannot even be formulated unless the above-mentioned distinction is made, for it rests on the statement that collectivities are not always coextensive in their action and their power dimensions. They may carry out more action than they control, or they may control more action than they carry out. Collectivities of the first type are dependent, while the second are parent collectivities.

In the following studies, two patterns of change are examined in the relationship between parent and dependent collectivities. In one, the dependent collectivity gradually becomes more self-controlling, building up its power and consequently reducing that of the parent collectivity. This process occurs in the relationship between parents and adolescent children; in a new military service (like the U.S. Air Force, for example, which was a wing of the Army and later became separated from it); between colonies and metropolitan societies (that is, national independence movements); and regional unification movements initiated by outside elites (for example, Britain and the Federation of the West Indies).[5]

There are several characteristic consequences of transitions of this type: (a) The gain in self-control of the dependent system tends to lead to conflict with the parent system, although the scope, extent, and degree of violence of the conflict differ, depending on the particular situation. (b) The increase in self-control reduces the ability of the dependent system to specialize. Specialization is here used not to refer to a concrete division of labor but rather as a functional term; for example, social or normative (integrative) specialization is curtailed as the actor is required to take charge of his own adaptive and allocative activities. (c) The transition involves a ritualistic phase that serves to reduce the stress generated by the increase in self-control and decline in integrative specialization.

[5] *Ibid.*, pp. 138ff.

Another pattern of change in the relationship between parent and dependent systems is one in which control is "generalized" from the member units rather than transferred from an outsider to one or more member units. *The parent-systems gradually become subsystems of the growing dependent system.* A regional community which is initially controlled by the member-states but is increasingly controlled by a community authority is a case in point. (Further theoretical discussion of this process is found in Chapter 2; additional illustrative material is included in Chapter 3.)

Finally, although outlined only in an exploratory way, the concept of future-system underlies both case studies, for they assume images of fully differentiated systems. One sees a fully differentiated kibbutz, the other sees a regional community as systems that would meet the four classes of functional requirements.

An alternative approach to dynamic functional analysis which has been attempted is to predict the direction of change of a system by studying the functions that are neglected or inadequately fulfilled by the existing system.[6] If, for example, the need for socially integrative mechanisms is ignored, an increase in incidences of violence would be predicted. This approach seems to us to be less fruitful than the concept of a future-system, for it essentially adds nothing to the conventional, "static" functional propositions (for example, a system needs to be socially integrated). It merely projects the dysfunctional consequences of not meeting the need into a point in time which is later than the dysfunctional cause (for example, neglect) but is still within the original system. Such analysis might delineate existing pathologies but is of little use for outlining new systems that might emerge from the transformation of the old one.

It is possible, though, to combine these two modes of analysis. The direction in which the strains in an existing system are likely to push that system, and the future-system that might be built if the expected alterations were to continue in the same direction, as well as the consequences of the introduction of planned change,

[6] This approach is reported by Alex Inkeles, *What Is Sociology?* (Englewood Cliffs, N.J.: Prentice-Hall, Inc., 1964), esp. pp. 37–39.

might be studied simultaneously. Such a combination could be particularly fruitful if a model of the kind Morton Kaplan has outlined for international systems were constructed for societies, and other social units. Kaplan suggests that international systems may take any one of six forms.[7] Hence for each system which has a form, the other five are its potential future-systems. Examination of a particular system's pathology might enable us to forecast the direction it will be likely to change as well as which of the potential future-systems it is most likely to evolve. Disintegration is always one of the potential future-systems but rarely the most probable one.

[7] *System and Process in International Politics* (New York: John Wiley and Sons, Inc., 1957), pp. 9–10. A more recent article on this subject is included in Etzioni, *Social Change*, pp. 476–481.

CHAPTER 1

The Functional Differentiation of Elites

---•◦•---

FUNCTIONAL ANALYSIS OF ELITES

Every social system, perhaps every system of action, is confronted with four basic functional problems. When simple social systems become more complex, four distinct subsystems emerge, each predominantly devoted to one of the major functional needs. Thus many processes of change can be analyzed as processes of functional differentiation. These ideas, formulated by Parsons in 1953,[1] have been fruitfully applied in the analysis of a large number of social as well as nonsocial systems, including the social structures of task-oriented groups,[2] of families,[3] and of economies;[4] the processes of socialization and social control;[5] and the history of culture, especially religion and the structure of the legal system.[6] We attempt here to show that with some minor

---

[1] See Talcott Parsons, "A Revised Analytical Approach to the Theory of Social Stratification," in R. Bendix and S. M. Lipset (eds.), *Class, Status and Power* (New York: The Free Press of Glencoe, 1953), pp. 92–128; and Talcott Parsons, Robert F. Bales, and Edward A. Shils, *Working Papers in the Theory of Action* (New York: The Free Press of Glencoe, 1953).

[2] Parsons, Bales, and Shils, *Working Papers*, pp. 63–268, esp. 111–161.

[3] Talcott Parsons, Robert F. Bales, *et al., Family, Socialization and Interaction Process* (New York: The Free Press of Glencoe, 1955).

[4] Talcott Parsons and Neil J. Smelser, *Economy and Society* (New York: The Free Press of Glencoe, 1956).

[5] Talcott Parsons, Robert F. Bales, *et al., Family, Socialization and Interaction Process* (New York: The Free Press of Glencoe, 1955), pp. 36, 38–39, 40–45, 140–41, 200–216.

[6] Discussions of Professor Parsons in a seminar, University of California, Berkeley, Cal., Spring 1958.

additions this conceptual scheme can be helpful in analyzing the social structure and the differentiation of elites. The discussion is based on a study of elites in communal settlements (kibbutzim) in Israel.[7]

The four universal functional problems are: (a) the need of the system to control the environment; (b) gratification of the system's goal; (c) maintenance of solidarity among the system units; and (d) reinforcement of the integrity of the value system and its institutionalization. In the rest of the discussion these functional problems will be referred to respectively as "adaptive," "goal-attainment," "solidaric," and "normative." Following Parsons' suggestion, the adaptive and goal-attainment functions will be labeled "external," and the solidaric and normative "internal."

Table 1.1

	Instrumental	*Consummatory*
External	A Adaptive	G Goal attainment
Internal	Latent (Normative) L	Solidarity I

The adaptive and normative will be labeled "instrumental" and the goal-attainment and solidaric functions "consummatory"[8] (see Table 1.1).

In every social system, some social situations, roles, or, in more complex structures, collectivities, are devoted mainly to one of the major functions. When the social systems become complex and internally differentiated, we expect to find in each subsystem

[7] For a fuller report, see the author's Ph.D. dissertation, "The Organizational Structure of the Kibbutz" (University of California, Berkeley, 1958). He is indebted to S. M. Lipset and Philip Selznick, and to Talcott Parsons for criticism of an earlier version, and especially to Y. Talmon-Garber. The data were collected at the Israeli Institute of Productivity.

[8] Talcott Parsons, "The Role of General Theory in Sociological Analysis" (paper presented to the American Sociological Society, Washington, D.C., 1957).

some roles or collectivities which specialize in initiating, directing, and/or regulating the activities of each subsystem. We refer to these roles and collectivities as "elites." Thus we expect to find four elites in each complex social system, one for each subsystem.

Our designations can be illustrated as follows: specialists or experts are adaptive elites; politicians or managers (depending on the context) are goal-attainment elites; the social leaders are the elite of integrative activities; and "cultural" (as defined by Parsons) leaders, including philosophers, ideologists, religious leaders, and others, are the elite of the normative subsystem. This nomenclature can be justified by showing that the activities of experts, managers, and social and cultural leaders, using these designations approximately as they are generally understood, are

Table 1.2

A		G
Universalism		Affectivity
Specificity		Performance
Quality		Diffuseness
Neutrality		Particularism
L		I

cognate with the activities of the four functional subsystems discussed above, if both types of activities are analyzed in terms of pattern variables. The pattern variables of the four subsystems have been specified by Parsons as shown in Table 1.2.[9]

We now specify the various elite activities in these terms. The experts are adaptive because their activities are specific and universalistic. They deal with knowledge, science, and technology. They are interested in the objective features of the environment from the point of view of the specific system problem they attempt to solve. The political or managerial elites tend to be affective- and performance-oriented. They direct activities toward the system goals (this is the affective element) and are interested in motion toward these goals rather than in maintaining the quality

[9] Parsons, Bales, and Shils, *Working Papers*, p. 182.

of the system (this is the performance orientation). The social leaders (often "informal leaders") are particularistic and diffuse in their orientation. Their focus of interest is the particular system of which they are leaders, and their influence as well as their involvement are not limited to segmental spheres of their group activity but encompass the whole group sphere of action. The cultural leaders deal with symbols and values which determine the normative quality of the system. Creation of new meanings, integration of new meanings with the old ones, reinterpretation of systems of meaning, creating and maintaining value commitments —all these activities undertaken by cultural leaders have one common requirement: some independence and detachment from the social system and a degree of neutrality toward it.

This typology of elites is an analytical scheme. Concrete elites can be analyzed according to the specific ways in which the analytical elements are combined. Thus industrial elites are often managerial-expert; many politicians are political-integrative (social) oriented, and the secondary orientations of many members of the cultural elites seem to be expert orientations (for example, most academicians). Thus a relatively more sophisticated classification of elites can be achieved only when the analytical scheme is applied at least twice and the predominant as well as the subordinate orientations of elites are determined.

THE PROCESS OF FUNCTIONAL DIFFERENTIATION

In a very simple and uninstitutionalized social system, as, for instance, friendship between two people who have about equal status and similar involvement in the relationship, there may be no elite positions. But in somewhat larger (for example, experimental groups) or more institutionalized systems (the family, for example), specialized roles of initiation and control tend to develop. At first, or at very low levels of complexity, these elite positions will tend to be *multifunctional*; that is, the same roleholders will initiate and control action in all major areas of activities. In friendship between a veteran and recruit, one, say the veteran, may be the "expert" on adapting to the environment (he knows the "ropes"), have a determining influence on the nature of the activities (to go have a beer or watch a movie), and at the same time be the one who maintains the harmony of the relationship (gives in) and reinforces its norms. Thus the veteran has a multifunctional elite position in the friendship system. In some primitive societies the chief and his court, seen as one unit, is such a multifunctional undifferentiated elite.

At somewhat more complex levels, elite roles and elite groups become differentiated. The separation of the religious elite from the political-bureaucratic elite is perhaps the most significant and well-known case to the student of modern societies. Industrial sociologists focus on a vital differentiation of line-staff functions (manager-expert functions) which emerges as industrialization develops. The formal-informal leadership distinction, essential to organizational sociology, is a differentiation between managerial-oriented and solidaric-oriented leaders.

We shall turn now to a detailed account of a case study of the process of functional differentiation of the elite of a community. The functional differentiation of the elite will be related to changes in the structure of a community which becomes more and more complex and more and more institutionalized.

NATURAL HISTORY OF THE KIBBUTZ AND ELITE DIFFERENTIATION

The elites we studied are the elites of the communal settlements in Israel, the kibbutzim.[10] There are about 225 kibbutzim, most of which follow a fundamentally similar life-pattern. The groups which eventually establish kibbutzim are conceived in the

[10] For general discussions of the kibbutz see Melford E. Spiro, *Kibbutz: Venture in Utopia* (New York: Schocken Books, Inc., 1963); M. Weingarten, *Life in a Kibbutz* (New York: Reconstructionist Press, 1955); Henrik F. Infield, *Cooperative Living in Palestine* (New York: Holt, Rinehart and Winston, Inc., 1944); Esther Tauber, *Molding Society to Man* (New York: Bloch Publishing Co., 1955); Ivan Vallier, "Structural Differentiation, Production Imperatives, and Communal Norms: The Kibbutz in Crisis," *Social Forces*, vol. 40, (1962), pp. 233–242; and Ben Halpern, "The Kibbutz Comes of Age," *Jewish Frontier*, vol. 16, (1949).

youth movements, grow up in the training camps, mature into autonomous young kibbutzim, and settle down to the routine life of an older kibbutz. We shall discuss the nature of the social system at each stage and then relate the process of elite differentiation to the changes in the nature of the social system. We shall attempt to find support for the following hypotheses: (a) with increasing complexity of the social system the elite becomes differentiated—that is, various functions are carried out by separate roles and different people; (b) differentiation is not random but follows a certain predictable pattern, multifunctional elites becoming differentiated according to functional lines; (c) once differentiated, a hierarchy of elites tends to develop, in which specialized (monofunctional) elites are at or near the bottom, dual elites are at the middle levels, and collectivity-oriented elites are at the top. We shall also relate analytically the process through which a new social system is created and gradually gains functional autonomy to the differentiation of the elites.

ELITES IN A PARTIAL SYSTEM

Most new kibbutzim grow out of groups of young people who are recruited from outside the kibbutz movement. Usually these groups crystallize in some collectivistic-oriented social movements like the pioneering youth movements in Israel and some Zionist youth movements in the Diaspora.[11] These young people generally live in their parents' homes, study or work during the day, and meet in the evenings and weekends in order to create a social group which later will become a kibbutz.

These youth-movement groups, called *garinim*,[12] are sporadic and partial social systems, dominated by normative and integrative orientations; sporadic, because between periods of activity the whole group becomes latent, and partial because they depend on parents, schools, workplaces, youth movement headquarters, and other external institutions for the fulfillment and regulation

[11] See J. Ben David, "Report of the Research Project on Youth Movement in Israel," *Transactions of the Second World Congress of Sociology* (London: International Sociological Association, 1954), vol. 1; S. N. Eisenstadt, *From Generation to Generation* (New York: The Free Press of Glencoe, 1955).

[12] Literally, "pits"; also "core." The term is used to designate that these groups are seeds of future kibbutzim.

of some basic functions. Particularly, the external functions of adapting to the environment (for example, making a livelihood) and allocating the available facilities among the group members are fulfilled for the group by members of outside social systems.

The group is a relatively autonomous system as far as the internal functions are concerned. Activities are mainly of two types: (a) normative—studying the writings of Marx, Lenin, Borkhov, and other European and Israeli socialists, and discussing kibbutz literature and Israel's politics—and (b) integrative—dancing, communal singing, and trips and parties. Much emphasis is put on holidays and various Boy Scout-like rituals. The groups are small, coeducational, and highly homogeneous in terms of age, ethnic and socioeconomic status, as well as educational background. This homogeneity, the lack of external functions, and the emphasis on internally oriented activities tend to create highly solidaric groups whose social structure is based almost completely on informal social control.

Elites at this stage are restricted to internal functions. Most external activities are initiated and controlled by elites in other systems. Parents determine when younger members can go to the youth-movement center, how much time they can spend, if they may join a trip, and so forth. Schools or employers have similar controlling functions. A youth guide nominated by the youth-movement headquarters directs and limits many of the activities conducted by the group. The garin has some "self-government" through two channels: elected committees and informal leadership. But the scope of this self-regulation is very limited. Informal leaders are easily co-opted, and committees tend to become inactive shortly after their election.

There is no elite differentiation at this stage. The youth guide controls both normative and integrative activities. The informal leaders, as far as we can tell, have similar positions in both realms of activity. Many local branches of the youth movements have only one committee which often discusses and decides on issues of both kinds, interchangeably.

ELITES IN THE TRANSITORY PERIOD

The second stage in the natural history of the kibbutz begins when the garinim leave their sheltered homes and city life for intensive training, usually after graduation from high school. There are several alternative training arrangements: some training takes place in agricultural colleges which are also boarding schools,[13] some in *moshavot*. Often the training for farm work and kibbutz life is combined with service in the army. In most cases the training takes place in an older kibbutz. We shall follow the development of the garin and its elites when this alternative is chosen.

With the transfer to the training place, the garin becomes a permanent social group called *hachshara*, which means "training." The group settles in one of the kibbutz quarters. Interaction becomes continuous, and contact among members is very frequent. For the first time the group obtains a common external base. All garin members work for the same "employer," an older host kibbutz, and are trained by its members. The members obtain all their supplies and accommodations from the communal services of the host kibbutz.

At the same time the hachshara becomes much more autonomous. It gains a high degree of self-control over internal functions and some control over externally oriented activities. The controlling functions of the youth guide are internalized. The group has to initiate and regulate by itself its social and cultural activities. Functionaries of the older kibbutz give some "expert" advice on these issues (for example, help in obtaining a lecturer) and set some limits to self-regulation (for example, a trip planned for Passover has to be delayed because the hachshara help is needed for an early harvesting). But, in general, the older kibbutz interferes only rarely in the hachshara's internal activities.

Externally oriented activities of the hachshara still take place in systems not under its control. The members work in the host kibbutz farm and services and receive accommodation from it. They are assigned to jobs mainly according to the kibbutz needs. A work-assigner usually determines which members will be assigned to what jobs, thus leaving the hachshara little control over the division of labor within it.

The increase in internal control is revealed in the considerable

<hr>

[13] These schools are discussed by Amitai Etzioni, "The Organizational Structure of 'Closed' Educational Institutions in Israel," *Harvard Educational Review*, vol. 27 (1957), pp. 107–125.

increase in scope and significance of committee activities. In the garin period most issues were decided through informal group discussions; in the hachshara it is done in the general assembly, which usually meets once a week and decides almost all the issues. It also elects committees which function in its name and report to it about their activities.

There is a cultural committee in charge of normative functions and also of some integrative functions.[14] It organizes lectures, a library, supply of newspapers and political information, etc., as well as parties and rituals on Friday and holiday evenings. There is a members' committee in charge of integrative and some normative activities. It has some judicial functions (for example, it settles serious conflicts among members). Its representatives hold intimate informal discussions with hachshara members who have "personal" problems, who are suspected of intending to leave the group, and who deviate from this or that kibbutz norm. At this stage the members' committee has only limited control over the allocation of material rewards, which are supplied by the host kibbutz mainly to individuals in the hachshara and not to the hachshara as a group.

There is a work committee which represents the hachshara to the host kibbutz work-assigner. It bargains with him over the ratio of hachshara members assigned to skilled and semiskilled jobs, reports about members who are sick, on applicants for vacations, and so forth. Thus at this stage it is a committee with an external-representative function.

The first signs of differentiation can be recognized at this stage. There is a role differentiation among the three or more committees but little differentiation among the elite personnel. While some members are considered to have greater aptitudes for this or that elite role, specialization is not encouraged. Active members are often switched from one committee to another and often are members of two committees at a time.

As noted, there are some signs of role differentiation on the

---

[14] The committees in the kibbutz are described and discussed in the studies mentioned above (see fn. 10) and in Maurice Pearlman, *Collective Adventure* (London: William Heinmann Ltd., 1938), and Ben-Shalom Avraham, *Deep Furrows* (New York: Hashomer Hatzair Organization, 1937).

elite level but very little specialization of elite personnel. In earlier stages of differentiation, tasks which have heretofore been organized in one role become separated and invested in two or more separate roles. Such role differentiation does not mean that parallel differentiation of personnel occurs automatically. The same people can go on carrying out the now separate tasks (this happens when the work unit becomes separated from the family unit), or there can be a high turnover among the carriers of the separate roles, so that most people will carry each role for some time, and only little specialization will occur. The young kibbutzim come close to this model for a short period, maintaining considerable differentiation of elite roles with little differentiation of elite personnel.

ELITES IN AN AUTONOMOUS COLLECTIVITY

The third step in the "natural history" of the kibbutz takes place when the training is completed. The hachshara leaves the host kibbutz and establishes a new one. Not all *hachsharot* (plural of hachshara) reach this stage. Some disintegrate, and some join an existing kibbutz. We shall follow the development of the elites where the hachshara establishes a kibbutz of its own.

The major change from hachshara to kibbutz is the internalization of control over the adaptive and managerial functions. At this stage members work in a farm at services which belong to and are controlled by them. The older kibbutzim often send a guide or two to help out during the first months, but they are generally considered strictly experts, sources of advice, and not partners in the structure of control. The general assembly controls production, division of labor, and allocation of material rewards (consumption), as it controlled the social and cultural activities in the hachshara.

The elite, which heretofore consisted of a few committees and informal leaders, expands rapidly and becomes much more elaborate and specialized. A whole organizational structure develops, with a center of decisions (the secretariat), division of tasks and authority, as well as some hierarchization. The first full-time functionaries are elected. A large number of new, mainly external-oriented committees are created, following the model of the older kibbutzim.

The most important new committee is the farm committee, which is in control of the externally oriented subsystem, the work system. It is a managerial-expert committee which plans and regulates the allocations of means of production, including labor, machines, other types of equipment, soil, water, fertilizers, technological knowledge, and financial means.

The work committee now distributes the workers according to the needs of their farm and its services as well as their personal needs; thus control over work becomes internalized. The farm committee is helped by various expert committees, including a planning committee for planning of the new kibbutz site, construction, and farm; a crop committee, which works out the details of the agricultural planning, including crop rotation; and some other committees which vary from kibbutz to kibbutz.

An important change takes place in the functions of the members' committee. In the hachshara days it had only integrative-normative functions (see above); now a new medium of integration is added. The committee determines the allocation of various material rewards and handles the integrative problems emerging from it.

The committees have limited significance compared with the functionaries, who are elected for the first time at this stage. While the committees meet once or twice per week after working hours, the functionaries are part- or full-time organizers who devote a considerable part of their working day as well as much of their leisure time to organizational activity. At this stage there are usually five functionaries: the general farm manager, usually also the chairman of the farm committee, who actually directs the work system of the kibbutz; the treasurer, who is the kibbutz representative in the city in financial and marketing matters; the shopping agent, who makes purchases for the kibbutz in the city; and the secretary, whose role is a combination of the clerk of the kibbutz, its representative to the authorities, and the only functionary active in internal activities. He is often chairman of the members' committee. Most of the new kibbutzim have also part-time work-assigners. In others, work is assigned by the work committee members in their free time. The last important addition are branch managers. The kibbutz' farm and communal services (communal kitchen, laundry, children's houses, clothing store, and so forth) are organized into work units called "branches." At this stage most branches are established, and branch managers are elected or nominated.

At this point a hierarchy of elites develops for the first time. At the top is the secretariat, to which all other committees are subordinated. Most functionaries are members of the secretariat; otherwise they are subordinated to it as well. The most developed hierarchy is found in the new organizational branch of the external activities. From bottom to top we find the following levels: workers, branch managers, farm committee and the general farm manager, the secretariat, and, finally, the general assembly.

By now, there is a considerable differentiation of elites as to role. The strongest differentiation is between the externally and internally oriented elites. On the one hand, we find the cultural committee, members' committee, and the secretary; on the other, the farm committee, other externally oriented committees, as well as four functionaries (all except the secretary) and the branch managers. There is some differentiation along the four functional lines. In the internal wing the cultural committee is predominantly normatively oriented, and the members' committee and the secretary are predominantly integratively oriented. (This differentiation basically existed already in the hachshara days, but it becomes more emphasized.) In the external branch the farm committee and the general farm manager are predominantly managerially oriented, and the advisory committees (the planning committee, the crop committee, and others) are predominantly expert-oriented. The branch managers of small branches are more expert-oriented; the branch managers of larger branches are managerial-oriented.

ELITES IN A COMPLEX SYSTEM

The change from a young kibbutz to an older one is a change from a relatively simple monolithic collectivity to a complex commune. The solidaric ties to the kibbutz as a collectivity are weakened with the increase of the significance of the solidaric ties to the subcollectivities. In earlier stages the kibbutz was mainly a group of young bachelors. By now most of its members have established a family, which becomes a significant unit of activity and loyalty.[15] A second focus of solidarity is often found in the new groups which join the kibbutz after the first years. The young kibbutzim are small (forty to eighty members), homogeneous groups. But soon the groups are not large enough for the various needs of the kibbutz, mainly for a rational organization of the farm and defense system. New groups join, unlike it in age, educational background, and/or ethnic origin and socioeconomic status. In most cases some social differentiation is maintained along these lines.[16] As the kibbutz becomes older, the children often constitute a social subcollectivity of their own. At last, to close the circle, the kibbutz plays host to a hachshara, which is preparing itself for the day it will establish its own kibbutz. In kibbutzim, where there is little differentiation of loyalties on status bases (for example, old-timers versus newcomers; ethnic origins), often loyalties are woven along functional lines of work units (called "branches").[17] But the elites themselves almost never constitute a basis for crystallization of a solidaric group (see below).[18]

The organizational structure itself does not change in any basic way, although it becomes considerably larger and more elaborate. At a relatively early stage an educational committee is added which is responsible for the socialization of the children, a normative function. As the number of the children increases, subcommittees for various age groups are introduced. In order to

[15] On the increasing significance of the family as a cohesive unit in the kibbutz see Y. Talmon-Garber, "The Family in Israel," *Marriage and Family Living*, vol. 16 (1954), p. 348, and Y. Talmon-Garber, "Jeunes et vieux dans les commaunautés israelliennes," *Esprit*, vol. 31 (1963), pp. 952–964. A relevant study is A. P. Hare, E. F. Borgatta, and R. F. Bales, *Small Groups, Studies in Social Interaction* (New York: Alfred A. Knopf, Inc., 1955).

[16] On the development of social differentiation in the kibbutz see Eva Rosenfeld, "Social Stratification in a 'Classless' Society," *American Sociological Review*, vol. 16 (1951), pp. 766–774; Yonina Talmon-Garber, "Differentiation in Collective Settlements," *Scripta Hierosolymitana* (Jerusalem: Hebrew University), vol. 3 (1956), pp. 153–178. See also Ivan Vallier, "Social Change in the *Kibbuz* Economy," *Economic Development and Cultural Change*, vol. 10 (1962), pp. 337–352.

[17] See Amitai Etzioni, "Solidaric Work-Groups in Collective Settlements," *Human Organization*, vol. 16 (1957), pp. 2–6.

[18] On lack of social ties between elite members see Y. Talmon-Garber, "Differentiation in Collective Settlements," p. 117. On the concept of social circulation see H. D. Lasswell, D. Lerner, and C. E. Rothwell, *The Comparative Study of Elites* (Stanford, Cal.: Stanford University Press, 1952), pp. 8–9.

maintain normative primacy of the committee, larger kibbutzim elect special educational subcommittees for administrative and technical tasks. The members' committee usually establishes an increasing number of subordinated committees which deal with specific allocations like a housing committee, an equipment committee, a health committee, and many others.

The number of functionaries and the time allocated to them are increased, but no new tasks are developed. Functionaries are first released from regular work for an hour a day (known in the kibbutz as an "eight," that is, eighth part of the working day). The time allocated for organizational activity is gradually increased. While in the new kibbutz usually only one or two functionaries have a full-time office, in the older kibbutz most functionaries are old full-time officers; in large kibbutzim two full-time functionaries fulfill tasks earlier carried out by one part-time functionary. Thus, *in toto*, there is mainly an increase in the volume of elite activity but little additional differentiation on the role level. The reason is, we suggest, that basic functional differentiation has already been reached at the earlier stage.

The main change as far as the elite structure is concerned lies now on a different level. Specialization takes place on the personnel level. Until now we saw a process of increasing differentiation on the role level, while elite members were switched frequently from role to role, although there was some concern about specialization of personnel, as noted earlier. At this last stage members are increasingly specialized in one function, yet elite members frequently hold more than one office, this being less true as the institution ages.

We studied the offices held simultaneously by elite members of two kibbutzim—a young kibbutz, COT, established in 1949, and an older COT—and forty-one "additional" offices in BAH (older kibbutz). By additional offices we mean the offices a member holds simultaneously with his basic office. From the point of view of the present argument and the statistics supplied, it does not make any difference which role is designated as "basic" and which as "additional"; what matters is the number of offices held by one person and the types of combinations.

Obviously, the number of cases is too small to allow for a fourfold functional analysis. But if we divide the offices into externally and internally oriented offices (we have suggested that the external-internal differentiation develops earlier), we can see significant differences between the two kibbutzim.

The data support the suggestion made above. In the younger kibbutz there are more members who hold offices in elites of different functional subsystems than in the older; while in the young kibbutz 33 percent of the combinations of offices are cross-functional, less than 10 percent are so in the older kibbutz. In support of this conclusion from other kibbutzim, it may be said that in Benjamin, a young kibbutz, the treasurer, who plays an adaptive-dominated role, was also the ideological leader of the kibbutz. In Simon (a young kibbutz) the general farm manager was at the same time also the chairman of the educational com-

Table 1.3 DISTRIBUTION OF ADDITIONAL OFFICES

	External-* External Offices	External-Internal or Internal-External Offices	Internal- Internal Offices
COT (young kibbutz)	8	6	4
BAH (older kibbutz)	27	4	10

* The first term designates the office of the elite member; the second, the additional offices. Thus external-internal, for instance, means that a member in an external committee (e.g., farm committee) is also a member of an internal committee (e.g., educational committee).

mittee. We do not know about any similar combinations in older kibbutzim. Some probably exist, but they seem to be considerably less frequent.

ELITES AND INSTITUTIONALIZED BRIDGES

Differentiated societies have separate subsystems devoted to the major functions. Thus the work system is devoted to adaptation, family and education to socialization (normative dominancy), the legal system mainly to integration, and what is often referred to as decision-making can be termed, in the conceptual frame of reference applied here, a managerial subsystem. The activities of these various subsystems have to be integrated if the system is to be maintained and its ability to reach its goals is to be preserved. To a degree this is performed by the regular functioning of the various subsystems, especially the integrative and normative subsystems. To some degree the ties among the various subsystems are maintained by special intersystem (interstitial) sectors. Some professions and many cross-class social groups and voluntary associations seem to have this function.

We would expect interstitial units to lack a dominant orientation and their structure to reflect the orientations of the subsystems they bridge. Thus, if we see a vocational school as a typical interstitial unit, we would expect it to combine the normative orientation of the family and primary school with the external orientations of the occupational system.

Among the most important categories of interstitial units are certain types of elites. While most are *specialized*, some are dual-oriented and others collectivity-oriented. The *dual* elites serve two subsystems simultaneously; the *collectivity*-oriented elites serve the whole. By integrating and coordinating differentiated activities, both contribute to the cohesiveness and effectiveness of the system.

We would expect to find specialized elites at the bottom or close to the bottom of organization and stratification structures, dual elites at the middle level, and collectivity-oriented elites at the top level. But while organizational structures almost always have one center of decision (that is, a top elite), in stratification and political structures of societies it varies considerably. While totalitarian states have a centralized top elite, in feudal societies and some democratic societies, notably the United States, top-level elite structure is much more complicated.[19]

The kibbutz gives us an opportunity to study a society which has a top collectivity-oriented elite which to a large degree coincides with the elites institutionalized in the organizational structure, and also gives us a chance to study a dual elite. The work

[19] See Raymond Aron, "Social Structure and the Ruling Class," in Bendix and Lipset (eds.), *Class, Status and Power*, pp. 567–577; C. Wright Mills, *The Power Elite* (New York: Oxford University Press, 1956); Talcott Parsons, "The Distribution of Power in American Society," *World Politics*, vol. 10 (1957), pp. 123–143.

committee in both the young and the older kibbutz is a dual elite; the secretariat is collectivity-oriented.

The work committee assigns members to jobs. Two types of considerations impinge equally on the decisions to assign members: the needs of the farm and services and the needs of the kibbutz as a solidaric unit. In pattern variables the first set of considerations is universalistic, specific, and performance- and neutrality-dominated. The factors taken into consideration are economic, technological, and physical requirements, aptitudes, managerial expediency, efficiency, and optimal distribution of means of production. The second set of considerations is particularistic, diffuse, quality and affectively oriented. The members' preferences about jobs, teammates, positions in the kibbutz, character, and similar factors are taken into account.

The task of the work committee is to work out solutions which will not undermine the work system, on one hand, and the integrative system, on the other—a difficult thing, since the conflicting needs of the two subsystems are considerable. Kibbutz members often refuse to serve on the work committee, especially to be work-assigners. While, in general, committee members are elected for one or two years, work-assigners are elected for shorter periods, in most kibbutzim for three months.

The interstitial character of the work committee is revealed by the hierarchical nature of the organization (Figure 1.1). Most elite roles in the organizational structure of the kibbutz are clearly in one line of authority, as the figure also illustrates. Thus the branch managers are subordinated to the general farm managers; the housing, equipment, and health committees to the members' committee; and the members of the educational sub-committees to the educational committee. But the work committee and work-assigner are not clearly subordinated to any committee and are often directly represented in the top committee, the secretariat (see below). While the work-assigner often works in close cooperation with the general farm manager and is under considerable influence from his managerial (universalistic) demands, he is also under pressure of the health committee, members' committee, and secretary to take into account "human factors." In some kibbutzim, one member of the work committee is an ex-officio representative of the members' committee. Former

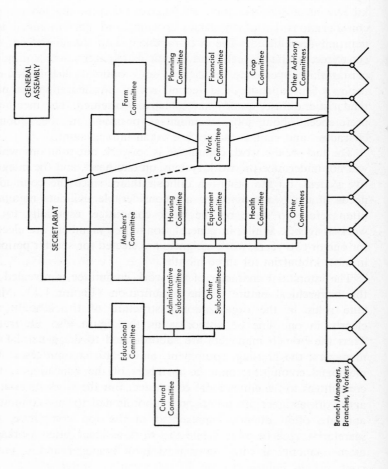

Figure 1.1 MODEL OF THE ORGANIZATIONAL STRUCTURE OF AN OLDER KIBBUTZ

members of the work committee seem to be more likely to become active members of internally oriented committees than holders of any externally oriented role, and former members of internal committees seem to be more like work-committee members than do those of any external committee.

Organizational structures are characterized among other things by a single center of direction. The nature of this top unit reflects to some degree the nature of the whole system. Thus, if the system is characterized by a dominancy of the normative function, for instance, we would not be astonished to find a strong representation of normative-oriented actors in the top elite of the system. But, on the other hand, the top elite of any organization cannot be a specialized elite in the dominant function of the organization, because other functions of the organization may be neglected. Since the organization is a social system, its effective functioning and, in the long run, its very existence depend on representation of all major functions—directly or indirectly—at the top level. Thus top management of successful industries includes "managers" as well as experts, engineers as well as salespeople, economists as well as accountants.

The top elite of the organization structure of most kibbutzim is the secretariat. It controls the whole organizational structure and is responsible before the general assembly for the functioning of the various committees and functionaries. In cases of conflict among the various committees, the issue is often decided by the secretariat or by the general assembly, which may act on recommendations submitted by the secretariat.[20] The agenda of the general assembly is prepared by the secretariat, and one of its members is the chairman of the general assembly in most kibbutzim. While members of the other committees often develop quite strong loyalties to one realm of activity, the secretariat is considered to be the "cabinet" of the whole kibbutz, and its members are particularly expected to have "the general welfare" of the kibbutz as their primary focus of interest and loyalty.

[20] On the democratic process in the kibbutz see R. D. Schwartz, "Democracy and Collectivism in the Kibbutz," in *Social Problems*, special issue on the kibbutz, S. Diamond (ed.), vol. 5 (1957). See also S. Landshut, "Self-Government in Communal Settlements," in *A New Way of Life, The Collective Settlements of Israel*, N. Bentwich (ed.) (London: Shindler & Golomb, 1949).

The secretariat is well adapted to its functions as a top, collectivity-oriented elite. All major functions are represented in it. It usually includes the treasurer, the general farm manager, the chairman of the members' committee, the chairman of the educational committee, and often the work-assigner. The secretary is the nominal chairman of the committee. In addition to the functional representatives, one or two members are usually elected to "represent the public." These are sometimes the most influential members of the secretariat. They are not committed to one function and thus help the secretariat to reach agreed-upon policies. Thus, while most committees include only specialists of one or two kinds, the secretariat includes representatives of all major functions and some unspecialized members. It is a multifunctional body which represents the collectivity as a unit versus the various subsystems.

DISCUSSION

Every stage of change (especially from the garin to the hachshara and from the hachshara to a young kibbutz) involves, on the one hand, an expressive crisis for the organization and, on the other hand, enhanced ritualistic activity. The crisis is expressed in considerable reorganization and in a relatively high number of members who "quit" by leaving the collectivity. The "rituals"—especially when a hachshara reaches maturity and a new kibbutz is established—are highly institutionalized.

Elites emerge and develop in a patterned process. First there are elite situations (informal discussions which include decision-making in the youth movement), then elite roles emerge. The third step occurs when elite roles differentiate, without a necessary parallel differentiation of the elite personnel taking place. Often a more or less parallel differentiation occurs later on the personnel level; this could be designated as specialization.

It was pointed out by Parsons that differentiation of social (and nonsocial) systems does not develop at random but takes place along predictable lines of the fourfold functional scheme. The differentiation of elites seems, in our case, to follow along these lines.

In analyzing the various elite roles and the process of change, we found that certain concepts and patterns of relationships have to be added to the scheme which was our starting point. We found that concurrently with the process of differentiation, a process of integration (not a process of merging) takes place. On the one hand, "primitive," multifunctional, undifferentiated elites give way to a set of specialized elites; on the other hand, interstitial elites emerge which integrate the activities of either two subsystems or of the collectivity as a whole. These elites function in the political and stratification structure of the organization and society studied here, so as to allow them, to some degree, to regulate the activities of the specialized elites and thus to integrate the whole system.

CHAPTER 2

The Epigenesis of Communities

———— ◆•◆ ————

This chapter presents an outline of the epigenetic model of social change, drawing for illustration primarily on the formation of international unions. The following questions are asked: (a) Where is the power located that guides the epigenesis process? (b) What form does the process itself take? (c) What sector is in the sequence first? (d) How does this affect subsequent development of sectors? (e) What sequences does the entire process follow? (f) What kinds of "products" do different epigenesis processes produce? It is essential to bear in mind constantly the peculiar system reference of this analysis: it is a system that does not exist but which the potential members are gradually building up. It is like studying the effect of social relations among students in terms of their post-graduate life before they have graduated.

POWER AND EPIGENESIS

Locus of Power: Elitism and Internalization

The main distinction between preformism and epigenesis is the function that new subunits serve; that is, old functions versus new ones. Determining the structural location of the power that controls the development of a social unit, especially that of new subunits, is essential both for distinguishing among units whose development follows one model and for differentiating between those of one model and those of the other. We need to know whether or not any one, two, or more elite units specialize in control functions; that is, whether or not control is equally distributed among all or most units. This will be called the *degree of elitism*. To the degree that there are elites, the question arises whether they operate from within or from without the emerging union. This dimension will be the *degree of internalization* (of control).[1]

Degree of elitism

Organizational analysis shows that there are two major ways of forming a new corporate body: An elite unit may construct the performance units, or several existing organizations that have both elite and performance units may merge. On the international level, a new community is formed in the first way when a nation more powerful than the other potential members "guides" the unification process. Prussia played such a role in the unification of Germany; Ghana, in the formation of the Ghana-Guinea-Mali union; Egypt, in the late United Arab Republic (UAR). The cases in which one nation played a central role are so numerous that Deutsch *et al.* suggest that unification requires the existence of one "core" unit.[2]

While many organizations and communities are established by one or a few elite-units, the control center of others is formed through a merger of several units, each contributing a more or less equal part. The power center of the emerging community is a new unit rather than an existing unit subordinating the others. One might refer to the first as elitist, to the second as egalitarian, unification. A study of the Northern Baptist Convention in the United States provides a fine illustration of egalitarian unification.[3] The development of the Scandinavian union appears to follow an egalitarian pattern also. While Norway was initially less supportive of the union than Sweden and Denmark, the differ-

---

[1] I found this dimension of value in analyzing the relationship between specialized units and parent organizations. See my "Authority Structure and Organizational Effectiveness," *Administrative Science Quarterly*, vol. 4 (1959), pp. 62–67.

[2] Karl W. Deutsch *et al.*, *Political Community and the North Atlantic Area* (Princeton, N.J.: Princeton University Press, 1957), pp. 28, 38–39.

[3] Paul M. Harrison, *Authority and Power in the Free Church Tradition* (Princeton, N.J.: Princeton University Press, 1959).

ences in their support to, and in their control of, the emerging
union (and the Nordic Council, its formal instrument) come close
to the egalitarian ideal type.[4]

The degree of elitism (or egalitarianism) should be treated as
a continuum. In some nation unions, one unit clearly plays a
superior role (England in the early Commonwealth); in some, two
or more countries are superior (Brazil, Argentina, and to a degree Chile, of the seven members in the Latin America Free
Trade Area); in others, participation, contribution, and power
are almost evenly distributed among all participants (as in the
Scandinavian union).

The degree to which one or more units control the unification
process versus the degree to which it is an effort of all participants
is closely related to the means of control used. At the elitist end
of this continuum we find mergers in which one country coerces
the others to "unify." It seems that on the international level cases
of elitist and coerced unification are much more frequent than
egalitarian, voluntary unions, especially if we regard the extensive
use of economic sanctions, not just military force, as resulting in
a nonvoluntary unification.[5] At the egalitarian end, use of normative means, such as appeal to common sentiments, traditions, and
symbols, plays a much more central role than coercive means or
economic sanctions. Economic factors operate here more in the
form of mutual benefits derived from increased intercountry trade
than sanctions or rewards given by one country to the others.

This raises an empirical question: How effective are the various
means of unification? One is inclined to expect that unification
that begins with coercion ends with disintegration. But the Roman
empire, despite its coercive techniques, lasted for about five centuries before it finally collapsed. Nor was the German union weak
or ineffective because of the methods employed by Bismarck to

---

[4] Frantz Wendt, *The Nordic Council and Cooperation in Scandinavia*
(Copenhagen: Mumsgaard, 1959), pp. 98–100. See also Norman J. Padel-
ford, "Regional Cooperation in Scandinavia," *International Organization*,
vol. 11 (1957), pp. 597–614, and Amitai Etzioni, "The Nordic Associa-
tional Web," in *Political Unification* (New York: Holt, Rinehart, and
Winston, Inc., 1965), pp. 184–228.

[5] The infrequency of voluntary unions is stressed in Crane Brinton,
From Many to One (Cambridge, Mass.: Harvard University Press, 1948),
pp. 49ff.

bring it about. Quite possibly the line that distinguishes effective from ineffective unification efforts lies not between coercion and noncoercion but between high coercion (of the kind used to keep Hungary in the Communist bloc in 1956 or to hold the Federation of Rhodesia and Nyasaland together in 1961) and less coercion.[6] Effectiveness seems also to be highly determined by the degree to which coercion is coupled with other means—for instance, with propaganda.

Degree of internalization

Collectivities whose developments follow an epigenesis model can be effectively ordered by a second dimension, namely, the degree to which the elite-unit (or units, if they exist) controls the emerging union from the outside or from the inside. This is not a dichotomous variable, for there are various degrees to which an elite-unit can be "in" or "out." An elite might be completely "out," encouraging or forcing the merger of two or more units into a union which it does not join, sometimes relinquishing control once unification is initiated. Colonial powers brought together, frequently unwittingly, subordinated units, only to have to withdraw once their union was cemented. For example, resisting the British control was a major force in bringing together the thirteen American colonies, the various tribes in the Gold Coast that became Ghana, and the Jewish colonies in Palestine that formed the Israeli society. On the international level, the United States required some degree of intra-European economic cooperation as a condition for receiving funds under the Marshall Plan; it encouraged the union of the six countries that formed the European Economic Community (EEC), and is now encouraging the EEC to include Britain, without having joined these unions. Britain was the major force behind the efforts to launch a Federation of the West Indies and the formation of the Federation of Nigeria. In all these cases the center of power was with a non-member, external unit.

In other cases, the elites that initiate and support unification

---

[6] For an outstanding discussion of the Soviet bloc from this viewpoint see Zbigniew K. Brzezinski, *The Soviet Bloc* (Cambridge, Mass.: Harvard University Press, 1960), chap. 12, and Andrezej Korbonski, "Comecon," *International Conciliation*, no. 549 (1964), pp. 3–62.

do not stay entirely out of the emerging community, nor are they a fully integral part of it. The United States, for instance, is an "informal but powerful" member of the Central Treaty Organization (CENTO). It signed bilateral pacts with Iran, Turkey, and Pakistan, the three members of CENTO, which in 1961 showed signs of becoming more than just a treaty.[7] Similarly, France, while not a member of the Conseil de l'Entente (a loose West African custom, communication, and, to a degree, military union of Ivory Coast, Upper Volta, Niger, and Dahomey), still is an active participant in this union through various treaties.[8] Finally, in still other cases, the elite is a full-fledged member of the union as Britain was in the European Free Trade Area and Prussia in the unification of Germany.

Power, Capability, and Responsiveness

The units that control the epigenesis of political communities differ not only in their degree of elitism and internalization but also in their communication capabilities and degree of responsiveness to the needs and demands of participant units.[9] Deutsch pointed out that when all other conditions are satisfactory, a unification process might fail because the *communication capabilities* of an elite are underdeveloped. This was probably a major reason why empires in medieval Europe were doomed to fail; they were too large and complex to be run from one center given the existing communication facilities.[10] Sociologists have concerned themselves extensively with communication gaps, but studies frequently focus on the interpersonal and small-group level (even in many of the so-called organizational studies of communica-

---

[7] The Ministerial Council of CENTO decided in its meeting in Ankara in April 1960, that a shared military command would be developed; intercountry roads and telecommunication improved; and economic and cultural ties increased (*New York Times*, April 29, 1961). Projects already completed include a new Turkish-Iranian railway, a new road linking the CENTO countries, as well as a microwave communication network (*International Organization*, vol. 15 [1961], p. 523).

[8] Immanuel Wallerstein, "Background to Paga," *West Africa*, July 29, 1961, p. 819, and August 5, 1961, p. 861, and Walter Schwarz, "Varieties of African Nationalism," *Commentary*, vol. 32 (1961), p. 34.

[9] Karl W. Deutsch, *Nationalism and Social Communication* (New York: John Wiley & Sons, Inc., 1953), pp. 65, 143.

[10] Karl W. Deutsch, *Political Community at the International Level* (Garden City, N.Y.: Doubleday & Company, Inc., 1954), pp. 13–15.

tion). Sociologists are often concerned with the structure of communication networks (two-step communication systems,[11] as against chain systems[12]) rather than with the articulation of these networks with the power structure.[13] For students of political systems and of complex organization, ideas such as "overloading" of the elite (presenting it with more communication than it is able to digest; requiring more decisions per time unit than it is able to make) is an interesting new perspective that connects communication studies with power analysis much more closely than the widespread human-relations type of communication analysis.

The concept of *responsiveness* further ties communication analysis to the study of power by asking to what degree the power center acts upon communication that is received and digested in terms of reallocating resources and rewarding the compliance of members.[14]

Thus to analyze epigenesis effectively, we must know not only who has how much power over the process but also what the communication capabilities are and the degree of responsiveness of the various power centers.

PERFORMANCE AND CONTROL: A DYNAMIC PERSPECTIVE

The performance, power, and communication elements of a social unit developing epigenetically do not always develop at the same rate. As the limbs of an infant develop before he has control over them, so new performances might be taken over by the accumulating unit before its power center gains control over them. Frequently, part of the performances of an accumulating unit are controlled by another unit, at least temporarily. The industrial capacity of colonies often developed before they gained political control over industry.

[11] Elihu Katz and Paul Lazarsfeld, *Personal Influence* (New York: The Free Press of Glencoe, 1955).

[12] Alex Bavelas, "Communication Patterns in Task-oriented Groups," *Journal of the Acoustical Society of America*, vol. 22 (1950), pp. 725–730.

[13] For one of the few studies that successfully tie the two, see R. H. McCleery, *Policy Change in Prison Management* (East Lansing, Mich.: Michigan State University, 1957).

[14] Deutsch, *Nationalism and Social Communication*, p. 143 (see also his *Political Community at the International Level*, p. 37).

New communities, whose development follows the pattern suggested by epigenesis rather than that of preformism, tend to develop new performance abilities first and to internalize control over these activities later.[15] Just as a child first learns to walk, then gains the right to decide when and where to walk, or as military units in basic training first learn to act as units under the control of the training ("parent") unit's instructor and sanction system before acquiring their own command, so some countries engage in some collective activity under the control of a superior, non-member power.[16] Later, control is internalized by the evolving supranational system, and a supranational authority is formed, which regulates collective activities previously controlled by the superior external power.

It is the existence of a supranational authority—at first limited, then more encompassing—that distinguishes *unions of nations* from *international organizations*. Unions have at least a limited power center of their own, whose decisions bind the members and are enforcible; they have internalized at least some control. International organizations, on the other hand, are run by intergovernmental bodies, whose "decisions" are merely recommendations to the members and are not enforcible.[17] They have, in this sense, no power of their own.

The special importance of the High Authority, a governing body of the European Coal and Steel Community (ECSC), is that its decisions directly bind the steel and coal industries of the six member nations and it can levy fines on industries that do not conform to its rulings (though national police forces would have to collect the fines, if they were not paid). Moreover, individuals, corporations, and states have the same status before the Court

[15] "Internalize" means here the transfer of power from external elites to internal elites.

[16] It should be pointed out that on the international level the power of a new union is more often generalized from its constituent units—"pooling of sovereignty"—than internalized from superior power. From the present viewpoint this distinction is not relevant; the question is: Who controls the collective action—the unit itself, or other units (without regard to whether they are outside or constituent units)?

[17] For an outstanding discussion of the differences between intergovernment and supranational decision-making bodies, see Ernst B. Haas, *The Uniting of Europe* (Stanford, Cal.: Stanford University Press, 1958), chaps. 12, 13. The following discussion of the High Authority draws on Haas's work.

of Justice of the ECSC; they all can sue each other, an individual suing a state, or the High Authority suing a member-state.[18]

Until the ECSC was formed in 1952, almost all European cooperation, such as the Organization for European Economic Cooperation (OEEC) and the North Atlantic Treaty Organization (NATO), was intergovernmental. In 1952 the High Authority was formed; this was the first major step toward self-control of the evolving supranational community. [Interestingly, this is also the year NATO developed a supranational authority with the formation of SHAPE (Supreme Headquarters Allied Powers Europe), which provided a supranational headquarters for the multination armies.] [19] In the following years functions and powers of the High Authority gradually increased. In 1957 the more encompassing common market (EEC) was established, which has its equivalent of the High Authority, the Economic Commission, except that its supranational powers cover more "performances"—much of the intercountry economic actions—than does the High Authority, which is limited to matters related to steel and coal.[20]

Attempts to develop supranational control over shared political activities, in which the members of the EEC do engage, have not yet succeeded. Whatever collective political action the Six take is based on intergovernment consultations of these countries, not supranational direction. Thus, in the development of this union of nations, *as in the epigenesis of many other social units, collective performances expand more rapidly than collective control.* (It should be noted that while performance accumulation frequently occurs before power internalization, the reversed sequence might occur, too. Power *capabilities* can be built up before performance. Modern armies, for instance, train groups of

[18] In March 1961, the Economic Commission—which is roughly, to the EEC, what the High Authority is to the ECSC—brought the Italian government before the court of the EEC for violation of an article of the Treaty of Rome concerning a ban on subsidies for trade in pork. This was the first such action taken since the formation of the EEC (*New York Times,* March 27, 1961).

[19] See Andrew J. Goodpaster, "The Development of SHAPE: 1950–1953," *International Organization,* vol. 9 (1955), pp. 257–262, and William A. Knowlton, "Early Stages in the Organization of SHAPE," *International Organization,* vol. 13 (1959), pp. 1–18.

[20] William Diebold, Jr., "The Changed Economic Position of Western Europe," *International Organization,* vol. 14 (1960), pp. 1–19, esp. p. 12.

officers in headquarters work before they are given command of military units.)

We saw that communities are built up by accumulation of *new* performances (military ones, for example) and control over them. We now turn to the dynamics of accumulation, recognizing three problems as basic to the analysis of all accumulation processes: (a) Under what conditions does the process start? (b) What factors contribute to its expansion and pace? (c) What is the sequence in which the functional sectors that make a complete community are assembled? The rest of this article is devoted to these problems.

INITIATION, TAKE-OFF, AND SPILL-OVER

BETWEEN INITIATION AND TAKE-OFF

The concept of take-off, borrowed from aerodynamics, is applied to the first stage of epigenesis to distinguish the initiation point from where the continuation of the process becomes self-sustained. The image is one of a plane that first starts its engines and begins rolling, still supported by the runway, until it accumulates enough momentum to "take off," to continue in motion "on its own," generating the forces that carry it to higher altitudes and greater speeds. The analogue is that through accumulation, while relying on external support, the necessary condition for autonomous action is produced. Also during "take-off" the pilot, released from airport tower control, gains control of his plane. (This control take-off might occur before or after the performance take-off.)

Economists use the above concept in the study of industrialization. In an underdeveloped country, for example, a certain amount of investment is necessary before that country's economy reaches the level at which it produces a national income large enough to provide for current consumption and for increased investment which, in turn, provides for additional growth of the economy.[21] An economy has taken off when additional growth is

[21] W. W. Rostow, *The Stages of Economic Growth* (Cambridge, Eng.: Cambridge University Press, 1960), pp. 4, 7–9, 36ff.

self-sustained; when no external investment or externally induced changes in saving, spending, or work habits are needed.

The concept of take-off can also be used in studying political, communication, and other social processes. A group of leaders, some labor unions, or "reform" clubs, join to initiate a new political party. Again, "to initiate" has two meanings, to which the concept of take-off calls attention: There is the day the leaders decide to launch the new party, a day that, if the launching is successful, will be known as the party's birthday. However, the new party initially draws its funds, staff, and political power from the founding leaders and groups. Gradually, as the party grows, it accumulates followers and contributors directly committed to it, and if it is successful, it eventually reaches the stage at which it can do without the support of its initiators and continue growing "on its own." While this point is far from being sharply defined, obviously it rarely coincides with the actual birth date. Much insight can be gained by comparing different polities with regard to the lapse between their initiation and their take-off points. For instance, the greater the lapse the more difficult it is for small or new groups to gain political representation. On the other hand, if the lapse is very small, entering the political competition becomes too easy, and it will be difficult to find a majority to establish a stable government.

In many countries there is a formal barrier that has to be surmounted before political take-off. Parties that poll less than a certain percentage of the votes are denied parliamentary representation. Frequently founders' support is given until the election day; then the party either gains representation and becomes a political factor in its own right or it flounders; it either takes off or crashes. One of the special characteristics of the American political system is that the take-off point for participation in national politics is remote from the initiation point. Many "third-party" movements that polled many hundreds of thousands of votes still could not continue to grow and to become permanent participants on the federal level.

Take-off is especially important for the study of social units that are initiated by charter, enactment of a law, or signing of a treaty. While sometimes these "paper" units might be an expression of an already-existing social unit, often the formal structure precedes the development of a social one. While it has often been pointed out that an informal structure is likely to evolve, turning the formal one into a full-fledged social unit, we do not know under what conditions these informal processes take off, as against those conditions under which they never reach such a point. Clearly not all formal structures become functioning social units. This applies in particular to international relations where the supranational take-off—that is, the transition from a formal, intergovernmental structure to self-sustained growth toward a political community—is quite infrequent.[22] Under what conditions, then, does take-off occur?

While these problems still require much research, there appears to be one central factor bringing unification movements to take-off: the amount of decision-making called for by intercountry *flows* (such as flow of goods) and by *shared performance* (for example, holding a common defense line) that, in turn, is determined by the scope of tasks carried out internationally. If the amount is large, intergovernment decision-making will prove cumbersome and inadequate and pressure will be generated either to reduce the need for international decision-making—by reducing the international tasks—or to build a supranational decision-making *structure*, which is a more effective decision-making body than are intergovernmental ones.

The central variable for the "take-off" of supranational authority is the amount of international decision-making required. This, in turn, is determined largely by the amounts and kinds of flows that cross the international borders (for example, tourists and mail) and the amounts and kinds of shared international activities (for example, maintaining an early-warning system). It should be stressed, however, that each flow or shared activity has its own decision-making logarithm. Some flows can increase a great deal and still require only a little increase in international decision-making; others require much more.[23] Moreover, the relationship

[22] See Deutsch *et al., Political Community and the North Atlantic Area,* pp. 85–87, on supranational take-off.

[23] Hence the fact that a mere increase in flows is not related to increase in supranationalism does not reject the hypothesis that these variables are positively related. Cf. I. Richard Savage and Karl Deutsch, "A Statistical Model of the Gross Analysis of Transaction Flows," *Econometrica,* vol. 28 (1960), pp. 551–572; Deutsch, "Shifts in the Balance of Communication Flows," *Public Opinion Quarterly,* vol. 20 (1956), pp. 143–160.

seems not to be linear; that is, some increases in a particular flow (or shared activity) can be handled by the old decision-making system, but once a certain threshold is passed, some supranational authority is almost inevitable.

It seems also that expanding the power and scope of a supra-national authority is easier than forming the first element of such an authority. Initially a supranational authority is often accepted on the grounds that it will limit itself strictly to technical, bureau-cratic, or secondary matters, and that the major policy decisions will be left in the hands of a superior, intergovernment body. This was the initial relationship between the High Authority and the Council of Ministers of the ECSC; between the Economic Com-mission and the Council of Ministers of the EEC; and between NATO's SHAPE and NATO's conferences of ministers.

Once such a bureaucratic structure is established, a process often sets in whereby full-time, professional bureaucrats tend to usurp functions and authority from the part-time, political, "ama-teur" superior bodies, thereby expanding the scope of the supra-national authority. At the same time, the very existence of supranational control in one area tends to promote such control in others. The concept of spill-over, or secondary priming, which is used here to study the epigenesis of nation unions, is applicable to the study of accumulation processes in general.

SECONDARY PRIMING OF CHANGE

"Spill-over" refers to expansion of supranational performances and control from one sphere of international behavior to another. It was introduced by Haas to refer to expansions within the sector in which unification originally started (for example, from coal and steel industries to transportation) and from sector to sector (for example, from the economic to the political).[24] Spill-over refers only to secondary priming, that is, to processes—in our case, unifications—that have been initiated or have taken off because of epigenesis in *other* social sectors. NATO, for instance, unifies the military organizations of fifteen nations, and the EEC inte-grates the economies of six of the NATO countries. While these processes probably support each other, only a little spill-over has

[24] Haas, *Uniting of Europe*, chap. 8.

taken place. Basically the military unification did not initiate the economic one or vice versa.[25] There was original priming in each area. Both unifications may have had certain common, and perhaps mutually supportive, sources (for example, the conflicts between the United States and Soviet Russia), but they did not trigger each other. On the other hand, the integration of the economies of the Six generates pressures toward integration of their governments, though so far political unification is mainly a "grand design."[26]

It follows that one can hardly understand supranational spillover without studying the internal structure and dynamics of the participating societies. This must be done from a dynamic perspective, for spill-over raises the following questions: Under what conditions and at what level of change does unification of one sector lead to the exhausting of its "degrees of freedom" and trigger unification in other sectors?[27] Which sector is likely to be affected first, second, and nth? Which sector will be affected most, second, and nth?

THE SEQUENCE OF EPIGENESIS

CLOCKWISE AND COUNTERCLOCKWISE SEQUENCES

The concept of take-off suggests that epigenesis has to gain a certain momentum before it becomes self-sustaining. However, it does not suggest in what sector the process takes off, or what the effects of the selection of a particular take-off sector are on

[25] Diebold, in *The Changed Economic Position of Western Europe*, points to the reasons why efforts to base economic integration on NATO have been unsuccessful. Kissinger, on the other hand, believes that NATO could serve as the basis of an Atlantic confederacy (*Reporter*, February 2, 1961, pp. 16–20). Deutsch *et al.* pointed out that where the initial unification efforts were based on military integration half of these efforts failed (*Political Community*, p. 28).

[26] On spill-over from the economic to the political area see essays by Paul Delouvrier and by Pierre Uri in C. Grove Haines (ed.), *European Integration* (Baltimore: Johns Hopkins Press, 1957).

[27] In other words, up to a point each institutional realm changes independently, but, once that point has been reached, further change affects another institutional realm.

the probability that complete unification will ensue. Similarly, the study of spill-over traces the relation between sectors once take-off in one sector has occurred, but it does not specify either in which sector epigenesis is likely to start or in what order other supranational sectors are likely to be built up (since it does not account for primary, simultaneous, or successive priming). To put it in terms of the epigenesis model, we still have to determine: Which part is assembled first, which ones later? [28]

A hypothesis defining the sequences most functional for the epigenesis of nation unions can be derived from an application of the Parsonian phase model.[29] Parsons suggests that the most functional cyclical fluctuations in the investment of resources, personnel, and time follow one of two patterns: either a clockwise sequence (adaptive toward normative), or a counterclockwise sequence.[30] The two patterns can be applied to the study of epigenesis. They suggest that it is most functional for a new community to assemble its subunits and its self-control from the adaptive to the normative, or the other way around; and that all other sequences are less functional.[31]

Before we turn to express this hypothesis in more substantive terms, the difference between the application of the Parsonian phase model to preformism and its application to epigenesis should be pointed out. The phase model, as such, concerns the

[28] Note that though sector spill-over occurs in the member societies, it leads to expansion in the scope of the supranational community.

[29] Parsons *et al.*, *Working Papers in the Theory of Action* (New York: The Free Press of Glencoe, 1953), pp. 182ff.

[30] The terms refer to the order in which the four functions are usually listed. (See Table 1.1). Here, as well as in an earlier work, I found it fruitful to apply Parsons' concepts with a certain amount of liberty. A long conceptual quibble seems unnecessary. The use of allocation instead of "goal attainment" and of normative integration instead of "pattern maintenance and tension-management" may serve as a reminder to the reader concerned with such conceptual subtleties that Parsons is not responsible for my way of using his scheme.

[31] This is one of those statements that sound tautological but are not. Since there are four phases in the system, the statement suggests that two modes of movement are more functional than twenty-two other possible ones. The first pattern—adaptive to normative—is referred to as clockwise because the convention is to present the four phases in a fourfold table in which the adaptive is in the upper left-hand box, the allocative in the upper right-hand box, the social-integrative in the lower right-hand box, and the normative in the lower left-hand box.

movement of an existing system, not its pattern of growth or change in its structure. Unless other processes take place, after a full round of the phase movement the system is the same as it started. Moreover, while each system is once accumulated or differentiated, the phase movement can continue ad libitum.[32]

Parsons also suggested a pattern for the analysis of social change, that of differentiation, according to which fused units bifurcate first into expressive and instrumental elements; then, each of these splits. Expressive elements are divided into social and normative ones; instrumental into adaptive and allocative ones. This, like all preformism models, is a pattern according to which functions that were served by one, fused structure, become structurally differentiated; that is, they gain their own subunits.[33] The accumulation model, on the other hand, knows no bifurcation, but suggests an order in which new structures serving new functions are conjoined. For example, countries that shared only a common market also establish a common defense line; that is, the union acquires a new function, not just a structural wing. The order we expect to be functional for unification movements to follow is either from the adaptive to the normative or the other way around.

In more substantive terms, the major question raised by the hypothesis concerning the sequence of accumulation is this: Is unification initiated in a particular sector more likely to lead to complete unification (to a political community)? If so, which is it: the military, economic, political, or ideological? Is the probability of success higher if accumulation follows a certain sequence? Which sequence (if any)? And is the most effective sequence the same for all types of unification?

On the basis of the study of ten historical cases, Deutsch and his associates reached the following conclusion:

[32] Note also that there is no one-to-one relationship between the pattern in which a system is built up (whether accumulated or differentiated) and the pattern in which it is maintained; for example, the epigenesis of a system might be counterclockwise and the system will "click" clockwise once its epigenesis is completed.

[33] For a later development of this model see Talcott Parsons, "A Functional Theory of Change," in Amitai and Eva Etzioni (eds.), *Social Change: Sources, Patterns and Consequences* (New York: Basic Books, Inc., 1964) pp. 83–97).

It appears to us from our cases that they [conditions of integration] may be assembled in almost any sequence, so long as all of them come into being and take effect. Toward this end, almost any pathway will suffice.[34]

They added, however, that:

In this assembly-line process of history, and particularly in the transition between background and process, timing is important. Generally speaking, we found that substantial rewards for cooperation or progress toward amalgamation had to be timed so as to come before the imposition of burdens resulting from such progress toward amalgamation (union). We found that, as with rewards before burdens, consent has to come before compliance if the amalgamation is to have lasting success.[35]

Deutsch's distinction between sequence and order in time seems unnecessary for our purposes. Especially after examining his forthcoming book, *Backgrounds for Community*, in which his historical material is analyzed in great detail and potency, we conclude that Deutsch suggests—if we push the freedom of interpretation to its limit—that the goal-attainment phase tends to come before the adaptive one (rewards before burdens); and that the normative phase (consent) tends to come before the solidaric phase (compliance). In other words, interpreting liberally, we find Deutsch suggesting that a counterclockwise sequence from normative to adaptive is most common.

Haas compares the findings of his study of a modern unification with the findings of Deutsch *et al.* on historical cases from this viewpoint.[36] He distinguishes between identical expectations (or aims) and converging expectations that make actors cooperate in pursuing their nonidentical aims. The distinction comes close to Durkheim's dichotomy of mechanic and organic solidarity and is similar to the dichotomy of expressive and instrumental elements.[37] Haas reports that the ECSC has followed a clockwise

---

[34] Deutsch *et al., Political Community and the North Atlantic Area,* p. 70.

[35] *Ibid.,* p. 71.

[36] Haas, "The Challenge of Regionalism," in Stanley Hoffmann (ed.), *Contemporary Theory in International Relations* (Englewood Cliffs, N.J.: Prentice-Hall, Inc., 1960), pp. 230–231.

[37] *Ibid.,* p. 229. In Haas's own words: "Converging expectations make for regional unity instrumental in nature rather than based on principle."

sequence in which convergent (or "external") expectations preceded the identical (or "internal") ones.[38] Interpreting Haas liberally, one could state that in the case of the ECSC adaptive integration (custom union) came first, followed by integration of economic goals (regarding coal and steel and later the formation of a common market). The union is now on the verge of political (or solidaric) integration (election of a European parliament; planning group for federal or confederal institutions) and at the beginning of normative integration. Actually, by the time Haas completed his study in 1957, there was hardly any supranational merger of normative institutions, and even attitudes had only started to change from convergent to identical.

Any effort to codify Deutsch's and Haas's findings for the benefit of further research on the question of the relative effectiveness of various sequences will have to take into account the nature of the merging units, the nature of the emerging unit (that is, the kind of union established), and the nature of functional statements.

MERGING UNITS

One might expect that supranational unification of societies that differ in their internal structure will proceed in a different sequence. If, for instance, the merging units are three newly independent states such as Ghana, Guinea, and Mali—states that in themselves are still in the process of building up their "internal" foundations—the emphasis on normative and solidaric sequences on the supranational level might be at first higher than when long-established and well-integrated states unify, as in the Scandinavian union, where the instrumental elements of unification are stressed. These observations support the far from earthshaking hypothesis that sector integration most responsive to the functional needs of the individual societies that are merging will come first in the unification sequence. After take-off, however, unification is expected to *proceed more and more in accord with the intrinsic needs of the emerging political union, less and less in accord with the internal needs of the merging units.*

[38] *Ibid.*, p. 230.

The preceding statements do not simply state that "political communities develop differently in different historical context"; that, for instance, one can account for the difference between Deutsch's findings and those of Haas by pointing to the fact that Deutsch deals with historical cases while Haas is concerned with a contemporary one. Such statements are frequently made by historians who believe that each context is unique, hence what needs explanation is not diversity but uniformity—if ever found. For the sociologist the "historical context" is a shorthand phrase referring to the values of a myriad variable; unless these are specified, little is explained by the statement that "the context is different." In our case the question is: Which contextual variables account for the difference in sequences and for how much of the difference? (Often numerous factors have an effect but a small number accounts for most of the variance.)

"Historical cases," for instance, are often preindustrial societies; hence it comes to mind that the level of industrialization might account for part of the difference; industrialized societies might tend to merge in an adaptive-first, normative-last sequence; nonindustrial ones, in a normative-first, adaptive-last sequence. This formulation seems suggestive because, if valid, it points to the direction in which these findings can be generalized. We would expect, for instance, contemporary nonindustrialized societies to unify in the "historical," not in the "contemporary," fashion. The hypothesis also calls attention to the special importance of historical cases in which unification came after industrialization. If these unifications followed a "contemporary" sequence, the hypothesis on the relation of industrialization to the sequence of unification would be strengthened.

Another variable to be teased out of the undifferentiated phrase, "historical context," is the degree of nationalism. There seem to be three major kinds of unions: pre-nationalist (for example, the Roman Empire); post-nationalist (such as the EEC); and unions that are themselves an expression of rising nationalism (for example, the unification of Italy). All other things being equal, we would expect the initial phases of pre- and post-nationalist unions to stress the adaptive aspect and follow the clockwise pattern; and those unions that express nationalism to be initiated on the normative side, following the counterclockwise sequence.

KINDS OF UNION

The sequence of unification is determined not only by the *initial* needs of the merging units (industrialization, for example) and the "period" (for example, advent of nationalism) but also by the function that the union fulfills for the various participant units as it is *completed*. Unions of nations differ greatly on this score. The most familiar type is that of custom unions, which keep up the level of international trade among member countries. The new Central American Union, formed in 1959, and the Latin America Free Trade Area, ratified in 1961,[39] are actually oriented at economic development, international division of labor, sharing of information, and even of capital, rather than increased regional trade.[40] Wallerstein points to still a different function of unions: Some serve as instruments of subordination, while others serve to bolster independence.[41] Thus the whites, who are stronger in Southern Rhodesia than in Northern Rhodesia and Nyasaland, used the federation of the three regions to hold the regions in which they are weak.

Functional analysis of social units that develop epigenetically is more complex than such an analysis of existing social units, for here we deal with functional analysis of change where the system itself is changing. Thus, as unification evolves, it comes to fulfill different (either additional or substitute) functions for the participant units and the emerging union. The West European unification might have been initiated in 1947 as a way of gaining capital aid from the United States to reconstruct the postwar economies; soon it acquired the additional function of countering Soviet military expansion; then it came to serve economic welfare and, with the

[39] See "The Emerging Common Markets in Latin America," *Monthly Review* (Federal Reserve Bank of New York), September 1960, pp. 154ff. See also Miguel S. Wionczek, "Latin American Free Trade Association," *International Conciliation* (Carnegie Endowment for International Peace), no. 551 (1965), pp. 3–62. Also see Ernst B. Haas and Philippe C. Schmitter, "Economics and Differential Patterns of Political Integration: Projections About Unity in Latin America," *International Organization*, vol. 18 (1964), pp. 705–737.

[40] This point was made by Lincoln Gordon in "Economic Regionalism Reconsidered," *World Politics*, vol. 13 (1961), pp. 231–253.

[41] On these unions see Immanuel Wallerstein, *Africa* (New York: Random House, Inc., 1962), chap. 7; and Rupert Emerson, "Pan-Africanism," *International Organization*, vol. 16 (1962), pp. 275–290.

"rebellion" of France since De Gaulle has returned to office, it even serves, to a degree, to countervail United States influence in the Western bloc.[42] (It should be mentioned in passing that at a given stage of development the same union may have different functions for different participants. Thus, Germany supported the EEC partially to overcome its "second citizen" status in the community of nations; allied control of German steel industry, for instance, was abolished when Germany entered the ECSC.[43] France supported the formation of NATO in part to gain some control over a rebuilt and rearmed Germany.)

All functional needs—those of individual members, those common to all members, and those of the evolving community—vary with the different stages of the unification process; and they all seem to affect the sequence in which the "parts" are assembled. It remains for future studies to relate differences in sequence to these functional variations, to validate two hypotheses: (a) The higher the degree of unification, the more its pattern of accumulation can be accounted for by common (identical or complementary) needs, rather than by the individual needs of member states, and by needs of the union rather than by common needs of the members. (b) Accumulation sequences, whatever their take-off sector, are more likely to complete the process of unification if they follow the clockwise or counterclockwise sequence than if they follow any other.

FUNCTIONAL AND "REAL" SEQUENCES

An important difference between the statements about sequences made, on the one hand, by Deutsch and by Haas and the statements made, on the other, by Parsons, his associates, and in the preceding discussion is that the former refer to actual occurrences (the ECSC followed this and that pattern) and empirical frequencies (nine out of ten historical cases followed this sequence), while the latter refer to functional sequences. Functional statements suggest that if epigenesis proceeds in a certain sequence, it will be most effectively completed; if it follows another sequence,

---

[42] Edgar S. Furniss, Jr., "De Gaulle's France and NATO: An Interpretation," *International Organization*, vol. 15 (1961), pp. 349–365.
[43] Haas, *The Uniting of Europe*, pp. 247–248.

certain dysfunctions will occur. The nature of the dysfunctions can be derived from the nature of the stages which are skipped (for example, high social strain is expected if the expressive elements are not introduced), or incorporated in a "wrong" order (for example, high strain is expected when gratification of goals is attempted before adaptation has been built up). The fact that a particular unification follows a sequence other than the one suggested by the epigenesis model does not invalidate the latter so long as it is demonstrated that the "deviation" from the model caused dysfunctions. In short, the test of the model lies in its ability to predict the course of action likely to be followed.[44]

In the construction of epigenesis models for the various kinds of nation unions, the use of two types of functional models must be distinguished: the crude *survival* model and the more sophisticated and demanding *effectiveness* model. The first specifies the conditions under which a structure exists or ceases to exist; the second also takes into account differences in the degree of success. In the case of nation unions, while many are likely to continue in existence, some will stagnate on a low level of integration while others will continue to grow in scope, function, and authority.

CONCLUSION

Sociological theories of change tend to be differentiation models and to study the structural development of existing social units. We presented some elements of an alternative, epigenesis model, which suggests that some social units acquire new subunits that fulfill new functions rather than just provide new subunits for functions served before in a less specialized manner. Since these new elements are incorporated from the environment, epigenesis models are much more concerned with input from and articulation with external units than differentiated models. Hence the first question we asked was: Where does the power lie that controls

---

[44] Note that the system this statement refers to is not the existing one but a future state—that of a complete unification—of a community. The use of a future-system reference might prove useful for the general development of the functional analysis of change.

the process—is it evenly distributed among the participant units or is it concentrated in the hands of elites? Are the power-holders members of the new emerging communities, or outsiders? Does increase in self-control of the union precede, follow, or coincide with the growth in its performances?

Turning from the powers that control accumulation to the pattern of accumulation itself, we asked: Where does the process start, what subunit is built up first? Which follows? What effect does the construction of one part have on that of the others? The concepts of take-off and secondary priming proved to be useful in understanding the initiation and progress of accumulating processes. An application of Parsons' phase model served us in formulating a hypothesis concerning the functional sequence of epigenesis.

The distinctness of epigenesis models should be emphasized: While differentiation models focus our attention on internal processes, epigenesis models are concerned with boundary processes; while differentiation models are interested in internal elites, epigenesis models ask about the changing power distribution between external and internal ones and their respective impacts on the process. Analytically speaking, preformist models see their subject units—even when undifferentiated—as functionally complete, whereas epigenesis models view their units as either partial (to varying degrees) or complete.

We emphasized the need to treat social units and their change as multilayer phenomena, including at least a performance, a power (or control), and a communication layer.[45] Whether we deal with a phase, differentiation, or accumulation model, we need not assume that changes on one layer are automatically concomitant with changes on the others.

[45] See my *A Comparative Analysis of Complex Organizations* (New York: The Free Press of Glencoe, 1961), chaps. 5 and 6.

Part Two

STRATEGIES OF CHANGE

Students of strategies employed by groups that seek a particular course of social change have focused on the aspect of "reform" versus "revolution." [1] The question repeatedly examined is: Can social change that is both broad in scope and rapid in pace be achieved without major violence?[2] Less often explored are the differences among strategies that seek *peaceful* change. To what extent is it possible to legislate change, and to what degree does such legislation need to be preceded, accompanied, and/or followed by a massive educational campaign? When faced with mounting opposition, is it best to slow down the process so that time is allowed to "work out" the resistance, or should the pace be accelerated to break the opposition? How far is it possible to progress following a piecemeal, gradual, step-by-step approach? Is there a point at which a showdown with resisting forces becomes inevitable, or can a full transformation be reached slowly by accumulation? If so, under what conditions would this occur?

A study of the ways in which the European Economic Community was initiated illuminates some of these questions. Efforts to form a federation of all Western European nations quickly and in one step failed completely, whereas attempts at gradual, piecemeal initiation succeeded. Thus far, the success is limited to the beginnings of a community; those who do not believe that major social change can occur without a violent showdown between its advocates and its opponents might still argue that sooner or later the evolution of the community will be blocked, or that what has already been achieved will be lost because the basis for success has not been assured.

It might be noted, however, that in the three years since our

[1] Richard T. La Piere, *Social Change* (New York: McGraw-Hill, Inc., 1965), esp. pp. 477–481.

[2] For a recent discussion of this question, see Albert O. Hirschman, *Journeys Toward Progress: Studies of Economic Policy-Making in Latin America* (New York: Twentieth Century Fund, 1963).

study of the EEC, its development has followed the pattern of success that was indicated in 1963. That is, additional tariff reductions were obtained ahead of schedule; much progress was made toward a common agricultural policy; and in March 1965 it was decided to merge the three executive authorities of the EEC, Euratom, and ECSC into one. It is, of course, too early to tell to what degree the Western European process of unification will continue to succeed. However, as far as initiation is concerned, the strategy employed, analyzed in some detail in Chapter 3, has been clearly successful.

Of special interest in studying the success of the EEC is that it is only in part the result of a deliberate design. At least as important is the fact that through trial and error and historical coincidence an environment was created in which the initiation of a European community became possible. For the student of strategy, it is important to note that some of these coincidences could be deliberately produced for similar efforts in the future. For example, to the degree that increased homogeneity of the membership enhanced unification, future elites favoring unification might deliberately attempt to encourage homogeneity, although in this instance it was not produced with the goal of unification in mind. Other changes in prerequisites will, of course, remain beyond the control of any elite, but greater awareness of their role might encourage the search for functional alternatives that can be more readily produced should such prerequisites be absent in future endeavors. And futile crusades, such as the 1946 "Federation Now" movement, might be avoided.

The second study deals with a much shorter and a much more limited phase of a strategy. In a sense, we have put the first segment of the gradualist strategy analyzed in the preceding chapter under a magnifying glass to concentrate on its details. It should be noted, however, that the context is not the same. In the case of the EEC, a strategy was employed among actors who are basically favorably disposed toward each other, even though this included France and West Germany in the postwar years. Here, various psychological and institutional devices paid off handsomely. In the second case, on United States-USSR relations, the actors were hostile to each other, as our case opens. While they had some common interests, they were suspicious of each other and reluctant to admit their shared interests. Hence psychological measures were believed to be needed, and a strategy was used to produce them, hopefully opening the door to more basic structural changes.

If the examination of the EEC deals with a strategy that initiated the building of a community, the study of United States-USSR relations in 1963 discusses a tactic to create some of the conditions under which the possibility of such initiation could be explored. Further, the community to be attempted—if and when the psychological strategy "worked"—was to be limited in scope compared to the one sought after in Western Europe. The strategy employed is piecemeal and gradual like the one used in Western Europe; it is more psychological and less "real"; like the one which initiated the EEC, it was successful as far as it went; and, similarly, whether or not it could have been further advanced and the degree to which it could be successfully applied in other contexts can only be most tentatively charted.[3]

Before we turn to an analysis of the strategies employed in the cases at hand, two conceptual comments are required. First, success is measured with regard to the degree to which the goal of a given actor is realized; no value judgment by the analyst is required. Second, while strategies are deliberately designed and employed policies, it is not a necessary assumption that those who employ them are aware a priori of all their consequences and ramifications. For instance, an actor might follow a moderate strategy and hence succeed in a situation where a more drastic strategy would have led to failure, without being aware that the chosen strategy was moderate or that the alternative course—not taken—would have been a calamity. The analyst, helped by hindsight, may nevertheless conclude that the success of the endeavor was due to the use of the strategy in question.

[3] For another study of this subject, see Richard E. Walton, *Two Strategies of Social Change and Their Dilemmas,* paper no. 95, Institute for Research on the Behavioral, Economic, and Management Sciences, Purdue University, 1964. For two studies in the same tradition as the present one, see Garth N. Jones, "Strategies and Tactics of Planned Organizational Change: Case Examples in Modernization Process of Traditional Societies," *Human Organization,* vol. 24 (1965), pp. 192–200; and Aslam Niaz, "Strategies of Planned Organizational Change," unpublished Ph.D. dissertation, University of Southern California, 1963.

CHAPTER 3

A Gradualist Strategy at Work

The successful initiation of the European Economic Community often has been hailed as the most important development of international relations in the West in the last century. Even if the EEC does not progress beyond the point it has already reached, it is probably the most integrated union ever to have been formed among nation-states. Moreover, observers have been impressed by the momentum the EEC has had until recently, leading most of them to expect that its level of integration will continue to rise and its scope of unification to grow. Much of the credit for the success of the EEC is often attributed to "background" factors, to the fact that the member countries share the same European tradition, have a sizable Catholic population, are in a similar stage of economic development, have a similar civilization, and so forth.

This homogeneity of background factors, it must be noted, had existed for many generations; it did not hitherto prevent these very countries from fighting each other. No less striking is the fact that earlier attempts to form unions of these same countries, in the years immediately preceding the formation of the EEC, failed. Part of the credit must hence be given not solely to the background conditions but to the way they were used, to the strategy of change employed by those who initiated and supported the EEC. These were often the same individuals and forces that participated in and learned from the earlier failures. We are not suggesting that any group of countries that employed this strategy would inevitably succeed in forming a common market. But when the background conditions are favorable and similar to those present in Europe in the 1950s, an effective strategy could make the difference between success and failure.

BUILDING UP HOMOGENEITY

The theory has often been stated that the more homogeneous a group of countries is, the more likely they are to form a union. Homogeneity is generally viewed as a set of given background characteristics; France and Italy have many characteristics in common which they do not share with Yugoslavia, and there is little that any of them can do about it. There is, however, one strategic consideration the initiator of a union faces that greatly affects the heterogeneity of the group with which he has to work, and that is what countries he invites or allows to join an attempt at unification. The surest way to reduce the heterogeneity is not by trying to make the countries more similar to each other—a painful and slow process—but by leaving out initially or subsequently screening out some of the countries, such as those that are most different, or a whole subgroup of countries that are quite similar to each other but different from the other subgroup(s), or those that most strongly resist unification. The development of European unification since 1945 followed all these lines of exclusion until a group homogeneous enough for effective unification was formed.

When in 1944 the leaders of the resistance movements of countries under Nazi occupation met in Geneva to discuss the formation of a United States of Europe after World War II, many still thought of including all the European countries, including those of Eastern Europe.[1] The initial invitation to benefit from the Marshall Plan funds and to cooperate in the planning of European reconstruction was sent to the Communist countries as well. This was done in part to embarrass Russia, which was unable to match American offers of assistance to these countries, and in part because the United States did not want to bear the onus for "splitting" Europe. But following the withdrawal of the Rus-

---

[1] Hans A. Schmitt, *The Path to European Union* (Baton Rouge, La.: Louisiana State University Press, 1962), p. 16.

sian delegation from the 1947 Paris negotiations, the circle was limited to non-Communist countries.[2]

The Organization for European Economic Cooperation (OEEC), the next station in the narrowing-down process, was formed in 1948, with sixteen members. The membership of the Council of Europe, another outgrowth of the postwar unification efforts formed in 1949, included fourteen countries, largely the same as those in the OEEC. Both organizations failed to "take off." That is, they made little impact on the international relations of the participant countries and did not trigger the expected process of either economic or political unification. NATO, with many of the same members and of similar size, scored somewhat better in attaining some degree of supranationality and integration with the formation of SHAPE in 1951, but it never led to the formation of an Atlantic community or even to an effective integration of the military establishments of the members.

The next attempts were made among a smaller group of countries considerably more similar in their background conditions. Six continental countries attempted to form the European Coal and Steel Community (ECSC) in 1952, and in 1954 the European Defense Community (EDC) and the European Political Community (EPC). The latter two failed for reasons discussed below, but the ECSC succeeded, serving as the forerunner of the EEC. Left out were all neutral countries (including those that had been members of the OEEC, such as Sweden and Switzerland); all countries that were low on the scale of commitment to unification (especially the United Kingdom); all countries that did not have a sizable Catholic population (especially Norway and Denmark); and all countries that were less developed, even if they were in NATO (Turkey and Greece) or were Catholic (Portugal and Spain).

Thus, the cause of European unification was pursued by a shrinking circle of participants, until a group of countries was left that was both less heterogeneous and more committed to unification than the earlier and larger groups. This might now seem an obvious course, but in the negotiations from 1955 to 1957 efforts were still made to keep a much larger number of countries in the unifying group—first, to include the United Kingdom in the

---

[2] *Ibid.*

Common Market, and then to form a European Free Trade Area including all or most of the OEEC members, as a substitute or supplement to the EEC. Only at this stage, as a reaction to the obstructionist position of the United Kingdom in the Council of Europe and in the OEEC and to the support its orientation found among the Nordic countries, did the need for a smaller circle become evident to the leaders of the European integration movement.[3]

What effects the present tendency to increase the number of members of the EEC, and therefore its heterogeneity, will have on the success of the union remains to be seen. While it appears as if the trend would hamper high integration, much can be said for the theory that once a union is established, its institutions molded, and its image crystallized, it can absorb more countries and withstand more heterogeneity than when it is being initiated.[4]

AIMING HIGH, SCORING LOW: AIMING LOW, SCORING HIGH

There is a strong negative relation between the level of ambition of various postwar European organizations and their degree of success: the higher the aim, the lower the score, and vice versa. We are not suggesting that the nature of the aim was the only factor, but it had considerable effect on the results of these earlier unification efforts. The highest aim was full political unification as the immediate goal of an inter-European effort. Political unification (the formation of a supranational parliament and executive) is "highest," since it affects all societal sectors from defense to education and from economy to foreign policy. Political unification hence means *ipso facto* wholistic unification. The slogans reflected the mood: "No Europe Without a Common

[3] On British orientation to unification, see a report by a Chatham House Study Group, *Britain in Western Europe* (New York, 1956). On Nordic support for the British position, see Frantz Wendt, *The Nordic Council and Cooperation in Scandinavia* (Copenhagen: Munksgaard, 1959), pp. 226–227.

[4] Amitai Etzioni, *Political Unification* (New York: Holt, Rinehart and Winston, Inc., 1965), pp. 247–269.

Sovereignty" and "Federation Now" were among the popular ones. This was the goal of the 1947 International Committee for a United Europe, the 1948 Hague Congress, and the European Movement that resulted from the Congress. The Hague Congress advocated setting up a European Assembly as a federal parliament and "other measures designed to unite Western Europe." [5] The score of these efforts was quite poor. They yielded the Council of Europe, which among all the postwar European organizations was probably the most anemic one or, as Goodspeed puts it, "little more than an experiment" and "a hybrid between a very loose-unit international parliament with purely advisory powers and a dignified international forum." [6]

A similarly ambitious plan was to form a military and political union of six countries under the EDC and EPC. The EPC aimed at forming "an indissoluble supranational political community, based on the union of peoples." Its parliament was to have a federal structure, and a European executive council responsible to this parliament. The EDC was to have multinational ("mixed") units and a supranational command, patterned after the High Authority of the ECSC. Neither of these ambitious projects was ever launched. The EPC treaty was not signed, and the EDC not ratified. One might point out that the EDC treaty was signed by all of the six countries and ratified by all but France; had it not been for the thaw in the Cold War and the death of Stalin, the French Assembly would probably have ratified it. But one must point out that, even if ratified, there is considerable doubt whether the EDC would have taken off. Other less ambitious military efforts, such as the Western European Union or NATO, despite the latter's Article 2, even in a period of intense Cold War never led to much political or economic unification or, for that matter, to extensive military integration.

An economic union is a much less ambitious goal than military or political unification. It does not require tackling the very institutional and ideological core of the nation-state: its constitution, government, parliament, its sovereignty. It is, initially, limited to one societal sector, the economy. Even if it eventually

[5] Stephen S. Goodspeed, *The Nature and Function of International Organization* (New York: Oxford University Press, 1959), pp. 588ff.
[6] *Ibid.*, pp. 589, 591.

leads to wide unification, it allows the illusion of sovereignty to be maintained unharmed, at least until the economic factors have rearranged themselves to accept and support unification and until various spill-over processes have been triggered in the ideological field (for example, increase in the power of the Economic Commission), and in the political sphere (for example, the formation of supranational interest groups and political parties).

The first attempt at economic unification, the OEEC, while less ambitious than the political ones, was still aiming too high in terms of membership and tasks. Economic cooperation and integration were to be attained among sixteen countries, including some countries that were partially devastated during the war (the Netherlands and Norway), countries that suffered considerably less (Denmark and Belgium), and countries that were unharmed (Sweden and Switzerland). The scope of economic cooperation attempted was broad; the OEEC was to cover from the outset all major economic sectors in which intercountry trade was conducted. Nevertheless the OEEC, while it did not serve as a take-off base for European unification,[7] achieved some limited economic goals, especially in the liberalization of intercountry trade and foreign exchange arrangements.[8]

The first fairly successful unification effort came of the less ambitious attempt to free the trade and harmonize the policies of two industries, coal and steel, rather than whole economies. Initially not much was expected to come out of the Schuman Plan.[9] Still it was the ECSC, as has often been pointed out, that

[7] "The intimate union of economies, which had been expected on both sides of the Atlantic, had not materialized under the OEEC" (Schmitt, *The Path to European Union*, p. 30).

[8] For an account of the achievements of OEEC, see M. Margaret Ball, *NATO and the European Union Movement* (New York: Frederick A. Praeger, Inc., 1959), pp. 217–252. It is important to keep in mind the criterion used here for defining an aim as "high" or "low," which is the amount of unification a given group of countries is willing and able to accept as compared with the amount aimed at by the charter of the organization in question. The goal of the OEEC, which was too high for its sixteen members, might well have been too low from some other viewpoint—for instance, for initiating a strong and wide enough spill-over process to bring about a United States of Europe.

[9] Some socialists thought it was just another cartel. See Erich Strauss, *Common Sense About the Common Market* (London: George Allen and Unwin, Ltd., 1958), pp. 76ff. See also George Lichtheim, *The New Europe* (New York: Frederick A. Praeger, Inc., 1963).

served as the take-off base for the EEC.[10] We should mention in passing not only that the aim of the founders of the ECSC was more modest, but also that it included fewer countries than the OEEC, that the initiation of this union was indigenous, while that of the OEEC was American—a condition for recipiency of Marshall Plan funds[11]—and that the ECSC was initiated after much reconstruction had taken place while the OEEC was faced with several countries preoccupied with maintaining mere subsistence. But in the same period, among the same countries that formed the ECSC, the more ambitious programs of the EDC and EPC failed. Thus, the nature of the goal chosen is clearly an important factor in determining the success of a union.

The founders of the EEC, six years later, were aiming higher than those of the ECSC, but the situation had changed; the EEC could benefit from the integrative forces formed or triggered by the success of the ECSC. Moreover, the goal of the EEC was *broken up into immediate, visible targets that were quite low and into more remote and less visible targets that were higher*. We cannot rerun history to prove that, had the long-term goals of the EEC been clear to the Six when the Treaty of Rome was ratified, one or more of the six parliaments might never have ratified it. But we can point out that those who consciously devised the strategy for the initiation of the EEC were very much aware of a need to aim lower in order to score higher; they had just failed in their effort to launch the more ambitious EDC and EPC, and they realized that the idea of European integration could not survive many more failures.[12] Here is the way one reporter depicts that period: "The European Movement had anything but clear sailing for the next several years. It suffered its worst setback in August 1954, when a proposal for a European Defense Community, aimed at integrating the armed forces of the Coal and Steel Community nations . . . was killed by the French National Assembly, which felt that to establish a common army with Germany would be going too far. After this blow—a really shattering

---

[10] Ernst B. Haas, *The Uniting of Europe* (Stanford, Cal.: Stanford University Press, 1958), pp. 109ff.

[11] Strauss, *Common Sense About the Common Market*, p. 19.

[12] It should also be pointed out that after the failure of the EDC and before the formation of the EEC, the less ambitious and more limited EURATOM was created.

one, since it showed how deep the old fears and prejudices still
ran—the European Movement abandoned its optimistic headlong
pace for a cautious step-by-step approach. . . . The problem was
to avoid risking another defeat—perhaps a final one."[13]

THE GRADUALIST APPROACH

The Treaty of Rome is a master example of a step-by-step or
gradualist strategy. It amplifies close targets and underplays more
remote (and more ambitious) ones; it breaks up, into small bits,
both the adjustments the parties have to make and the loss of
sovereignty they have to endure; it allows "stretch-outs"; and it
follows a multi-path approach. At the same time it also provides
for acceleration, a locking-in system, and the build-up of an integrative center that is stronger than the one provided in the
text of the Treaty itself. Each of these principles requires some
elucidation.

AMPLIFY THE CLOSE; UNDERPLAY THE REMOTE

Now that the EEC is safely launched, its president and many
of its initial designers state that its aim is political unification,
not merely economic.[14] But this is not quite what the parties emphasized in 1957. The preamble of the Treaty includes some vague
phrases, such as "to establish the foundation of a closer union
among European people," which can be interpreted to mean anything from a federation to a free trade area. It is put in a clearer
context in the first articles of the Treaty, which stress the economic focus of the European Economic Community. The crucial
Article 2 reads: "It shall be the aim of the Community, by establishing a Common Market and progressively approximating the

---

[13] John Brooks, "The Common Market," *New Yorker* (September 22,
1962), p. 56.

[14] "It is only now that the political implications of this [economic union]
are beginning to appear." Roy Pryce, *The Political Future of the European
Community* (London: John Marshbank, Ltd., 1962), p. 9. See also *The
Spectator* (October 5, 1962), p. 464.

economic policies of Member States, to promote throughout the Community a harmonious development of economic activities, a continuous and balanced expansion, an increased stability, an accelerated raising of the standard of living and closer relations between its Member States."

The Treaty goes on to spell out in hundreds of articles how these economic goals are to be obtained. No political goals are suggested, other than that hidden in one subclause at the end of a paragraph about "closer relations between the Member States." No mention is made of the method for progressing toward political unification, while the service of the economic goals is spelled out in great detail. Even in regard to organizing the shared economic activities, the use of the term "supranational" is avoided— though a supranational commission is provided for by the Treaty. In short, if the goal of the initiators and most enthusiastic supporters of the Treaty was a United States of Europe, as Monnet's Action Committee title suggested, little was done to make that goal visible between the 1955 meeting in Messina where negotiations over the EEC Treaty were initiated and the 1957 meeting in Rome where it was signed.

This should not be understood as implying that the European Movement conspired to enroll the governments of the Six in a political union under the guise of an economic one. Politicians in Europe could not fail to recognize the goals of the European Movement and the devotion of people like Spaak, who played a crucial role in designing the Treaty, or Monnet, to these goals. But the important point is that this time the "Europeans" were going to rely on spill-over effects and a gradual process rather than try to make their way by a headlong attack on the windmills of sovereignty. They did not conceal their long-range desire, but they neither emphasized it, focused their efforts on it, nor insisted on including it in the Treaty.

PHASING OF ADJUSTMENTS

Practically all the changes, adjustments, and sacrifices that the member countries were expected to make under the Treaty were broken into many small steps. Although after fifteen years no one may be able to tell the difference, it is one thing to inform a government that it will have to give up its control of international trade, flow of labor, and level of employment as of the first of next year, that it will have to form a monetary, tax, investment, planning and social policy—in short, economic policy—in harmony with six other governments with decisions made by a weighted majority in a supranational body, and quite another thing to tell the same government that it will have to reduce its tariffs to some countries by 10 percent next year, and that similar reductions will have to be introduced in the following twelve to fifteen years, and that this will require the development of common economic policies sometime in the next half-generation.

Specifically the Treaty of Rome called for: (a) elimination of tariffs among the member countries over a period of twelve years; (b) gradual removal of qualitative trade controls (such as quotas) during the same period; (c) step-by-step harmonization of external tariffs over twelve years; (d) formation of a common agricultural policy at the end of the first stage (see below); (e) formation of shared economic policies on matters vaguely defined, at times not specified; (f) formation of a community organ, the Economic Commission, with power to initiate and formulate proposals, but leaving the sole power of approval in the hands of the intergovernmental Council of Ministers. That is, the Commission was given, on paper, considerably less supranational power than the High Authority of the ECSC.

PHASING SUPRANATIONALITY

The varied and complex voting patterns of the Treaty need not be explored here. Of great interest, however, is the fact that these patterns lead to more supranational decision-making as the union advances from stage to stage. The Treaty does not use the term, but a trend toward supranationality is implied in that many kinds of decisions which must be reached by unanimous vote in the first stage are to be made by a qualified majority in the second stage and by a qualified majority in the third stage. This allows for some development of Community institutions, sentiments, and vested interests before supranationality is built up (though some of it is introduced from the onset by the very establishment of the Economic Commission).

"STRETCH-OUTS"

As a further device for easing the adjustment pains, the Treaty institutionalized "stretch-outs" in which the participants can extend the period of adjustment beyond the envisioned twelve years. The Treaty implementation is broken into three stages of four years each; at the end of the first stage, the member states can agree by a majority vote to extend the first stage by two years. Further extension of this stage or of the second and third ones can be obtained through a unanimous vote of the Council of Ministers, but the total adjustment period cannot be extended over more than fifteen years. While a total of three years of "stretch-out" is not very great, it still provides another measure to lure the timid into trying the Common Market way. The fact that the "stretch-out" provision has not been used at the end of the first stage and seems unlikely to be used later supports Monnet's often quoted "theory of change"—that nothing moves governments better than having started them moving; hence the main effort should be one of initiation.

MULTI-PATH APPROACH

The Treaty of Rome goes farther than the instruments drawn up for either the Council of Europe or the European Defense Community in allowing for a large variety of institutional arrangements. Kitzinger effectively pointed out this quality of the Treaty of Rome: "The system [set up by the Treaty] is neither one of centralized public planning, nor one of laissez-faire competition; it is neither one of nationalization nor one of purely private enterprise. . . . For atomic energy the system contains strong elements of public ownership and public control. For agriculture it is one of state support and quality [sic] control. For under-developed regions it is one of public finance and public encouragement of private capital. For transport it is one involving central plans and a mixture of European, national and private enterprise. . . ."[15]

[15] U. W. Kitzinger, *The Challenge of the Common Market* (Oxford: Oxford University Press, 1962), pp. 21–22. For another example of the efficacy of the multi-path approach—in this instance, to international

PROVISION FOR ACCELERATION

The Treaty does more than ease the adjustment and lure the timid; it also provides ready-made outlets for the eventuality that a momentum evolves that is greater than was initially anticipated. Provision for acceleration ensures that the more supportive sectors will not be frustrated by cautious arrangements originally designed to get the Community started. The Treaty allows for the timetable of various unification processes to be accelerated. These provisions turned out to be of much use when the members found that they wanted to accelerate the build-up of the Community because they wanted to make it irreversible in view of external pressures to dissolve the EEC in a large union; because the first steps seemed not only undisruptive, but quite beneficial to the participants; and because anticipation of a free market at a later stage led many industries to expand their production capacity and become anxious to gain full access to the larger market.[16] Thus, tariffs were twice reduced ahead of schedule, in 1961 and 1962, and quotas were abolished in four years instead of twelve.

LOCKING-IN SYSTEM

A little-emphasized provision of the Treaty provides for a system that locks in integration that has been attained and makes regression difficult. The transition from the first to the second stage requires a unanimous agreement of the six members; the transition from the second to the third stage and from the third to completion of the whole adjustment process requires no decision whatsoever—it is automatic. Only a unanimous decision of all the Six can delay the initiation of stage three or the completion of the process. Thus, no one has a veto power on progress, and everyone has a veto against regression; any one party can prevent a legal retreat once the first stage is completed, which it was in 1962.

---

stabilization of prices of primary commodities—see Jan Tinbergen, *Shaping the World Economy* (New York: Twentieth Century Fund, 1962), pp. 74ff.

[16] Leon N. Lindberg, *The Political Dynamics of European Economic Integration* (Stanford, Cal.: Stanford University Press, 1963), pp. 201ff.

PROVISION FOR INSTITUTIONAL SPILL-OVER

The Treaty of Rome was constructed to allow its institutions to increase the scope of the subjects regulated or controlled by them —of the power they apply in general, and, in particular, of the power they apply supranationally—without having to return to the national parliaments for ratification of changes or amendments of the Treaty. From this viewpoint it is of interest to compare the Treaty of Rome with that of the ECSC. The High Authority of the ECSC is given more supranational power than the Economic Commission, but the usages to which this power might be applied, the goals to be pursued, and the policy to be followed are carefully spelled out. The Treaty of Rome, on the other hand, as Lindberg pointed out in his keen analysis, is a permissive or framework treaty.[17] It provides the Economic Commission with fewer supranational powers than the High Authority, but it provides much less specific goals to the Community institutions (for example, agricultural policy). Actually, while it specifies some matters (for example, amount and timetable of tariff reductions) and leaves the implementations of some other specific goals to the Community institutions (for example, agricultural policy), it leaves almost completely open many questions of economic policy. This provision for institutional spill-over turned out to be valuable because the Commission sought and acquired more authority and more power than was specifically assigned to it without violating or revising the Treaty.

The significance of this point should be spelled out. The Commission cannot, even under a permissive rather than a prescriptive treaty, introduce proposals that are in great conflict with those which the national governments are willing to support; the governments may not only refuse to approve or even discuss proposals in the Council of Ministers but also can refuse to reappoint the Commissioners when their four-year term is up. The importance of permissive treaty structure is twofold: (a) it leaves the Commission free to take the initiative in bringing about greater consensus among the national governments than they might reach without the Commission's prodding; and (b) there is no need to go through the cumbersome and risky process of

[17] *Ibid.*, part I.

ratifying a treaty revision when the governments or the Council of Ministers are willing to delegate more power and tasks to the Commission—as they did several times, for instance, in matters concerning acceleration and agricultural policy. The Treaty of Rome leaves it largely to the discretion of the Ministers when to delegate their power to the supranational Commission.

NO REALLOCATION BEFORE INTEGRATION

While it cannot be documented here, one of the central factors that precipitated the breakup in 1961 of both the United Arabic Republic and the Federation of the West Indies was the attempt to reallocate economic assets and the anticipation of more reallocation among units whose community ties were not yet built up.[18] Communities, whether national or international, are composed of units whose assets are never equal. Taking from the rich and giving to the poor is a common mode of reallocation in modern communities; in national ones it is often achieved through a progressive income tax and a regressive allocation of welfare services—that is, the rich pay more taxes and the poor receive more services. Such reallocation of assets is acceptable to the richer units (for example, New York State) only *after* they conceive of the poorer units (for example, Mississippi) as part of the same community. In the same way, reallocation in favor of labor was not carried out as long as the British middle class saw labor as another "nation,"[19] but it became the rule once the labor force was seen as an integral part of the British national society. Attempts to use resources of the comparatively better-off islands, Jamaica and Trinidad, to finance the developments of the much poorer remaining eight islands of the Federation of the West Indies before the community of the West Indian islands was firmly established was one cause of the breakup of that union.[20] In the

[18] The conditions under which these, as well as two other contemporary unions, developed is the subject of a comparative study by the author entitled *Political Unification*.

[19] Disraeli's book on the relations between the middle class and the laboring class was entitled *Sybil, or, The Two Nations* (New York: Alfred Knopf, Inc., 1934).

[20] David Lowenthal (ed.), *West Indies Federation* (New York: Columbia University Press, 1961).

UAR, the 1961 acceleration of the efforts by the Egyptians to change the allocation within Syria in favor of the farming and working classes and to transfer to Egypt the control of Syrian commerce, industry, and army—again before the sense of community had jelled—helped to precipitate that union's collapse.[21]

The EEC deliberately minimized reallocation in the first stage. Efforts were made first to build up community sentiments, institutions, and integrative forces; reallocations were to be left to later stages. The continuation of a strong prosperity, high employment (and increasing employment in Italy), accelerated economic growth (better than 5 percent per annum), and the continuous increase in intercountry trade (85 percent in the first five years) served as a general rewarding background. Whether the EEC can be credited with all these achievements is an open question; the facts remain that it did not stop prosperity and almost surely contributed to it and that most people thought it contributed much more to prosperity than it probably did. Thus, in addition to the reward of real economic success, it acquired the myth of success which was supportive to the EEC institutions and gratifying to its supporters.

Many specific interests of national economic groups were expected to be satisfied through unification. Italian labor expected free access to other countries' employment sources; France, Italy, and the Netherlands increased export of their agricultural products to Western Germany; Western Germany developed a larger free market for its industry, and so forth. Labor was at first somewhat suspicious of a Community to be governed by a Christian-Conservative majority to which business was committed, the forerunner of which appeared to be a steel and coal supercartel. But labor's support of European unification was secured through the policy of an *upward leveling* of the working conditions started by the ECSC and continued by the EEC. According to this policy, the best working conditions of each member country—the wage rate of Luxembourg, paid vacations in Belgium, equal pay to women and men in France, and so forth—were to be the standard the whole Community would strive to attain.

The only major sector that seemed likely to suffer was the farm sector, and there seemed to be no way to satisfy the others without depriving it. As in other modern economies, the agricultural sector

21 See fn. 18.

in the EEC countries is inefficient, but through political pressures the farmers obtain various state subsidies and other aids which in effect reallocate the national income in their favor. The formation of the Community, dedicated to raise the standard of living of all citizens, provided both a new urge and a new opportunity to reduce the most inefficient sector of these countries. This, however, would involve considerable adjustment pains if not outright loss of income and power to the farmer. Typically, whatever effect the EEC will have on rural-urban relations was not made explicit before the Treaty was signed, nor is it stated in the Treaty. Despite the fact that three members, especially France, were greatly interested in including agriculture in the Common Market, it was agreed to delay the formation of a common agricultural policy until the end of the first stage—that is, until integrative powers were built up. Moreover, what was to happen at the end of the last stage was left most vague. All the Treaty stated was that a common agricultural policy had to be formed, and, as one writer added, "that farmers should receive as much money as possible and consumers get their food as cheaply as possible, and that these two desirable but conflicting objectives should be brought about by almost any known method."[22]

Since the number of farmers varies in each country ranging from 10 percent of the active labor force in Luxembourg to 41 percent in Italy, and since the German farmers are considerably less efficient, because of their smaller holdings, than the French,[23] a major crisis occurred when the EEC came around to forming an agricultural policy. Since by now both industry and labor were solidly behind the EEC, and their expectations of higher trade, continued prosperity, full employment and, to a lesser degree, upward leveling had been fulfilled, the union was hardly endangered.

As these lines were written, it was far from clear what the common agricultural policy of the Community was going to be. While it has been agreed that the Community will collect levies on imported foodstuffs and use the income to finance in part sub-

[22] Brooks, "The Common Market," p. 47.
[23] On the agricultural problems and policy of the EEC, see J. F. Dewhurst, J. O. Coppock, P. L. Yates, and associates, *Europe's Needs and Resources* (New York: Twentieth Century Fund, 1961), *passim*.

sidies to the farmers, gradually replacing the varied national subsidies, it is not clear yet what the level of these subsidies will be. If they are high, most of the burden of adjustment will be shifted to outsiders (American farmers, for example), who will be driven out of the German market to make room for the French and other EEC farmers' products. If they are low, the EEC farmers in general, and in particular the more inefficient ones, will have to shift to different occupations to earn their living. In one case, reallocation will be largely between outsiders and insiders; in the second, between farmers and other sectors, or farmers of one member-country vis-a-vis others. Again, one cannot rerun history, but there can hardly be any doubt that attempts to form a reallocation policy (especially an internal one) before the Treaty was signed, before integration was actually initiated, and before the Economic Commission was formed, might well have prevented the initiation of the union. In at least one other case, that of the Nordic Common Market, the lack of consensus on agricultural policy was one of the major factors that prevented its establishment.[24]

It is of interest to note in passing that when the EEC began to formulate its agricultural policy at the end of 1961, it still could not squarely face the question of reallocation; it phased it. First, it was agreed that the subsidies to farmers would be continued; second, that the subsidies would be given by the Community rather than the national governments and would be under the supervision of the Commission, thus taking the question out of national power centers that are subject to direct pressure from the farmers. It was decided to determine the level of support at a later date.

CUSHIONING

The "no reallocation before integration" principle works on two assumptions: (a) The marginal alienation of the groups from which benefits are taken is going to be greater than the marginal

[24] Wendt, *The Nordic Council*, pp. 165ff.

gratification of the groups to which benefits are given. For instance, the alienation of those farmers who will lose subsidies is greater than the gratification of the taxpayer who will pay less taxes or buy cheaper food. (b) The alienation of the deprived groups will be more concentrated and politically better articulated than the gratification of the others. Major reallocations are hence deferred. But if unification is to be initiated, complete avoidance of adjustment by any group is impossible. For instance, although the gains to be derived from increased intercountry trade are universal for all industrial countries, some adjustment, such as the closing of the most inefficient plants and some shifting of workers, is inevitable. Actually, the EEC has faced relatively little need for such adjustment because of the high level of employment of resources and labor force that was maintained. Three devices, however, were built into the Treaty and used to cushion these adjustments and thus to reduce their negative political repercussions.

1) *A Social Fund* was set up. It pays for the retraining of workers and their resettlement as well as some unemployment benefits for the adjustment period. The fund is financed by the EEC budget—that is, all members pay to ease the adjustment of some industrial workers. But unlike the major adjustment of the farm sector, here only small groups and hence small sums are involved. The total budget of the fund for 1958–1961 was $26 million.[25]

2) A *European Investment Bank* was set up that has a cushioning function similar to that of the Social Fund except that it is intended to help less developed regions, like the Italian South, rather than specific occupational groups. Again, the assistance was limited in time and amount. It has not smoothed major adjustments but has rather eased those of small sectors which were expected to be especially hard hit if left to their own devices.[26]

3) Finally, there are the *Escape Clauses* built into the Treaty which enabled the Commission to allow an industry or country to delay the reduction of a particular tariff or other protectionist

[25] Kitzinger, *The Challenge of the Common Market*, p. 43.

[26] A third fund, that for overseas development, is not discussed since it would require an analysis of the relations between the EEC and the African nations, which is beyond the scope of this article.

device, to stretch out the transition period. This device, on the surface, costs the Community nothing in the sense that no funds need to be raised to pay for the adjustment; it is "paid" by losses to the other industries or countries whose removal of protection is not reciprocated, but those are less visible as long as this device is not employed too liberally. The EEC allowed the use of escape clauses to help the adjustment of some industries—including the Italian shipbuilders and the French paper-pulp industry—but, all in all, it was not widely applied. Thus, unlike the "stretch-out" clauses that allow the delay of the whole process, the escape clauses serve those especially injured, or those that require special concessions because of humanitarian or political considerations; in this way they help the continuation of unification rather than cause its delay.

DOMESTIC STRATEGY: GOVERNMENTS OR PEOPLE?

So far we have explored strategies followed on the international level—the nature of the Treaty, the role of the supranational institutions, and so forth. The question that remains to be answered is what strategy is followed within the member countries. We should like to comment on three major decisions made by the supporters of European unification and on the effects of these decisions, which are of interest to sociopolitical theorists and to the federalists and participants in the minimalist-maximalist controversy.[27] The supporters of unification, a great many of whom are federalists, faced three problems: Should they focus their efforts on winning the support of the wider publics or that of national governments? Should they seek to advance their cause through legislation, education, and propaganda, or through "direct action"? How many societal sectors should be tackled first—all of them at once, only a few, or one at a time?—and which

---

[27] For a most effective review of this controversy, see Inis L. Claude, Jr., *Swords into Plowshares* (New York: Random House, Inc., 1961), pp. 407–432.

ones should they be if not all were included in the first round? Not all of these are mutually exclusive alternatives, but there is always a question of emphasis and arguments over relative efficacy.

The initial tendency of the European Movement in the late 1940s was clearly to focus on the people rather than on governments, on education and propaganda, and on wholistic unification through political integration. The federalists are, in general, suspicious of governments and put their trust in the good judgment and common sense of the informed citizen. After World War II, in which many European governments showed their weakness by succumbing to Nazi Germany, a much higher value was placed on the assent of the people than on that of governments. Although the European Union idea received the blessing of heads of governments from Churchill to Adenauer, the focus of the initial unification efforts was on a popular movement headed by citizens' "action committees" and on informing the people of the value of a united Europe. It was following the clamor of this movement, which called for a United States of Europe, that the abortive Council of Europe was set up, a high-level forum in which the Grand Debate continued.

In sharp contrast was the initiation of the successful Schuman Plan designed in secrecy in the French Planning Office by Jean Monnet and his staff. He is reported not to have discussed it with the German authorities, or for that matter with those of any other country, although he did privately consult some American acquaintances in Paris.[28] When the draft of the plan was completed on May 3, 1950, it was brought before French Foreign Minister Robert Schuman, whom Monnet expected to be more willing to surrender some economic jurisdiction to a supranational body than the ministers in charge of economic affairs. Schuman informed Dean Acheson, the American Secretary of State, on May 7; the French Cabinet approved the plan on May 8; German contact and assent were obtained on May 9; and the plan was made public later that month.[29]

The drafting of the Treaty of Rome was less shrouded in secrecy, but it proceeded on the same high level of governmental

[28] Schmitt, *The Path to European Union*, pp. 59–61.
[29] *Ibid.*

planning and negotiations, with the public being informed at later
stages. The central "European" figures, like Monnet and Spaak,
exercised their influence largely through their governmental positions and contacts in the various administrations and parliaments.
Monnet's influential Action Committee was formed on the basis
of this principle; it includes some forty political leaders of the six
countries of "Little Europe." The membership covers the full
political spectrum with the exception of the extreme right or left;
each member is there not just as an individual but as a representative of his organization.[30] The committee issues public statements
from time to time but works chiefly out of the public eye. In short,
the initiators of the ECSC and the EEC focused on governments
rather than on people, on national legislation rather than on
public education, and on the economic sector rather than on the
political one.

This is not to imply that the federalists and their efforts at
public instruction had no effect on the evolution of European
unification. They did much to spread the European idea, which
had little sociological force before World War II. They established some of the public support for the ECSC and EEC, both of
which needed parliamentary ratification once they were announced. Still, it was more through the tapping of deep national
interests of the six countries (for example, Germany's desire to
abolish the International Ruhr Authority, one of the institutions
through which its status as an occupied country was maintained)
and the economic interests of major national pressure groups (for
example, labor, through the promise of "upward leveling" of working conditions) that these plans gained support, than through the
federalists' call for supranational executives and legislators. Even
today the Economic Commission studiously avoids identification
with the federalists, although it benefits from their maximalist
demands in the European Parliamentary Assembly in its negotiations with the comparatively minimalist Council of Ministers.
When a European parliament is directly elected by the European
people and has full control over a European executive, it will be

[30] The Latin America Free Trade Area was initiated in a similar fashion
—that is, an intercountry political pressure group was created under the
leadership of Raul Prebisch. See Andrew Shonfield, *The Attack on World
Poverty* (New York: Random House, Inc., 1960), p. 42.

much more an expression and result of economic, military, and political integration than its prime mover, as federalist theory implies.

THE LIMITS OF THE STRATEGY

The limits of this strategy are those common to all strategies; the most they can do is to make effective use of a given set of circumstances. A gradualist approach cannot be used by the Black Muslims to make the United States government grant them a state for themselves, or by the Women's Christian Temperance Union (WCTU) to reintroduce prohibition, or by the United Nations to unify Israel and Egypt. It is only when the background conditions are ripe, and the goal, high or low, is in line with the basic values of the participants, that a gradualist strategy can be effectively employed.

As a typical reform orientation rather than revolutionary approach, it is geared to gradual adjustment or improvement rather than speedy change in international relations or political structure. Hence, it serves best when the political structure itself is stable and when it is not undermined by a national defeat, wild inflation, deep depression, or civil war. It serves best those who have some access to power or are in power, as Monnet, Hallstein, Spaak, and Schuman had or were, and will not do for those who have no foothold on the power pyramid. It serves best those who have the patience and the time to wait for gradual change. Those who are in a hurry, like those who wanted a United States of Europe in 1946, will have to try more sweeping attacks. Moreover, the fact that the gradualist approach served to initiate effectively the unification of Europe does not ensure its continued success. But whatever the future of the EEC, the strategy used to launch it will remain of much interest. Further study of this strategy and the conditions under which it can be effectively used must inevitably face such questions as whether this strategy can be usefully employed in tackling greater problems, such as forming unions or communities larger than Little Europe, strengthening the United Nations, and advancing the cause of general and complete disarmament.

CHAPTER 4

A Psychological Approach to Change*

The pattern of events between June 10 and November 22, 1963 provided a partial test of a theory of international relations. The essence of the theory is that psychological gestures initiated by one nation will be reciprocated by others with the effect of reducing international tensions. This tension reduction, in turn, will lessen the probability of international conflicts and wars.

Examining this theory in light of the 1963 experiment, we ask: (a) What are the main propositions of the theory? (b) What initiatives were actually taken by the United States in the experiment period, and how did the Union of Soviet Socialist Republics react? (c) What were the effects of these initiatives and responses on interbloc relations, and to what degree did these effects conform to the expectations of the theory? (d) What other factors, not accounted for by the theory, could have produced all or part of these effects? (e) What factors limited both the scope and the extent of the experiment, and under what conditions could it be replicated or extended?

A PSYCHOLOGICAL THEORY OF INTERNATIONAL RELATIONS

The theory views the behavior of nations as basically that of persons who have strong drives that motivate their pursuit of goals,

* This article grew out of my work at the Institute of War and Peace Studies at Columbia University. I am grateful for the research assistance

influence their choice of means, and distort the communications they send and receive. (The person-like behavior of states is sometimes explained by the fact that their leaders are subject to the behavioral patterns of persons in general.) It suggests that nations, when in conflict, tend to be caught in a spiral. The hostility of one as perceived by the other evokes his hostility, which in turn is perceived by the first side, further increasing *his* hostility. Arms races, in which the participant countries increase the level of their armaments because the other countries are doing so, are viewed as an expression of such upward spiraling of hostile reactions.

Psychological analysis of international behavior has been so discredited[1] that most political scientists as well as members of sister-disciplines might well find their patience severely tried when asked to examine such a theory. It should therefore be stressed from the outset that the evidence provided below, although partial, provides some new support for some elements of the psychological approach. While the more extreme interpretation of the theory remains unsupported, a more moderate interpretation is strengthened enough to stand among the major hypotheses on international behavior that are to be further explored. After a brief recapitulation of the theory and its two versions, the evidence speaks for itself.

According to both versions of the theory, a high level of hostility generates psychological blocks that prevent the sides from facing international reality. Various defense mechanisms are activated: for one, a high level of tension tends to produce a *rigid* adherence to a policy chosen under earlier conditions, whether or not it is suitable for the situation at hand. The sides increase armaments and hold to a hostile posture ("Cold War"), though armaments have been procured beyond the level of military needs,

---

of Sarajane Heidt and Robert McGhean. Since this article was written, two books have appeared which provide additional documentation for the points made but seem not to affect the conclusions reached: See Theodore C. Sorensen, *Kennedy* (New York: Harper & Row, Publishers, 1965), esp. chap. 25; and Arthur M. Schlesinger, Jr., *A Thousand Days* (Boston: Houghton Mifflin Company, 1965), esp. pp. 888–923.

[1] See, for example, Kenneth Waltz, *Man, the State, and War* (New York: Columbia University Press, 1959), ch. 3. Cf. Otto Klineberg, *The Human Dimension in International Relations* (New York: Holt, Rinehart and Winston, Inc., 1964).

and hostile feelings are no longer justified in view of changes in the character and intentions of the opponent.[2] These changes are *denied*, another mode of defensive behavior, to make the continuation of the earlier policy psychologically possible.

Further, fears of nuclear war, *repressed* since they are too threatening to be faced, express themselves in stereotyping and paranoia, indications of which are found by advocates of the theory in the conduct of nations locked in a state of international tensions. *Stereotyping* is represented by the division of the world into black and white, good and bad nations,[3] and the manipulation of information by selecting among and distorting the content of communications, so that positive information about one's adversary is ignored and negative information about one's own side disregarded. Blocked or distorted communication between the sides thus prevents "reality-testing" and correction of false images.

Stereotyping is often accompanied by *paranoia*. Whatever the adversary offers is interpreted as seeking to advance his own goals and as a trap for us. If the Soviets favor complete and general disarmament, this in itself brings Americans to point to disarmament as a Communist ruse.[4] The possibility of a genuine give-and-take is ignored. The same repressed fear, the psychological analysis continues, causes even reasonable concessions to the other side, although they are made as part of a give-and-take, to be seen as submission or, to use the political term, appeasement. The labeling of bargaining behavior as disloyal or treacherous impedes negotiations that require open-mindedness, flexibility, and willingness to make concessions while not sacrificing basic positions and values.

What could a therapy be? How, the psychologists ask, can the

[2] Gabriel A. Almond, *The American People and Foreign Policy* (New York: Frederick A. Praeger, Inc., 1960), p. 16.

[3] Urie Bronfenbrenner, a psychologist, found that when American schoolchildren were asked why the Russians planted trees alongside a road, they responded that the trees blocked vision and "made work for the prisoners," whereas *American* trees were planted "for shade." *Saturday Review*, Jan. 5, 1963, p. 96. See also Urie Bronfenbrenner, "The Mirror Image in Soviet-American Relations: A Social Psychologist's Report," *Journal of Social Issues*, vol. 17 (1961), pp. 45–56.

[4] On disarmament as political gamesmanship, see John W. Spanier and Joseph L. Nogee, *The Politics of Disarmament* (New York: Frederick A. Praeger, Inc., 1962), chap. 2.

vicious circle of hostile moves and counter-moves be broken? The answer is similar to psychoanalytic technique—increased and improved communication. Communication can be increased by visits of Americans to Russia and Russians to America, by summit conferences, exchange of newspapers, publication of American columns in Soviet newspapers and vice versa, and the like.[5] Communication will become less distorted and tensions will be reduced if one of the sides begins to indicate a friendly state of mind. While such indications will be initially mistrusted, if continued they will be reciprocated, reducing hostility which in turn will reduce the counter-hostility, thus reversing the Cold War spiral. Once the level of tension is reduced, and more communication is received from the other side, there will be an increased ability to perceive the international reality as it is, which will further reduce tensions. Joint undertakings are also favored because psychological experiments with children have shown that the introduction of shared tasks helps to reduce hostility.[6] International cooperative research, joint exploration of the stars, oceans, and poles, joint rather than competitive development aid, are hence favored.[7]

There are significant differences in the extent to which this theory claims to explain international behavior. Strongly put, it suggests that the "world is just a stage," "war starts in the minds of man," and "the situation is what we define it to be." In this interpretation, the causes of war are psychological and can be fully explained on the psychological level of analysis. Arms are merely an expression of these attitudes of mind.[8] If attitudes are

---

[5] These ideas are also held by non-psychologically oriented writers. For example, see C. Wright Mills, *The Causes of World War III* (New York: Simon & Schuster, Inc., 1958), pp. 103ff.

[6] A study often cited in this context is Muzafer and Carolyn Sherif, *Groups in Harmony and Tension: An Integration of Studies on Intergroup Relations* (New York: Harper and Row, Publishers, 1953).

[7] See discussions of the International Cooperation Year—for instance, the *Washington Post*, March 7, 1965.

[8] In a statement typical of this line of argument, Erich Fromm points out: "This time the choice between violent-irrational, or anticipatory-rational behavior is a choice which will affect the human race and its cultural, if not its physical survival.

"Yet so far the chances that such rational-anticipatory action will occur are bleak. Not because there is no possibility for such an outcome in the realistic circumstances, but because on both sides there is a thought barrier

modified, arms will either not be produced or have no threatening impact. The people of New Jersey, it is pointed out, do not fear nuclear arms held by New Yorkers.

More moderate versions of the theory view psychological factors as one aspect of a situation that contains economic, political, and military dimensions as well. Just as triggers without hostilities do not make a war, so hostilities without arms cannot trigger battles. Moreover, even if armaments were initially ordered to serve a psychological motive, once available they generate motives of their own to propel hostile postures and wars. Thus one can hold the psychological theory with varying degrees of strength.[9] Osgood, in most of his writings on this subject, has advanced the stronger version,[10] while this author subscribes to the more moderate one.[11]

A second line of variation centers on where the blame for triggering the spiral is placed. Some writers tend to view the sides as equally at fault with no "real" reason for a Cold War other than misunderstanding. For example, Stalin only wished to establish

---

built of clichés, ritualistic ideologies, and even a good deal of common craziness that prevents people—leaders and led—from seeing sanely and realistically what the facts are, from recognizing alternative solutions to violence. Such rational-anticipatory policy requires . . . a serious examination of our own biases, and of certain semipathological forms of thinking which govern our behavior." Erich Fromm, *May Man Prevail?* (Garden City: Anchor Books, 1961), p. 8. See also H. Cantril (ed.), *Tensions That Cause Wars* (Urbana, Ill.: University of Illinois Press, 1950); M. Deutsch, "A Psychological Basis for Peace," in Q. Wright, W. M. Evan, and M. Deutsch (eds.), *Preventing World War III: Some Proposals* (New York: Simon & Schuster, Inc., 1962), pp. 369–392; O. Klineberg, *Tensions Affecting International Understanding* (New York: Social Science Research Council, 1950).

[9] For a discussion of various versions of this approach, see Arthur I. Waskow, *The Worried Man's Guide to World Peace* (Garden City, N.Y.: Doubleday & Company, Inc., 1963), pp. 74–82.

[10] Charles E. Osgood, *An Alternative to War or Surrender* (Urbana, Ill.: University of Illinois Press, 1962), esp. chap. 3. See also John H. Kautsky, "Myth, Self-fulfilling Prophecy, and Symbolic Reassurance in the East-West Conflict," *Journal of Conflict Resolution*, vol. 9 (1965), pp. 1–17; Raymond A. Bauer, "Problems of Perception and the Relations Between the United States and the Soviet Union," *Journal of Conflict Resolution*, vol. 5 (1961), pp. 223–230.

[11] Amitai Etzioni, *The Hard Way to Peace* (New York: Collier Books, 1962), esp. chap. 4, and *Winning without War* (Garden City: Anchor Books, 1964), esp. pp. 21–26, 62–68, 209–212.

weak friendly governments on his Western borders, which the West misperceived as expansionistic. Others tend to put more of the blame on the West or on the East. All of these interpretations can be coupled with the psychological analysis on the grounds that regardless of the initiator and whether the initial cause was real or imagined, the same process of psychological escalation is at work. The therapy, hence, remains the same. To insist that the side that triggered the process be the one to take the initiative to reverse it, is viewed as immature behavior.

Next, there are important differences in the steps suggested to break the cycle. It is generally agreed that measures which require multilateral negotiations are not appropriate for the initiation of tension reduction. The high level of hostility and mutual suspicions invariably disrupts the negotiations, and the mutual recriminations that follow increase rather than reduce the level of international tensions. Unilateral steps are therefore needed. The important differences between the two versions of the theory concern the nature of these steps. Jerome Frank, for instance, stresses that the initiatives must be clear, simple, and dramatic to overcome the psychological barriers,[12] for any minor concession will be seen as a trap to encourage the opponent to lower his guard. Actually, in Frank's judgment, unilateral renunciation of nuclear weapons might well be the only sufficiently large step to break the vicious cycle.[13] More moderate interpretations call for significant reductions of arms as initiatives; still more moderate interpretations seek to restrict the unilateral steps to purely symbolic gestures not involving any weakening of the military strength of the initiator even though some arms reduction, such as the cutting of arms surpluses, might be recommended.[14]

Finally, there are those who believe that the transition from a "Cold War" to a "stable peace" would be achieved by a chain of unilateral initiatives followed by reciprocations by the other side, while others believe that such exchanges would open the way to effective multilateral negotiations. The unilateral-reciprocal approach, it is suggested, is needed to create the atmosphere in which

---

[12] Jerome D. Frank, "Breaking the Thought Barrier: Psychological Challenges of the Nuclear Age," *Psychiatry*, vol. 23 (1960), pp. 245–266.

[13] *Ibid.*, pp. 262ff.

[14] Etzioni, *The Hard Way to Peace*, esp. chap. 7.

important international accommodations such as broad-based arms-reduction schemes can be introduced, but those in themselves cannot be introduced in this way because the unilateral-reciprocation approach can carry only comparatively simple communications, and the sides are unlikely to make major arms reductions unless those of the other side are made simultaneously.[15]

AMERICAN INITIATIVES

The Kennedy experiment can be viewed as a test of a moderate version of the psychological theory that seeks to use symbolic gestures as unilateral initiatives to reduce tension in order to get at other factors, leading toward multilateral negotiations.

The first step was a speech by President John F. Kennedy at the American University on June 10, 1963, in which he outlined "A Strategy of Peace." While it is not known to what degree the President or his advisors were moved by a psychological theory,[16] the speech clearly met a condition of this theory—it set the *con-*

[15] *Ibid.*, pp. 95–98. Others view unilateral-reciprocation as a much more encompassing measure. Schelling points out another difference in the policy's use—as a communication method (which can convey hostility as well as good will) and as a treatment of international conflicts. His approach is that of a communication method. Thomas C. Schelling, *The Strategy of Conflict* (New York: Oxford University Press, 1963). Also, Schelling, "Signals and Feedback in the Arms Dialogue," *Bulletin of The Atomic Scientists*, January, 1965, pp. 5–10. Another major difference is among those who favor continuing unilateral concessions if the other side does not reciprocate and those who would stop after awhile. Sibley favors continuing, even if this would involve unilateral disarmament. See Mulford Sibley, *Unilateral Initiatives and Disarmament* (Philadelphia: American Friends Service Committee, 1962), pp. 19–28. Osgood (*An Alternative to War or Surrender*), who expects reciprocation, is not completely clear on this point. See also Arthur Herzog, *The War-Peace Establishment* (New York: Harper & Row, Publishers, 1965), pp. 144, 159. Etzioni favors stopping after several steps (the number depends on the scope of each step). See *The Hard Way to Peace*, pp. 99ff. It is surprising to learn that Levine finds Etzioni unclear on this point on p. 56 [Robert A. Levine, *The Arms Debate* (Cambridge, Mass.: Harvard University Press, 1963] though he reports Etzioni's position correctly on p. 228.

[16] There were several meetings between advocates of this theory and the President and his advisors. Those are reported in a study now in progress by Kathleen Archibald.

text for the unilateral initiatives to follow. As any concrete measure can be interpreted in a variety of ways, it is necessary to spell out the general state of mind these steps attempt to communicate.[17]

The President called attention to the dangers of nuclear war and took a reconciliatory tone toward the Soviet Union in his address. He said that "constructive changes" in the Soviet Union "might bring within reach solutions which now seem beyond us." He stated that "our problems are man-made . . . and can be solved by man." This might not sound very strong in a détente atmosphere, but coming eight months after the 1962 Cuban crisis, when the United States and Russia stood "eyeball to eyeball," such statements marked a decisive change in American attitudes. United States policies, the President added, must be so constructed "that it becomes in the Communist interest to agree to a genuine peace," which was a long way from the prevailing sentiment that there was little the United States could do, so long as the Soviet Union did not change. Further, there was doubt that the Soviet Union was capable of a genuine interest in peace. Nor did the President imply that all the blame for the Cold War rested with the other side; he called on Americans to "reexamine" their attitudes toward the Cold War.

Beyond merely delivering a speech, the President announced the first unilateral initiative—the United States was stopping all nuclear tests in the atmosphere and would not resume them unless another country did. This, it should be noted, was basically a psychological gesture and not a unilateral arms limitation step. The United States at that time was believed to command about five times the means of delivery of the Soviet Union and to have them much better protected, and had conducted about twice as many nuclear tests, including a recent large round of testing. American experts believed that it would take about one to two years before the information from these tests was finally digested,

---

[17] Both the speech and the build-up had been advocated. *The Hard Way to Peace,* p. 96. The importance of the context is overlooked by Levine (*The Arms Debate,* p. 327). Levine, belittling the role of gestures, argues that they have taken place "for years." He refers, of course, to such isolated acts as the closing of a military base or reducing travel restrictions which took place in a Cold War context without the context provided by a "strategy for peace."

that in all likelihood little was to be gained from additional testing even after that date,[18] and that if testing proved to be necessary it could be conducted in other environments, particularly underground. Thus, in effect, the President used the termination of testing as a psychological gesture.

The steps that followed had much the same quality. Kennedy's speech, delivered on June 10, was published in full during the next few days in the Soviet government newspaper, *Izvestia*, as well as in *Pravda*, with a combined circulation of 10 million, a degree of attention rarely accorded a Western leader. Radio jammers in Moscow were turned off to allow the Russian people to listen without interruption to the Voice of America's recording of the speech, a fact that was reported in the United States and therefore had some tension-reduction effect on both sides. Premier Khrushchev followed on June 15 with a speech welcoming the Kennedy initiative. He stated that a world war was not inevitable and that the main danger of conflict stemmed from the arms race and the stockpiling of nuclear weapons. Khrushchev reciprocated on the psychological-military side by announcing that he had ordered that the production of strategic bombers be halted. The psychological nature of this step is to be seen in that the bombers were probably about to be phased out anyway and no verification was offered for cessation of production. The main step here was the announcement rather than a change in military capabilities.

In the United Nations, the Soviet Union on June 11 removed its objection to a Western-backed proposal to send observers to war-torn Yemen. The United States reciprocated by removing, for the first time since 1956, its objection to the restoration of full status of the Hungarian delegation to the United Nations.

Although the United States had proposed a direct America-Russia communications link at Geneva in late 1962,[19] the Soviets finally agreed to this measure on June 20, 1963, and the "hot line" went into operation on August 30.

Next, attention focused on the test ban. Following the United

[18] Jerome B. Wiesner and Herbert F. York, "National Security and the Nuclear-Test Ban," *Scientific American*, vol. 211 (1964), p. 27.

[19] Richard D. Stebbins, *The United States in World Affairs 1963* (New York and Evanston: Harper & Row for The Council on Foreign Relations, 1964), p. 84.

States' example, Russia reciprocated by not testing in the atmosphere, so that until the treaty was signed, both sides refrained from such testing under an understanding achieved without negotiation but rather through unilateral-reciprocal moves. This (in accord with the moderate version of the theory), coming after several earlier rounds of symbolic "exchanges," led in July to multilateral negotiations in Moscow toward a treaty which was signed on August 5, 1963. The signing of the treaty was followed by a number of new proposals for East-West agreements. Foreign Minister Gromyko, in a speech before the General Assembly of the United Nations on September 19, 1963, called for a "non-aggression pact between the members of the Warsaw Treaty (*sic*) and the members of the North Atlantic bloc" and asked for a peace treaty with Germany. President Kennedy came before the United Nations and dramatically suggested, on September 20, 1963, that the United States and the Soviet Union explore the stars together. Also mentioned repeatedly in the front page news in those weeks were the possible exchange of observer posts at key points to reduce the danger of surprise attack; expansion of the test treaty to include underground testing; direct flights between Moscow and New York; and the opening of an American consulate in Leningrad and a Soviet one in Chicago.

The next step actually taken came in a different area—a symbolic reduction of the trade barriers between East and West. As part of the Cold War, the United States and, following its guidance, other Western nations had sharply limited the trade between East and West. Not only was trading of a long list of strategic material forbidden, but trade in other materials required an export license that was difficult to obtain. Restrictions were also imposed on the credits Russia could obtain. There were occasional violations of these bans, especially by traders in Western countries other than the United States, but the total East-West trade remained very small.

On October 9, 1963, President Kennedy approved the sale of $250 million worth of wheat to the Soviet Union. The almost purely psychological nature of this step is not always understood. As the test ban treaty had, for reasons mentioned above, only a limited military significance, so the wheat deal had very little commercial importance. The barriers to East-West trade were *not* removed, credit and license barriers were maintained. The President himself said that this decision did not initiate "a new Soviet-American trade policy,"[20] and such trade remained in 1963 a fraction of the total Soviet foreign trade. The total value of the wheat the United States actually sold was a minuscule $65 million. (Russia, at the same time, bought wheat worth $500 million from Canada and grain worth $200 million from Australia. These transactions were made against American wishes and therefore did not serve the American policy of tension reduction.) The United States had at the time 1.2 billion bushels of surplus wheat at an annual storage and related cost of $290 million in fiscal year 1963. The main values of the deal were hence a gesture and the educational effect of the public debate which preceded the Administration's approval of the deal.

October brought another transformation of a unilateral-reciprocal understanding into a binding, multilateral formal agreement. This time it concerned the orbiting of weapons of mass destruction and, once more, though it appeared to be a military measure, it was largely a psychological one. The United States had formally decided, after considerable debate, that it was not interested in orbiting nuclear bombs;[21] the Soviet Union, as far as could be determined, had reached a similar conclusion. Thus neither side orbited such weapons, but it was carefully watching the other side. At one point the United States offered to introduce a formal ban on such orbiting, gaining little Soviet response. But now the atmosphere was more favorable. On September 19 Gromyko suggested such a pact, and Kennedy indicated that the United States was still willing. An agreement in principle was announced on October 3, and the final resolution was passed in the General Assembly on October 19 with the approval of both powers. Its im-

---

[20] *Documents on American Foreign Relations* (New York and Evanston: Harper & Row for the Council on Foreign Relations, 1962), pp. 182–193.

[21] Mainly because these bombs are more difficult to deliver on target than when carried by air or missile. See Donald G. Brennan, "Arms and Arms Control in Outer Space," in Lincoln P. Bloomfield (ed.), *Outer Space* (Columbia University: The American Assembly, 1962), p. 129. See also Amitai Etzioni, *The Moon-Doggle* (Garden City, N.Y.: Doubleday & Company, 1964), pp. 118ff. Sorensen points out that it is "a measure with no immediate military consequences for either nation but a sign, nevertheless, of easing tensions." Theodore C. Sorensen, *Kennedy* (New York: Harper & Row, Publishers, 1965), p. 743.

mediate effect was to publicize and formalize an area of agreement that had in effect existed in the preceding years.

Another measure, psychological in nature, was an exchange of released spies. While spies had been exchanged under a variety of circumstances in the past, the October 1963 exchange served the new policy, because it was not an isolated event but a measure that fitted into a wider context, if it was so planned or not. The Russians released two Americans accused of spying (Rev. Walter Martin Cizzek and Marvin William Makinen) and the Americans released two Soviet citizens from a similar charge.

In late October and in the first three weeks of November, there was a marked slowdown of American initiatives, and reciprocation to such Soviet initiatives as proposals for a nonaggression pact, a German peace treaty, and disarmament, almost completely stopped. The reasons were many: the Administration felt that the psychological mood in the West was getting out of hand, with hopes and expectations for more Soviet-American measures running too high;[22] allies, especially West Germany, objected more and more bitterly;[23] and the pre-election year began, in which the Administration seemed not to desire additional accommodations. The present posture seemed best for domestic purposes. There had been some promising signs for those who favored disarmament, and no matters of grave enough importance were involved, so that even if all went sour—if the Soviets resumed testing, orbited bombs, and so forth—no credible "appeasement" charge could be made by Republicans. There was an expectation that moves would be renewed after the elections. For the election year, however, the slogan was "go slow"; even such

[22] Max Frankel wrote on October 25, 1963 that "there is real concern here [in Washington] about the decay of the vigilance so carefully developed in the non-Communist world and about the erosion of barricades erected against the spread of Soviet influence." *New York Times*, October 25, 1963, p. 6.

[23] Adenauer, then still West German Chancellor, said of the détente that "only the stupidest calves choose their own butcher." *New York Times*, October 6, 1963, p. 6. For German objections to the treaty, see *Documents on American Foreign Relations*, 1963, nos. 26, 27; *Department of State Bulletin* (Washington: G.P.O., September 2, 1963), pp. 353–355; United States Senate, *Executive Report 3* (on Executive M), 88th Congress, 1st Session, September 3. Sorensen, on p. 743 of *Kennedy*, reports that "the Adenauer government still took an alarmist attitude about the whole matter."

measures as air and consular treaties were delayed.[24] (The experiment was actually resumed after the election; the factors that prevented its success merit a study in their own right.)[25]

SOVIET RESPONSES

One of the prevalent criticisms against the unilateral initiatives theory is that the Soviets might not respond to such initiatives.[26] The Soviets, it is said, are Marxists and quite aware of the difference between real moves and symbolic ones. The whole policy of symbolic gestures would appeal only to people who think in Madison Avenue terms and not in political, military, and economic ones. Major increases in trade might be effective, but the symbolic selling of a few bushels of wheat would not. Arms reduction might have important consequences, but conciliatory speeches and the like would be perceived as empty gestures.

The evidence on this point is fairly clear. For each move that was made, the Soviets reciprocated. Kennedy's "Strategy for Peace" speech was matched by a conciliatory speech by Khrushchev; Kennedy's unilateral declaration of cessation of tests was matched by a cessation of the production of strategic bombers; spies were traded for spies, etc. The Russians evidenced no difficulties in understanding the gestures and in responding to psychological initiatives; they participated in a "you move—I move" sequence rather than waiting for simultaneous negotiated, agreed-upon moves. Further, they shifted easily to multilateral-

[24] *New York Times*, December 18, 1964, p. 1.

[25] This was indeed the case. On December 17, 1964, air and consular convention negotiations were reopened. Further, on January 3, 1965 the United States and the Soviet Union expanded their cultural exchange agreement. On February 2, 1965 the United States unilaterally announced a new cutback in production of enriched uranium for atomic weapons. On February 5, 1965, as a "symbolic step toward curbing the spread of atomic weapons," the United States placed one of its reactors under international inspection. Also on February 5, the liquidation of 129 missile sites was announced, following an earlier announcement of the closing of other bases. This sequence, however, was simultaneous with the American escalation of the war in Vietnam in early 1965.

[26] Robert A. Levine, "Unilateral Initiatives: A Cynic's View," *Bulletin of the Atomic Scientists,* vol. 19 (1963), p. 22.

simultaneous arrangements once the appropriate mood was generated, as reflected in the test ban treaty and outer space resolution.

Another "danger" that critics of unilateral initiatives raised was that the Soviets might reciprocate "below par" and thus accumulate an advantage. While one might not convince a skeptical judge, as these matters are not readily measurable, it seems that the Russian reciprocations were "proportional" to the American ones. Khrushchev's speech might have been somewhat less elegant than Kennedy's, but it would be difficult to defend the proposition that announcing a halt to the production of bombers is lower in value than the declaration of cessation of tests, both basically psychological gestures. The spies were exchanged for spies; the test treaty and the space ban involved substantially identical, strategically similar commitments. In short, neither side seemed to have made a disproportionate gain.

While the warnings of the critics were not realized, a danger that seems not to have been anticipated in Washington did materialize: the Russians responded not just by reciprocating American initiatives but by offering, in the spirit of the détente, some initiatives of their own.[27] Washington was put on the spot: it had to reciprocate if it were not to weaken the new spirit, but it could lose control of the experiment. The first test came at the very outset, when Russia took the initiative and suddenly removed its objection to the sending of United Nations observers to Yemen. The United States reciprocated, as previously mentioned, allowing the restoration of full status to the Hungarian delegation to the United Nations. The United States also responded handsomely to Russia's initiative on a space ban. It found it more difficult, however, to respond to the other Russian initiatives. The United States agreed to the wheat deal, but only after hesitation that was sufficient to reduce the gesture's value. It never quite succeeded in making a good case of its objection to a nonaggression pact between the North Atlantic Treaty Organization and the Warsaw Treaty Organization. (The argument that this would involve a recognition of East Germany was a thin one, for several wordings

---

[27] Etzioni, *The Hard Way to Peace*, p. 107. This could have been anticipated on the basis of previous Soviet conduct. For Russian moves that were not reciprocated by the United States, see Stebbins, *The United States in World Affairs 1963*, pp. 76–77.

were suggested that would circumvent this difficulty.) It was felt that a nonaggression pact between these two was already covered within the United Nations charter, which would be weakened if the message were rearticulated in another document. In other cases the United States was unconcerned about such duplication, for instance, between the Organization of American States and the United Nations.[28] The United States hesitated in responding to the Soviet initiative on an air treaty, as well as more encompassing moves regarding Germany and disarmament. Despite this reluctance, however, there were enough initiatives and reciprocations as well as multilateral measures within the three months to allow a partial testing of the theory. What was the effect of the gestures and counter-gestures?

THE PSYCHOLOGICAL IMPACT

The first steps in June 1963 did not produce what later became known as the Soviet-American détente or the 1963–1964 thaw in the Cold War. In accord with the preceding psychological analysis, they were rather received with much ambivalence and suspicion. The *New York Times* seems to have reflected accurately the mood the author observed in Washington at the time, when it stated on June 16, 1963, that

. . . there was a new threat of international peace in the air this week, the kind of threat that leaves sophisticates smirking and the rest of us just dumbfounded. The "accommodators," as outraged Republicans call them, were simply delighted. The "cold warriors," as the accommodators call them, regarded conciliation as a shrewd new tactic.[29]

Thus even the initiating side was not convinced that there really was a new line, and, if we may assume that the Russian authorities read the *New York Times,* they too could hardly have been immediately persuaded.

[28] Bryce Wood and Minerva M. Morales, "Latin America and the United Nations," *International Organization,* vol. 19 (1965), pp. 714–727.
[29] *New York Times,* June 16, 1963.

In line with the theory, Kennedy's initiation speech included recognition of Russia's achievements ("We can still hail the Russian people for their many achievements—in science and space, in economic and industrial growth, in culture and in acts of courage") and suffering ("And no nation in the history of battle ever suffered more than the Soviet Union suffered in the course of the Second World War"). These statements seemed to have weakened the rigid image that was typical of the Cold War period.

The impact of the speech was felt outside the seats of government. In the United States, "from around the country came a generous flow of messages echoing all these responses, but more approving than not. And from around the globe came new bursts of hope kept alive by quick signs of interest in Moscow."[30] A *New York Times* correspondent in Moscow reported that "the ready approval of its contents by ordinary Russians was evident in the reactions of Muscovites who lined up at kiosks to buy newspapers."[31] But the main turning point came when the test treaty—considered an important "breakthrough"—was successfully negotiated. The fact that at first hopes for a treaty ran low, and that it took great effort to obtain, only increased the significance of its ratification.

The treaty to partially ban thermonuclear tests was the central gesture of the Kennedy experiment. Until it was reached, gestures and counter-gestures were met with caution, if not skepticism. When in early July Khrushchev offered a ban on tests in seas, air, and space (as was ultimately agreed), but coupled this offer with a suggestion to sign a nonaggression pact between the North Atlantic Treaty Organization and the Warsaw Treaty Organization, the *New York Times* referred to the offer as "Another Booby Trap?"[32] A week later, discussing the test treaty negotiations, the same source reflected the mood in the capital: "If these talks are successful, it is generally believed that a new chapter in East-West relations will open. But there are grave doubts on all sides that such a new chapter is indeed at hand."[33] Thus, a test ban was viewed to have major tension-reduction potential, but there was

---

[30] *Ibid.*
[31] *Ibid.*
[32] *New York Times,* July 7, 1963, p. 1E.
[33] *New York Times,* July 14, 1963, p. 1E.

much doubt whether it would be achieved. A Washington reporter still refers to the détente at this point with a question mark and explores at length the possibility "that the Soviet Union did not really want an agreement"[34] (that is, was negotiating in bad faith). An American report from Moscow indicated that "a successful negotiation [of a test treaty] might lead to a détente in the cold war" and that "Mr. Khrushchev would also hope that conclusion of a partial test-ban treaty would create an atmosphere in which he could negotiate other advantageous agreements, especially on Germany."[35]

The treaty was negotiated in July, signed in August, and ratified in September. Thus, for more than two months, it served as the focus for discussions about Soviet intentions, the possibilities for peaceful coexistence, and the dangers of nuclear war; and the Senate hearing helped to keep the debate alive. Its ratification was therefore not merely one more gesture in an international sequence of pseudo-events,[36] but a major educational act. The American public that entered the period with ambivalent reactions to a test ban treaty, remembering the arbitrary resumption of testing by the Soviet Union in 1961 after three years of voluntary moratorium, as well as the 1962 Cuban crisis, was now strongly in favor of the agreement. Louis Harris reports that a national poll taken in July, before the negotiations on the treaty had begun, found that 52 percent of the population strongly supported a treaty. This percentage had risen to 81 percent by September when the treaty was ratified.[37] A hope for more moves was built up.

The tone of the press changed; there was now an "official amity" between the United States and the Soviet Union,[38] although only a few weeks earlier, few commentators believed that a treaty was to be signed. Now, while some newspapermen, accustomed to sudden shifts in international winds, continued to be cautious, a report from Moscow stated:

[34] *Ibid.*, p. 5E.
[35] *Ibid.*
[36] This concept was introduced by Daniel J. Boorstin in *Image* (New York: Atheneum Publishers, 1962), esp. pp. 9–12. A pseudo-event has the following characteristics: it is not spontaneously initiated; it is manufactured largely for publicity purposes; and it is intended to be a self-fulfilling prophecy, to create its own consequences.
[37] *Washington Post*, September 16, 1963.
[38] *New York Times*, August 4, 1963, p. 1E.

As Secretary of State Rusk left the Soviet Union today, after six days of discussions with Soviet leaders, it appeared almost certain to Western observers here that a surface of calm would descend on East-West relations. . . . The prospect, it is believed, is for a long period of manifold negotiations at all levels and in many cities and countries on all sorts of issues. . . . The feeling is that the Russians are generally interested in maintaining the current state of improved relations with the West. They are believed to be hoping for a minimum of friction.[39]

The correspondent who had reported smirking and dumbfoundedness over any possible thaw in June now stated that "We have cleared the air and cleared the atmospheres and warmed the climate and calmed the winds."[40] The test-ban treaty had allayed many of the doubts about Russian intentions.

Following the signing of the treaty came a number of new proposals to improve East-West relations and further extend the détente. While none of these materialized in this period, the repeated and frequent offering of various tension-reduction measures had some effect in itself. Actually, hopes rose so quickly that late in August, Secretary of Defense McNamara warned that it was perilous to relax in a "euphoria," and Kennedy cautioned in September that the test ban was "not the millennium."

By late October, almost no new American initiatives were taken, and those of the Soviet Union were not reciprocated. The press referred to a "pause in the thaw"; there was a marked slowdown in tension reduction though efforts continued, as we shall see, to preserve the measure of détente that had been achieved. The assassination of President Kennedy and the beginning of the election year ushered in a year of more or less stable semi-détente.

What are the conclusions from this brief and incomplete test of the theory? Certain of the central hypotheses were supported:

1) Unilateral gestures were reciprocated.
2) Reciprocations were proportional.
3) Unilaterally reciprocated gestures reduced tensions.
4) Unilaterally reciprocated gestures were followed by multi-lateral-simultaneous measures, which further reduced tensions.

[39] *New York Times*, August 11, 1963, p. 3E.
[40] *New York Times*, September 22, 1963, p. 8E.

5) Initiatives—especially concerning the test ban—were "suspect," but, when continued, they "got across."

6) The gestures and responses created a psychological momentum that pressured for more measures, a reversal of the Cold War or hostility spiral.

7) When measures were stopped, tension reduction ceased. (We shall see the significance of this point below.)

8) The relatively more consequential acts were initiated multilaterally or were transformed from an initially informal, unilaterally-reciprocated basis to a formal, multilateral one.[41]

Not all the assumptions and derivations of the theory were as clearly supported. Most important, it is impossible to tell, without rerunning history for "control" purposes, whether multilateral negotiations could have been successfully undertaken without the "atmosphere" first having been improved by unilateral steps. The fact, however, that both the test treaty and the space ban were first introduced on a unilateral-reciprocal basis and that even in the reduced tension condition these measures were hard to defend before Congress suggests that, if not preceded by tension reduction, either they might have failed, or the risks of failure would have been sufficiently high for the Administration to refrain from introducing them. (Attempts to introduce the test ban in earlier periods failed.)[42]

Also, the Kennedy experiment was only a partial application of the theory: the gestures were not the clear signals a full test of theory would require. Thus, for instance, in order to gain the Senate's consent for a test-ban treaty, its value for American security was stressed.[43] It would allow, it was said, stopping of testing while we were ahead both in number of tests and weapons technology. Further, President Kennedy made it clear that the United States would "vigorously and diligently" pursue its underground nuclear test program.[44] The wheat deal was interpreted in

[41] Etzioni, *The Hard Way to Peace*, pp. 99ff. That this was necessary was a point of some debate. See Waskow, *The Worried Man's Guide to World Peace*, pp. 75ff.

[42] Spanier and Nogee, *The Politics of Disarmament*, chap. 6.

[43] United States Senate, Committee on Foreign Relations, *Nuclear Test Ban Treaty: Hearings on Executive M, 88th Congress, 1st Session Aug. 12–17* (Washington: G.P.O. 1963), pp. 97–109.

[44] *Documents on American Foreign Relations*, 1963, no. 27.

a similar fashion,[45] that is, a show of Russia's weakness. Further, during the whole period, American observers provided various interpretations of the gestures as other than efforts to communicate a desire for peaceful coexistence (for example, the détente exacerbates the Soviet-Sino rift). While a policy is often supported by a large variety of arguments, and the self-serving ones are usually emphasized when facing Congress, their preponderance could not but have had negative side-effects on Soviet-American relations. Also, the same gestures would have been more effective had they been introduced with less hesitation, and if Soviet initiatives had been met with less ambivalence.

Above all, since the process was halted, one cannot tell whether psychological measures open the door to "real" give-and-take or are essentially meaningless in the absence of unilateral concessions such as unilateral renunciation of nuclear arms. The fact remains, however, that gestures that were almost purely psychological in nature led to an American-Soviet semi-détente lasting from June 1963 until the escalation of the war in Vietnam, in 1965.[46] Whether more of the same could have brought about more fundamental changes cannot be learned from this case.

ALTERNATIVE EXPLANATIONS

Even though the adoption of the measures advocated by the theory yielded the expected psychological results, there still remains the possibility of spuriousness; in other words, that the result was produced by factors other than those specified by the theory. The question then becomes, what other simultaneous processes could account for the détente? We shall examine the two alternative sources of the tension reduction most often cited and show why they do not invalidate the claims that the unilateral-initiatives approach deserves credit for the détente. It should be noted, however, that it always is possible to claim that still another

[45] *New York Times*, October 14, 1963, p. 1E.
[46] Max Frankel, "Vietnam Tension Wiping Out Gains in U.S.-Soviet Ties," *New York Times*, June 20, 1965. See also James Reston, *ibid.*, June 23, 1965.

factor was at work; there is no final test against spuriousness. But until it is shown that an alternative factor has actually caused a given effect, we are justified in holding to the statement that the theory has been strengthened by the Kennedy experiment. This is especially so because, as we shall see, we can trace directly the contribution of the unilateral initiatives to the détente.

The first alternative explanation is that of catharsis. According to this theory, the door was opened for a détente after the Cuban blockade discharged a large amount of frustration that Americans had accumulated over the Cold War years. Traditionally, Americans' foreign policy expectation is that periods of war will be short, and that wars will end with an American victory followed by the restoration of peace. In contrast, the Cold War required a continual state of mobilization and prolonged tensions without the prospect of victory. The resulting frustration was deepened by the widely held belief that the Communists were more successful than the West in Asia, Latin America, and Africa. Under the pressure of these frustrations, it is often suggested, efforts to reach accommodation with Russia became viewed as showing weakness, and a "tough" *verbal* position gained much popularity. The establishment of a Communist government in Cuba, Soviet successes in space, the fiasco of the 1961 Bay of Pigs invasion, and the positioning of Soviet missiles in Cuba in 1962 all further increased American frustration. While initially the 1962 blockade raised many fears, once it proved not to lead to war and to yield a Soviet retreat, it became the first American victory in a long time. While the blockade's successes were widely viewed as supporting the "tough" line, suggesting that power politics could be used in the nuclear age, the psychological effect was one of cathartic release; hence, it is said, the Cuban showdown increased the American public's willingness to accept arms control negotiations with the Soviet Union.

The other interpretation associates the initiation of the détente with the unfolding of a different psychological process—the effects of the increased visibility of the disintegration of the blocs. In 1962 Communist China attacked the Soviet Union publicly, criticizing Soviet involvement in Cuba as "adventurism" and its retreat as "defeatism." Russia, like America, continued its economic and military support to India when it came under Chinese attack in 1962. At about the same time, the American-French dispute forced itself on the public's attention.

Initially, the popular American press, apparently reflecting the opinion of the public at large, tended to ignore or regard as a "put-up job" the split in the East and to underplay the rift in the West. But the rifts finally gained recognition with the hostile rejection of Mao and of De Gaulle partially replacing that which was focused on the USSR. The Soviets now seemed "reasonable" and "responsible" compared to Communist China, for Russia appeared willing to share with us the concern over nuclear proliferation and dangers of war provoked by over-eager allies.

Some evidence to support the effect of this bifurcation of the bloc images in generating the détente can be seen in the fact that the newspapers, reporting Soviet-American negotiations, regularly reported the latest rounds in the conflict in the East and in the West in the same place. A typical *New York Times* Sunday review of the news of the week ran the following captions: "Conflict in East," "Russia vs. China," and "U. S. vs. France"; and last—"East vs. West."[47] Direct reporting of the relationship between changes in the intrabloc situation and those which were interbloc was also common. For example:

The answer seems to hinge on whether Premier Khrushchev really wants a test ban. One school of thought is that he does. The argument runs that Moscow's relations with Peking have reached the point virtually of open rupture. Consequently, Premier Khrushchev is thought to be willing to deal with the West, especially if one result of such dealings might be increased difficulty for Peking in acquiring nuclear capability.[48]

It is not implied that the only effect of the decline in the solidarity of the blocs was to bring the two superpowers closer to each other. In reality, the Soviet Union was occasionally reluctant to agree to American proposals so as not to lose points in its fight with China over control of the Communist movement in third countries. Similarly, the United States was not always eager to agree to Soviet initiatives for fear of displeasing West Germany and thus playing into the hands of France. But the very conscious-

---

[47] *Ibid.*, and *New York Times*, July 7, 1963, p. 1E.
[48] *Ibid.* See also August 14, 1963, p. 1E and August 25, 1963, p. 4.

ness of deep differences of interest within the blocs, even when preventing agreement between them, had the psychological effect of reducing interbloc tensions, at least in the short run. The recognition of the splits in the alliances undermined the prevailing simplistic image of the forces of light fighting the forces of darkness. Both camps seemed to have "gray guys," and the sharp differences between the camps appeared smaller. As a result, it is suggested, the ideological fervor of the international atmosphere declined, tension was reduced, and détente was enhanced.

Such a weakening of ideological fervor is important for the initiation of negotiations with give-and-take, because otherwise politicians find it hard to face their voters with the outcomes of the negotiations. As long as any give-and-take, even when completely symmetrical, tends to be viewed as a concession, if not outright appeasement or treason, ideological disarmament allows the public to see that some genuine bargaining is possible, and that certain kinds of accommodation serve both sides to the disadvantage of neither.

At the same time, bifurcation of the bloc images shifted the focus of the xenophobia. Regarding the Communist camp, Red China, with considerable disregard of its actual foreign policy, became the villain; in the West, the focus of American self-righteousness was now De Gaulle. These two replaced the previous preoccupation with Soviet Russia. Hate, it is suggested, was rechanneled rather than reduced. (Or, more technically, a new object was substituted rather than the drive being extinguished or significantly weakened.)

All these psychological processes might have been feeding into each other. In other words, catharsis, bifurcation of images, and unilateral initiatives might all have contributed to the détente as well as to each other. For instance, catharsis might have eased the initiation of a policy of unilateral initiatives, and in turn the resultant reduction of interbloc tensions accelerated bifurcation of the bloc images, which made less difficult the reduction of tensions through additional unilateral initiatives.

We still remain with the difficult question of the relative weight of the three processes in bringing about the détente. While it is impossible to answer this question with precision, it seems that while catharsis and bifurcation might have helped, they were not necessary prerequisites to the resultant situation; unilateral initiatives alone could have produced the effect. The best evidence for this is found in the examination of two other occasions in which a thaw was achieved—the 1959 Camp David spirit, and the 1955 Geneva spirit. These cannot be analyzed within the limits of this study, but they seem to show the validity of the assertion that unilateral initiatives can bring about a détente without the support of the two other psychological processes.

It also should be noted that the 1963–1964 thaw did not immediately follow the end of the Cuban crisis, in the sense that no détente existed between November 1962 and June 1963 (though this still would not rule out the role of catharsis as a preparatory condition). Similarly, while the bifurcation of the bloc images was accelerated in 1962, it existed before, and it was accelerated by the détente as much as it caused it. Above all, the effect can be most directly traced to the unilateral initiatives; it started with them, grew as they grew, and slowed down only as they decreased.

THE EFFECTS OF SABOTAGE

Sabotage is a traditional tool of foreign policy, going back at least to the Greek states. In the age of mass democracies, one of its forms is that of creating international pseudo-events to affect the psychological atmosphere in a direction counter to that of the prevailing policy. In some formulations of the psychological theory, this problem is disregarded, for nations are conceived as analogous to individuals, thus able to shift policies such as a man changes his mind.[49] In formulations which take into account the existence of vested interests in the continuation of inter-bloc tensions, both overt opposition to tension reduction and sabotage are expected.[50] The lesson of the U-2 flight which triggered the termination of the 1959 thaw was analyzed before the 1963–1964 détente took place. It showed the need to realize that

[49] Asked by a journalist if he believes that "nations act like people," Osgood is quoted to have answered, "I do." Herzog, *The War-Peace Establishment*, p. 158.

[50] Etzioni, *The Hard Way to Peace*, p. 104.

many governmental activities have a communicative value, and that if a government seeks to communicate that it has shifted to a new posture, measures are to be taken to ensure that no activities are continued that conflict with the new posture. This point should be emphasized, as some inconsistency is often present in the foreign policy of many countries. For example, U.S. policy on MLF (multilateral nuclear force) for a while attempted to assure the Russians that there would be no proliferation of arms while at the same time encouraging the West Germans to hope for some control of nuclear weapons. But when one engages in psychological campaigns, consistency has a high value because "out-of-character" steps largely undermine the effect of the campaign on recipients who, the psychological theory suggests, are suspicious to begin with.

The preceding discussion assumes that the U-2 flights were continued due to an oversight (neglecting to cancel this hostile activity as the change in posture came), or were a planned attempt to reap the benefits of continued violations of Soviet territories on one level, while trying to reduce tensions on another. If they were an act of sabotage, it would suggest that the ability of the American government to follow such a road to peace would require tightening of internal controls.[51]

The lesson of the U-2 incident is that it is necessary to anticipate both unwitting and deliberate sabotages and prepare a proper response. Some observers suggested that Premier Khrushchev was, for domestic reasons, looking for a way out of the 1959 détente and that the U-2 just provided an excuse. But the possibility that the Russian premier was really embarrassed before his fellow members of the powerful Presidium, some of whom objected to the détente, cannot be ruled out. This would suggest that he had not foreseen an act of sabotage and was not prepared to act in a way that would reduce its chilling effect on the thaw. Further, Eisenhower's insistence that he personally ordered the flight and his refusal to make apologetic comments, behavior which is common in such circumstances, made Khrushchev's accommodation in favor of continuation of the détente more difficult if he desired

---

[51] This has also been suggested as an explanation for the "tailgate" incident outside Berlin in October. See Jean E. Smith, "Berlin, The Erosion of a Principle," *The Reporter*, November 21, 1963, pp. 32–37.

to continue, and gave him a ready excuse if he were looking for one. While it is true that sooner or later he might have found one anyway, it must be noted that the fact that Khrushchev was not willing to terminate the Camp David atmosphere without such an excuse, suggests that he was not particularly anxious to terminate it at all. Moreover, had time been gained by not providing an excuse, the pro-détente motives and forces might have prevailed. Drawing on all this, we suggested in 1962 that unilateral initiatives be guarded against sabotage, and, if it did occur, the sabotage should be rapidly defused rather than allowed to damage the détente.[52]

We have already seen that domestic forces and politics as well as allies prevented the United States from giving a clear signal of a shift to a Strategy for Peace. Several leading Democratic Senators and important representatives of the military objected to the test-ban treaty; the wheat deal was made with much hesitation and debate; and various tension-provoking interpretations were given to the détente policy. Steps "out of character" and direct acts of sabotage also occurred, but their effect on the détente was much more limited than the U-2 flight, for they were treated more in accord with the theory.

An example of steps "out of character" is found in a note struck by President Kennedy himself, when, during a speech at West Berlin's City Hall on the 26th of June, he not only described himself as a Berliner and repeated the usual statements regarding America's commitment to Germany's defense but added, in tones familiar to the pre-détente period:

There are many people in the world who really don't understand —or say they don't—what is the great issue between the free world and the Communist world. Let them come to Berlin.

There are some who say that Communism is the wave of the future. Let them come to Berlin.

And there are some who say in Europe and elsewhere—"We can work with the Communists." Let them come to Berlin.

And there are even a few who say it's true that Communism is an evil system but it permits us to make economic progress. Let them come to Berlin.

Khrushchev, giving a counter speech a few days later in East

[52] Etzioni, *The Hard Way to Peace*, pp. 104–105.

Berlin on the occasion of Ulbricht's birthday, chose not to reciprocate in kind and thus the incident was soon forgotten.

The "tailgate clash" on the route to West Berlin between
October 10 and 12 came closer to being in conflict with the Kennedy experiment. Briefly, what happened was that the Americans
riding in a convoy to West Berlin refused to dismount for a head
count, and the Russians would not allow them to pass. The Russians claimed that they usually were granted the right to count the
passengers, but the West claimed that this was the case only if
more than thirty soldiers were involved, and there were fewer
this time. (When fewer, the Russians looked over the tailgate,
hence the name of the incident.) When the Russians countered
that there were more than thirty, the United States answered that
the balance were civilian drivers who did not "count"; the Russians claimed that they did. The Americans tried to break through;
the Russians blocked the route with armed carriers. Headlines
around the world projected for two days an image of two sides
standing "eyeball to eyeball," finger on the trigger, in a typical
Cold War test of will lacking in any détente-like spirit. Finally, the
crisis was resolved, and at noon on October 12 the convoy was
allowed to pass.

Although who was to blame for the incident is by no means
clear, this is of little importance to the analysis of its effect on
American-Russian amity. It clearly was a setback, as tensions
mounted rather than declined, and to most American newspaper
readers the fault lay completely with the Russians, and the sense-
lessness of the act amidst a détente heightened their suspicions of
Russia's good faith. The *New York Times* declared that "the pro-
vocative Soviet behavior on this matter has set back the cause of
the détente, reinforcing Western suspicion of Moscow."[53] The
Herald Tribune's editorial on October 12 was entitled, "The Soviet
Mask Slips." It said that

The wholly unjustifiable display of Soviet pettifogging at the en-
trance of Berlin, then, will be taken by the American government and
people as an indication that the protestations of Mr. Khrushchev and
of Mr. Gromyko concerning Russia's desire for more friendly relations with the U.S. are just a mask.

[53] *New York Times*, October 13, 1963, p. 8E.

But once the incident was settled, the explanation encouraged by Washington was that there was a "misunderstanding" about the rules and not a new Soviet pressure on the West or a shift in Russian policy away from détente.[54] Others attributed the incident to abuse of authority by low-ranking Soviet officers. One reliable American journal published an account that provided evidence suggesting that the issue was largely caused by an American officer.[55] A second interpretation, seeking to defuse the incident, was that Berlin was an "abnormal" situation, excluded from the general détente the Russians were seeking with the West.[56] While the incident left the détente marred, especially as it was about to be slowed down anyway, these interpretations, encouraged by Washington and London, succeeded in restricting its damage. This was in sharp contrast to the impact of the U-2 flight.

A second incident, which occurred on October 31, 1963, had almost exactly the same pattern. An American scholar, Frederick C. Barghoorn, was arrested in Moscow on espionage charges. President Kennedy stated that the charges were "unwarranted and unjustified" and that they "badly damaged" Soviet-American relations. Western newspapers again asked if Russia were shifting away from the conciliatory "Spirit of Moscow," and the conservative press sounded its "I told you so" horns. The professor was released, and it was almost immediately suggested that "the arrest might have been carried out by security officers . . . anxious to throw a monkey wrench into Premier Khrushchev's policy of 'co-existence' with the West."[57] Khrushchev chose not to identify with the arrest but let the professor go because of the "personal concern" of President Kennedy.[58] Later, although the incident had left its mark, its impact was, once again, defused. American sources further helped to dissipate the resultant tensions by suggesting that "they still found it conceivable that something had occurred to arouse their [the Russians'] suspicions about the professor."[59] In each case, then, a dissonant note was sounded but

---

[54] *New York Times*, October 20, 1963, p. 6E.
[55] *The Reporter*, November 21, 1963, p. 36.
[56] *New York Times*, October 20, 1963, p. 6E.
[57] *New York Times*, November 17, 1963, p. 1E.
[58] *Ibid.*
[59] *New York Times*, November 16, 1963, p. 3.

was soon softened and modified to protect the main theme. Thus, both the fragility of the détente and the mechanisms to safeguard it were demonstrated.

PSYCHOLOGICAL VERSUS "REAL" FACTORS

By far the most difficult question to answer is: What gains can be achieved from a détente in other than psychological terms? The 1959 détente was the shortest and yielded nothing; the 1955 détente was longer and brought about the neutralization of Austria, one of the very few instances since World War II in which territory held by the Red Army was released to a society with Western institutions. There is a widely held belief that the 1955 amity could have yielded much more, possibly an arrangement regarding Germany and Berlin, but this must remain a speculation. The 1963 détente led to a partial test ban and a ban on the orbiting of weapons of mass destruction, both steps of largely psychological value. Whether or not it will prepare the ground for additional steps is as yet unknown.

There remains a more general question which is of a different order from the analysis of any one period and its psychology: how important are psychological factors in affecting international behavior? Answers range from theories that imply that these factors are all-important to those which view the determinants of international relations to be exclusively "real" factors. The correct view probably lies somewhere between the extreme positions. Certainly factors other than psychology are relevant, and it can easily be demonstrated that psychological factors have "real" consequences. The question then is one of the *relative* importance of these factors.

While we are unable to provide a definitive answer to this question, several comments can be made. First, the advent of nationalism and mass armies has increased the importance of the role of psychological forces. Second, their consequences seem to have increased further with the introduction of nuclear deterrence forces because deterrence is itself a psychological concept and is therefore affected by such factors as credibility, fear, and misperception.

In addition, the present study suggests that psychological forces are most important when the sides wish to *initiate* a change in policy but seem not to be strong enough to *sustain* the change when it is not supported by other factors. When other processes agitate for change (for example, a new congruence in Soviet-American interests with regard to the spread of nuclear arms), a modification of psychological variables in the same direction makes the new policy easier to introduce. Moreover, the psychological forces might get somewhat "out of hand" and bring about some changes in policy above and beyond what other considerations seem to suggest. (For example, in 1958 the United States sought to *negotiate* a moratorium on nuclear testing but not to bring about its initiation. When Russia suddenly declared a moratorium unilaterally, the United States felt it had no choice but to reciprocate. This did not, however, lead to additional measures.) On the other hand, it seems that the psychological factors are basically well in hand; they cannot be used to bring about a policy that is a major departure from the policy other forces favor. Thus, in general, psychological factors have significant *auxiliary* and *limited* independent effects.

A study of the actors who are affected by psychological dimensions might in large part illuminate the reasons for the preceding statement. Most statements about "international tensions" are actually referring to states of mind of citizens rather than relations among nations or among the governing elites of the nations.[60] The kind and degree of influence of the citizenry on foreign policy is a complicated question that cannot be explored here. But it might be suggested that to a great extent *the effect of psychological factors on the international behavior of a state results from the impact of such factors on the citizens, who in turn influence foreign policy-making elites*. In the pre-nationalist stage, the mass of the citizens had little effect on foreign policy, and psychological factors were, therefore, relatively unimportant. In totalitarian societies, citizens have less influence on foreign policy than in

---

[60] For a study of psychological factors affecting international relations by effecting the interaction of national representatives, see Bryant Wedge and Cyril Muromcew, "Psychological Factors in Soviet Disarmament Negotiation," *Journal of Conflict Resolution*, vol. 9 (1965), pp. 18–37.

democratic ones; hence psychological factors are relatively less consequential there.

In democratic societies, public opinion is determined through a complicated process in which the public, its local leaders, the mass media, the national elites, and various social and economic processes are working on each other. In the short run, one of the most outstanding features is that the national leadership is confronted with the public opinion it helped to crystallize at earlier points in time. Once a context (or *gestalt*) is established, there is a demand for consistency. Seeming inconsistency activates various psychological processes, such as the feeling of betrayal. Thus, at various points American administrations have felt that they could ill-afford politically to support the admission of Communist China to the United Nations, because the American public was educated against it, and the Administration believed that no amount of short-run explanation could change public opinion to make the political costs low enough. In that sense, it seems correct to suggest that the Kennedy experiment was much more oriented toward the American people than the Russians or any international "tensions."[61] Its primary purpose, it seems, was not to directly affect international relations but to increase the range of options the Kennedy Administration could take up without running high political risks from a public steeped in Cold War psychology. Thus the policy of unilateral initiatives can be said to have worked, and the experiment to have been successful. A wider range of foreign policy was made politically possible.

[61] To the degree it was oriented to international tensions, those between the Soviet Union and Communist China were at least as much a target as United States-USSR relations.

Part Three

CONSENSUS FORMATION

The often-repeated dichotomy between harmony and conflict is not a very useful one, for all systems contain elements of both, no system can be based purely on one or the other, and some conflict is a foundation for whatever harmony exists. A more fruitful approach is to ask under what conditions various kinds and degrees of conflict emerge, or—the other side of the same question—under what conditions various kinds and degrees of conflict-limitation occur.

The specific process of change in scope and degree of conflict studied here is one of consensus formation among divergent units. In the first study (Chapter 5), there is much hostility among the units, and wide areas of conflict exist. Encapsulation refers to the process by which these conflicts are modified so that they become limited by a set of agreed-upon rules. The second study (Chapter 6) deals with relations among units that have more shared interests and are less hostile toward one another. Consensus on a wider range of issues is then possible even to the extent of initiation of supranational communities.

Many of the sociological analyses and much of the data accumulated in other fields are relevant to the problem at hand. Our endeavor, therefore, is more one of extrapolation of existing theory to a new field than of construction of a new theory. The effort is, however, different from most extrapolations in that the transferring of theorems is not only from one substantive field to another on the same analytical level but also involves a shift in the level of analysis.

The first kind of extrapolation occurs when, for instance, theorems are transferred from the study of one kind of complex organization to another. The process then becomes one of abstraction and respecification. For example, we find that the more workers view their foreman as a father-figure, the more likely they are to view the profit-making enterprises of the factory as being just. We generalize from this particular situation and state: the more low-ranking members of an organization identify with those higher in rank, the more likely they are to view the organizational goals as legitimate. We then respecify and apply this proposition to another organization—the army, for instance—and state that we expect that the more soldiers view their officers as father-figures, the more likely they are to view the war effort as a just one. This proposition, like others so derived, seems to have a greater likelihood of being found to be valid than those constructed in other ways.

In moving theorems from one level of abstraction to another, the same procedures are followed except that it becomes necessary to add (or subtract) one or more emergent properties. This involves a greater reformulation of the propositions and thus provides a potentially higher theoretical bonus, but the probability of mistaken extrapolation is also increased.

In constructing a theory of consensus formation, a sociologist will tend to transfer theorems about mechanisms that limit conflict *within* a society to the relations *among* societies. This is then justified on the grounds that the emerging system is becoming more like an existing one. But in this way the central analytic difficulties are deferred only one step: from analyzing the future-system to explaining the transition from a pre-societal to a societal stage. The search for a theoretical model of this transition cannot build on extrapolation from *intra*-unit processes. In the following discussion, we present some propositions regarding the ways in which a greater degree of consensus is achieved in *inter*-unit relations and interaction.

The first study raises the question of what attributes of ongoing conflicts (for example, between racial groups, labor and management, or nations) *in themselves* generate forces that lead toward the formation of rules that limit the conflicts, and advance the formation of organizational structures (or "machinery") that enforce these limitations. The second study approaches the same problem from a different perspective. Starting with the proposition that broad consensus is difficult to attain in highly heterogeneous units, it charts a sociological structure that might be able to overcome this dissensus factor and asks under what conditions such a structure might emerge.

CHAPTER 5

On Self-Encapsulating Conflicts

THE BASIC CONCEPT

Encapsulation refers to the process by which conflicts are modified in such a way that they become limited by rules (the "capsule"). The rules exclude some modes of conflict that were practiced earlier (or at least not ruled out), while they legitimize other modes. Conflicts that are "encapsulated" are not solved in the sense that the parties become pacified. But the use of arms, or some usages of arms, are effectively ruled out. Hence the special interest of this process to the student of international affairs. Most observers do not expect the Communist and the capitalist views to become reconciled and hence suggest that the political basis for disarmament is lacking. They see only two alternatives: two (or more) powers that are basically either hostile or friendly. Encapsulated conflicts point to a third kind of relationship. Here feelings of hostility, differences of belief or interests, and a mutually aggressive orientation might well continue, only the sides rule out some means and modes of conflict. In this sense encapsulation is less demanding than pacification, since it does not require that the conflict be resolved or extinguished but only that the range of its expression be curbed; hostile parties are more readily "encapsulated" than pacified.

At the same time encapsulation tends to provide a more lasting solution than does pacification. When pacified, the parties remain independent units that, after a period of time, might again find their differences of viewpoint or interest provoked, leading to new conflicts or renewal of the old one. Once encapsulated, the parties lose some of their independence by being tied and limited by the capsule that has evolved; it is this capsule that limits future conflicts, though the possibility of breaking a capsule—that is, undermining the rules and bonds formed—can by no means be ruled out.

Capsules differ considerably in their scope and hence in their strength. Some minimal rules govern even the most unrestrained conflicts, such as the use of the white flag, the avoidance of poison gas, and the treatment of prisoners of war. In the present context these minimal capsules are of little interest since by themselves they obviously do not provide a basis on which an international community capable of significantly curbing interbloc conflict can grow. The following discussion is concerned not with capsules strong enough to rule out certain kinds of wars (for example, all-out nuclear wars), the concern of strategists of limited war,[1] but with capsules that might be able to rule out war altogether— the disarmer's hope.[2]

The most difficult requirement the disarmer's proposition has to meet is for the process of encapsulation to be *self-propelling*. Once a third superior authority is assumed, the rabbit is put into the hat and all the fascination that remains is limited to the particular way it is going to be pulled out. Once a world government or a powerful United Nations police force is introduced, an authority exists which can impose rules on the contending parties and thus keep their conflicts limited to those expressions allowed by the particular capsule. But the unavoidable fact is that such universal superior authority is not available, and hence the analysis must turn to *conflicts that curb themselves,* and in which, *through the very process of conflict,* the participants work out a self-imposed limitation on the means and modes of strife.

[1] See Morton H. Halperin, *Limited War in the Nuclear Age* (New York: John Wiley & Sons, Inc., 1963).

[2] The relationship between the reduction of armed conflicts and the growth of global community is explored in part III of Etzioni, *The Hard Way to Peace* (New York: Collier Books, 1962).

HISTORICAL ANALOGUES

Combing history for a precedent, scanning the sociological treasures for an illustration, the patient student finds several *imperfect* cases: three are imperfect in that encapsulation was not fully self-propelled, and the fourth was not fully encapsulated. Still, they do provide some insight into the dynamics of self-encapsulation. It is not our purpose here to do justice to any of these cases but to describe their basic features for illustrative purposes.

Shortly after Uruguay gained its independence in 1830, the country was torn by civil strife between two gaucho armies, named after the color of their insignia—*Colorado* (red) and *Blanco* (white). The first president of Uruguay was Rivera, the head of the Colorado; his army-party held the upper hand for most of the years that followed. But the Colorado was never able to defeat the Blanco decisively; this kept the country in the torment of war that flared up sporadically over the next two generations, as the two neighboring powers of Argentina and Brazil were feeding the fire. Various limitations on warring were introduced over the years, such as limiting the arena (excepting the cities) and the means of war, under the pressure of business groups, professional groups, and ranchers, whose losses were heavy and who were tired of the continuous strife. At the turn of the century the government turned civilian and, pressed by a dissenting Colorado wing, allowed the Blanco to participate in the elections. These were initially quite fraudulent and led to a short but bloody clash between the sides in 1904. Though the election was won by the Colorado, it was followed by several reforms that allowed more genuine participation in political life for all sides and much advanced the shift of the conflict between various societal groups to political-constitutional channels.[3] Armed confrontation between the sides disappeared. Now the Colorado and the Blanco (renamed Nationals) are two parties which fight each other with ballots, leaflets, campaign promises, and the like, but not with

[3] For a brief discussion of Uruguayan constitutional developments, see Philip B. Taylor, Jr., *Government and Politics in Uruguay*, Tulane Studies in Political Science, vol. 7 (1960), pp. 11–22.

arms. Encapsulation first limited the warfare and now rules it out.[4]

Labor-management relations in most modern capitalist societies knew an earlier period of considerable violence which was gradually ruled out and is today practically excluded. In the United States, for instance, in the first half of the nineteenth century labor organizations were viewed as conspiracies and fought with all the instruments management could marshal, including the local police, militia, strikebreakers, and professional spies. The workers, in turn, did not refrain from resorting to dynamite and other means of sabotage nor from beating the strikebreakers. The Haymarket riot of 1886[5] and the Homestead strike of 1892[6] are probably the most often cited battlegrounds of American management and labor. At the end of the nineteenth century labor gradually won some rights of organization and collective bargaining, though the process of ruling out violence on both sides continued well into the 1930s.[7] While sporadic violence still erupts, by and large the power of the sides in a conflict is assessed without resort to force, and the means of conflict are largely limited to peaceful strikes, public relations campaigns, appeals to government agencies, and so on. The typical representative of the side is a lawyer, not a strong-arm man or an agitator. While there never was a state of all-out war between American labor and management, there is no question but that over the last two generations their means and modes of conflict have become much more institutionalized and constitutional, and violence as a means of conflict has largely been excluded.[8]

These two cases, different in practically every aspect, have one characteristic in common: both occurred within a national society, an already existing community, and hence could to some

[4] Russell H. Fitzgibbon, *Uruguay, Portrait of a Democracy* (New Brunswick, N.J.: Rutgers University Press, 1954).

[5] For details of this conflict, see Henry David, *The History of the Haymarket Affair,* rev. ed. (New York: Russell and Russell, Inc., 1958).

[6] Arthur G. Burgoyne, *Homestead* (Pittsburgh: Rawsthorne Engraving & Printing Co., 1893) provides a detailed contemporary account, written from the labor union point of view, of the Homestead strike.

[7] Robert Dubin, "Industrial Conflict and Social Welfare," *Journal of Conflict Resolution*, vol. 1 (1957), pp. 179–199.

[8] S. Perlman, *A History of Trade Unionism in the U.S.* (New York: The Macmillan Company, 1922).

degree draw on it; in both, the sides were under some pressure from the society to curb their conflicts. In this sense encapsulation was not self-propelling and provides a poor analogue for the study of intersocietal conflicts. Actually the limitation is not as severe as it might first seem, since initially labor was not a recognized part of society; the relations between the industrial and the working classes were referred to as those between "two nations." Part of the process of encapsulation was indeed the integration of labor into American society,[9] and the relationship between management and labor in the industrial context benefited from the evolution of the bond between them as classes in the realm of the national society. For instance, it made it possible for both sides to work out some of their differences by turning to the legislature, which was initially responsive only to one of them.

The same point can be made about Uruguay. It is not as if a full-fledged national society existed to begin with; actually it evolved in part out of the process of encapsulation and in the effort to contain the conflict between the Whites and the Reds. In this sense encapsulation here was more self-propelling than in the case of labor-management relations. In capitalist societies it was a question of admitting into the national community a new social group; in the case of Uruguay it was more a question of creating such a community.

The encapsulation case most often cited is that of the religious wars; this case seems more relevant since it was "international," transgressing the boundaries of any one society. The history of the religious wars, waged in Europe between the Catholics and Protestants in the sixteenth and seventeenth centuries, is highly complex.[10] Its main feature, though, is that somehow the contest was transformed from a war of armies to a competition between churches. Missionaries replaced knights, orders replaced the columns of warriors, and persuasion replaced violence. The

[9] Robert Franklin Hoxie, *Trade Unionism in the United States* (Des Moines, Iowa: Appleton-Century-Crofts, 1917; 2d ed., 1923). See especially chap. 3, "The Essence of Unionism and the Interpretation of Union Types," and chap. 7, "The Law in Relation to Labor."

[10] For a brief chronology of this encapsulation, see Norman Bentwich, *The Religious Foundations of Internationalism*, 2d ed. (New York: Bloch Publishing Co., 1959), chap. 5, "From the Reformation to the French Revolution," pp. 111–136.

transition, to be sure, was gradual. First, some areas were excepted; Richelieu, for instance, allowed the Huguenots to pursue their Protestant religion in their part of Catholic France. The rule of *cuius regio eius religio* also limited the extent of violence for a while, though a fuller limitation of the conflict followed only when tolerance evolved for both religions in each territory.

Encapsulation here was self-propelling, since there was hardly an encompassing society that could impose limitations on conflict between Catholic and Protestant states; initially the conflict was universal, in terms of the then relevant universe, and the limitations on it—whose evolutions (in particular the role of nationalism) have yet to be studied—must have grown largely out of the conflict itself. Still, even this analogue is less than completely satisfying, not only because it took many years of violence to tire the parties to the extent that they became ready for encapsulation, but also because their mutual tolerance seems to have grown only as secular conflicts, those of nationalism, replaced the religious ones. The parties were rearranged and war continued under different flags. In this sense, the European encapsulation did not advance enough to provide a helpful analogue.

AN ECONOMIC ANALOGUE

To close this long quest for a model, I find by far the most rewarding analogue in quite a different area; namely, in the avoidance of price wars in certain industries. To obviate the necessity of discussing a multitude of irrelevant details, a hypothetical case will have to suffice. Imagine two superfirms competing over the car market; one firm seeks to capture a larger and larger share of the market; the other firm is trying to hold on to its share. The competition is waged (let us assume, in order not to complicate matters unnecessarily) through changes in quality and in prices; that is, the expanding company attempts to cut into the market of the other one by offering automobiles of higher quality for lower prices. The defensive firm counters by matching the offers of the expanding firm. Both companies realize that an all-out price war might well be ruinous for both sides,[11] and the small price markdowns might easily lead one side or the other to offer larger ones, soon passing the point at which cars are sold above cost and thereby undermining the economic viability of both firms. Quality contests, in which each firm tries to excel over the other, are also expensive; but for reasons that are not completely clear, quality contests are much more self-limiting and much less likely to ruin the companies.[12]

For these reasons it is more "rational" all around to limit the interfirm competition to quality contests; indeed, years pass without a price war; the companies seem to have implicitly "agreed" not to resort to this devastating means of conflict. But any day a price war might erupt. The expansionist firm, set on gaining a larger share of the market, any day might turn to a price war if it finds that it is making no progress in the quality contest. The defensive firm, on the other hand, attempting to make the other firm accept a duopolistic sharing of the market, feels it must not allow even a small fraction of the market to shift to the other one; even a small encroachment would reward and thus encourage expansionist efforts. The defensive firm, it is hard to deny, might have to initiate a price war to counter encroachments on its share of the market. Both firms realize that by resorting to price war they might undermine their own viability, but both hope that the price war will be limited and that they will be able to use it to show their determined commitment to whatever policy they favor, be it expansionist or duopolistic. Theoretically, there are several ways out of this tense and potentially ruinous situation; in practice it seems the range is much more limited.

The solution advocated by the defensive firm is to formalize and legalize the existing allocation of the market; each firm will hold on to its part, and thus *both price* and *quality* contests, the conflict *in toto*, would be stopped once and for all. The expan-

[11] Ralph Cassady, Jr., *Price Warfare in Business Competition*, Occasional Paper no. 11, Bureau of Business & Economic Research, Michigan State University, 1963—esp. pp. 81–90, "Price Warfare & Armed Conflict: A Comparative Analysis."

[12] John G. Fuller, *The Gentlemen Conspirators* (New York: Grove Press, Inc., 1962), provides an example of an encapsulation whose machinery was quite formal but extra-legal—the electrical industry's price-fixing attempts.

sionist firm finds it difficult to accept this duopolistic solution; such freezing of markets provides no outlet for its ambition and it feels that some buyers, given a free choice, would prefer its product. Whether its ambitions are justified or its feelings valid does not matter; in either event it refuses to accept the duopolistic settlement and there is danger that the implicit curbs on the conflict will be eroded.

The tension thus generated—either firm might suddenly find that a price war has begun—has led several executives on both sides to consider an all-out price war to drive the other firm to bankruptcy; but this, the cooler heads on both sides point out, requires taking some rather forbidding risks, actually endangering the survival of both firms. Economics is not enough of a science, and the information about the resources of the other firm is not adequate, to provide any assurance about the outcome of such a showdown. In short, while this alternative is constantly considered, it has been avoided so far because it is believed to be too risky.

Still another approach, favored only by a few, is to form a monopoly by merging the two superfirms. But practically everybody realizes that the two firms could never agree who the president of the merged corporation should be, what it should produce, how to share the profits, and so forth. This solution may not be dangerous but it seems unfeasible.

Finally, the existing precarious "encapsulation" might be extended not by imposing new arrangements but by building an extension of existing relations between the two firms. This would involve making an explicit *agreement* to avoid price wars and setting up limited *machinery* to enforce the agreement, while allowing—within very broad limits—*free competition* through quality. The goal here would be to formalize an implicit accommodation toward which the firms have moved by themselves; to provide both sides with reliable assurances that there will be no regressions; to relieve the psychological strains and the economic cost of fear. Unlike the duopolistic approach, encapsulation does not rule out continuation of the competition: while some means of conflict (price wars) are ruled out, others (quality improvements) are legitimized.[13] *It should be emphasized that this conflict-*

---

[13] Cf. Lewis A. Coser, *The Functions of Social Conflict* (New York:

under-rules, or competition, is not far removed from the existing relationship between the firms, which was in effect limited to quality contests and avoidance of price wars but which involved no explicit agreement. The question is not whether the conflict is or is not imposing limits on itself, that is, encapsulating, but whether the capsule formed is to remain implicit or to be further strengthened by being made explicit.

Among the conditions under which the firms are likely to be willing to shift to explicit curbs on conflict are the following: both firms have to realize that (a) their chances of driving the other into bankruptcy (winning a total victory) are minimal; (b) unless explicitly and effectively ruled out, price wars may occur and would very probably be ruinous to both—that is, implicit encapsulation is too weak; (c) the expansionist firm has to accept the limited outlet for its ambition provided by competition in quality, on the assumption that trying to satisfy greater ambitions is too dangerous and that the only other alternative offered is a duopoly in which there would be no safe outlet at all; (d) the defensive firm has to be willing to forego its desire to frustrate completely the drive of the other firm, because it realizes that in the long run such an effort is unlikely to succeed, if only because buyers like to shift, and the other firm would probably not agree to pacification through a duopolistic division of the market. At the same time, the defensive firm has to feel able and *be* able to compete in quality, to feel that losses of buyers will be at worst limited, probably temporary, with some real possibility of regaining customers lost earlier. Thus competition will jeopardize the defensive firm's control of its present share of the market, but it will also open the door to potential gains.

AN INTERNATIONAL APPLICATION

The international analogues to the interfirm model are too obvious to need spelling out. The Western response to the Communist challenge is largely dominated by the sharp distinction be-

The Free Press of Glencoe, 1956), pp. 121–128, "Conflict Binds Antagonists."

tween parties in conflict and parties in peace. East and West are in conflict; resolution through the formation of a world government or all-out war is seen as either unfeasible or immoral, or both. The main Western approaches are "protracted conflict"[14] and a search for pacification. The first approach foresees no accommodation with the Communist system and hence prepares for many years of conflict. The other approach implies a hope of full resolution as the Communist system mellows. A third alternative—open competition in some spheres coupled with a prohibition of conflict in others, through effective international machinery—is not now being viewed as a realistic goal or as the direction in which East-West relations are actually shifting.

The fusion of containment and deterrence, policies that still form the essence of contemporary American strategy, reflects this conception. For the advocates of "protracted conflict" it means holding the line, buying time, though it is never quite clear for what this time is to be used. For the advocates of pacification, this strategy offers a solution reminiscent of the stalemate of the Anglo-French conflict over Africa in the 1890s. It suggests, in effect, a duopoly dividing the world into two spheres of influence along the containment line; each side is deterred from challenging the other's sphere by nuclear, conventional, and subconventional arms. If such an arrangement were acceptable to the other side, then both could live happily ever after in a state of peaceful co-existence.

Duopoly, in this as in other cases, is a stance favored by the challenged side which seeks to preserve its sphere of influence; it is one of the least attractive alternatives for the expansionist side, requiring it to give up its ambitions and its drive and settle for whatever it had gained before the agreement. The central question is whether there is any other approach that would be more attractive to the USSR and still be in line with the basic values and objectives of the West. The disarmer's answer is encapsulation of the interbloc conflict so as to allow full and open competition in unarmed capabilities and effectively to rule out armed competition.

There is an important psychological difference between duopoly

---

[14] For a further discussion of this concept, see Robert Strausz-Hupé, et al., *Protracted Conflict* (New York: Harper & Row, Publishers, 1959).

and encapsulation. Duopoly seeks to extinguish the expansionist drive by frustration: if the Soviets are confronted with an "unalterable counterforce at every point where they show signs of encroaching upon the interests of a peaceful and stable world,"[15] they will gain nothing, and sooner or later stop trying. Encapsulation, by contrast, draws upon both negative sanctions and positive rewards. Violations of the rules must be frustrated, but the use of "allowed" means of conflict is rewarded. This approach provides a legitimate outlet for ambition. In this sense encapsulation builds on sublimation, not on extinction.

This difference in psychological quality has some significance for the West, too. The combination of containment and deterrence is not only hindering the Communist efforts but also frustrating the West. Ever since Korea, this policy has faced domestic political difficulties because it offers no accommodation except protracted conflict or because the expected accommodation—peaceful coexistence—has not yet been achieved, half a generation after the policy was initiated. Our state of continuous half-mobilization is alien to democracies in general and to the American tradition in particular; the psychological pressure is toward either a rush strike or appeasement, though effective leadership has so far countered both. Encapsulation would allow an end to the psychological state of war and, in peaceful competition, provide an outlet for Western drives as well, since unarmed efforts would have no geographical limits. Trade with Poland, cultural exchange with Outer Mongolia, and so forth, might be forerunners of broader efforts.

Encapsulation requires drawing a sharp line between permissible and nonpermissible means, but *where* the line is to be drawn is a different question altogether. Theoretically it can be drawn between all-out and limited wars, nuclear and conventional wars, inner and outer space, and the like. There are considerations of political feasibility, inspection technology, and the assessment of the dangers of escalation of permissible into nonpermissible conflicts. Here we will explore the characteristics of an encapsulated conflict where the line falls between armed and unarmed means, where war is tabooed but competition in aid, trade, and ideas is

[15] George F. Kennan (X pseudonym), "Sources of Soviet Conduct," *Foreign Affairs*, vol. 25 (1947), pp. 566–582.

fully accepted. One may ask whether the East and the West do not already, in effect, rule out nuclear war and most other kinds, and focus their sparring on a space race and a development race, that is, unarmed competition.

In effect they do, but the analogue of the two rival firms highlights the difference between an implicit and unenforced limitation on conflict and an explicit and enforced one. The present interbloc accommodation is of the first type. Whatever limitations have been introduced are based on expedient and probably transient considerations. There is little in the present system to prevent either party from exploiting some major technological breakthrough (for example, in the field of anti-missile defense) by means of an all-out blow against the other. Secondly, since the existing limitations on the conflict are self-imposed and have never been explicitly negotiated and agreed upon, they are vague and ambiguous. Khrushchev, for instance, may not have anticipated the American reaction to his Cuban missiles; yet the United States saw them as a major violation of the status quo which it thought the USSR had gradually come to accept. Thus violations *might* be quite unintentional and still trigger the spiral of responses and counter-responses that would split open the capsule of implicit limitations.

Thirdly, since there is *no effective machinery for adjusting* the implicit curbs on conflict, the main way of seeking to reduce or extend their scope is to commit violations; these efforts are highly volatile and endanger the whole capsule. The lack of effective machinery also means that arbitration procedures are worked out each time on an *ad hoc* basis. Lastly, practically *no machinery is evolved for validation and enforcement* of the rules. The sides rely almost completely on their partisan reporting for validation and on the threat of retaliation for enforcement. Thus they always hover only one step away from unlimited conflict. (Among the exceptions are the mutual inspection privileges included in the Antarctica agreement and the 1963 treaty for partial cessation of nuclear tests.)[16]

[16] A third example of situations in which conflict seems to be anticipated and measures taken to decrease it is provided by Soviet-American space agreements. See Lincoln P. Bloomfield (ed.) *Outer Space* (New York; Columbia University, The American Assembly, 1962), esp. chap. 7, "The Prospects for Law and Order."

SUPPORTING FACTORS

There are two factors, one obvious and one less obvious, that exert pressure on both the United States and the USSR to move toward a higher international order, toward a more explicit and enforceable limitation of interbloc conflict. One lies in the technology of weapons, the other in the change in bloc solidarity.

When the basis of our current "duopolistic" strategy was formulated in 1946–1947 there were only four atomic devices in the world, while by 1964 the United States alone commanded more than 40,000 atomic and nuclear weapons. Their dangers have often been listed, including unintentional nuclear war growing out of mechanical accident, unauthorized behavior, miscalculation, escalation, technological breakthrough, and the spread of nuclear capabilities to other countries. These dangers weigh heavily on both the American and the Soviet leadership. In themselves they do not suffice to produce a movement toward a new international system, but they do constitute a background factor that keeps alive—if not active—an interest in ways of curbing the conflict.

Less often discussed in this context is the impact of the disarray of the two camps, which is still often viewed as transient. Actually it seems that neither the USSR nor the United States will reestablish in the foreseeable future the kind of superpower hegemony they enjoyed during the 1950s. The rising power and foreign-policy independence of France, of Communist China (which makes up with resolve for part of its lack of resources), of Britain to a degree, and soon of West Germany, make for changes in the basic international constellation, and these changes tend *to favor more effective and far-reaching encapsulation.* In the more nearly bipolar world of the 1950s the rules of the game could be left implicit and much reliance could be placed on the fact that the blocs were stalemating each other. As long as there were only two camps, the room for maneuvering was small and the moves highly predictable.

The rebellion of bloc-lieutenants opens the international arena to many new combinations. The Germans, French, and Chinese fear an American-Russian deal at their expense; the United States fears a German, or French, or German-French deal with Russia. France recognized Communist China; Britain was refused a hookup on the American-Soviet "hot line"; Canada and Britain broke the policy of economic isolation of Cuba; and so forth.

Both superpowers are now challenged by junior competitors and threatened by the prospect of nuclear anarchy. Unable to solve these problems on their own, they resort increasingly to the joint imposition of universal rules. The direct communication line between the White House and the Kremlin, completed in September 1963, is one measure. Its heralded function is to prevent accidental war, but it may also allow the United States or the USSR to dissociate itself from a provocation by one of its allies. Thus it warns the other powers to heed the big two and respect the order they establish—or else be left out on a limb. The limited ban on nuclear testing is another rule set by the big two for global adherence. If this trend continues, the order-by-blocs may be *in part* replaced by regulation through universal rules backed by the two superpowers (and smaller powers). American and Russian support of India against China, U.S. curbs on Cuban exiles, and Russian curbs on Castro agents in Latin America—all these fit the new mold.

AN OPTIMISTIC PROJECTION

If both sides should continue to seek joint or coordinated acts, and encapsulation continued to advance, to what areas might the attention of the superpowers turn next? The disarmer's way of putting the same question would be this: assuming an "optimistic scenario"—that is, under the best circumstances that can realistically be expected—in what ways might the presently limited encapsulation be extended? There seem to be three major areas: (a) the reduction of armed capacities, without which little credence can be given to conflict curbs in other areas; (b) expansion of unarmed capacities as these become, even more than before, the center of the global competition; and (c) strengthening the line that separates the unarmed conflicts from the armed ones, thus making unarmed competition less volatile.

The following discussion spells out some of these possibilities. It may seem very much like a trip into a never-never land unless the reader keeps in mind that it represents the optimistic limit of the range of possible developments and that measures which seem impossible one day are often implemented the next day.

REDUCTION OF ARMS

In the last decade and a half, both sides have tried to increase their strategic force by qualitative and quantitative improvements. Each side has responded to the achievements of the other by fresh efforts of its own. But as both sides acquire fully protected second-strike (retaliatory) forces, which will make any additional buildup unjustifiable, this upward arms spiral is expected to slow down and even halt.[17] American production of nuclear bombs and long-range bombers has slowed down already; the production of missiles is expected to be curtailed later on.[18] If the USSR does likewise, once having protected its strategic forces, the strategic arms race may for the first time find a plateau—especially if there is no major technological breakthrough.

An effective ban on deployment of weapons in outer space, which can be comparatively readily verified, would be a natural correlate; it would prevent the arms race from spilling over into a virtually limitless area.[19]

Many experts believe that some reduction of strategic forces could be initiated at this stage, to be verified without inspection—through intelligence, destruction of weapons at a neutral spot, and other devices.[20] Additional reductions would require considerable inspection of the member countries by outsiders and are, in my judgment, not to be expected in the near future. But reduced forces geared for retaliation would suffice to provide a much more congenial environment for encapsulation.

[17] Robert S. McNamara, Testimony before the House Armed Services Committee, January 30, 1963.

[18] *Ibid.*

[19] The present ban covers only weapons of "mass destruction," usually understood as nuclear. For additional measures needed, see chap. 7 of Etzioni, *The Moon-Doggle* (Garden City, N.Y.: Doubleday & Company, 1964).

[20] Institute for Defense Analysis, *Verification and Response in Disarmament Agreement* (Washington, D.C.: Woods Hole Summer Study, 1962).

The need to reduce conventional and subconventional forces (those used for subversion and counter-subversion) is usually underplayed, but it seems to me of the utmost importance. All the armed clashes in the last fifteen years involved conventional arms and took place in the large underdeveloped territory, or "third world," which has become the focus of the interbloc contest. It is here that the pattern for unarmed competition is molded, as both the United States and the USSR are sending aid, technical assistance, cultural missions, and the like to the same group of countries (for example, Indonesia, India, Egypt). Claims of superiority for their respective technologies, economies, methods of administration, industrialization, and so forth, can thus be tested according to the underdeveloped nations. This is the kind of competition that any fair-minded observer cannot help but bless. The problem is, though, that the limits of this unarmed contest are neither fixed nor guarded; it constantly threatens to spill over into limited armed confrontations, brush-fire wars, that both hinder encapsulation and threaten to escalate.

A step toward understanding between the two camps would be to treat the whole underdeveloped world as a big Austria out of which both sides would keep their armed forces, both overt and covert.[21] Such a multicontinental embargo on the shipment of forces and arms, if it could be effected, would have the following virtues: (a) it would avoid the dangers of escalation by keeping the superpowers out of local conflicts; (b) it would enhance encapsulation by providing a large arena in which the two blocs could compete peacefully to their heart's desire; (c) it would allow revolutionary forces in these countries to run their course without big-power intervention—in other words, the fate of governments would be decided by the people of those countries rather than by "big brothers." There is good reason to believe that this would encourage governments that are more development-oriented and responsive to their people than are the present ones; and this in turn is probably the best way to forward their commitment to freedom and social justice.

Under most circumstances, such an extension of the "Austrian"

[21] See Hans Kohn, "The Future of Austria," Foreign Policy Association's *Headline Series,* no. 112.

system to scores of countries will not be feasible. It is likely only if the dangers of unintentional war and nuclear anarchy are more fully recognized, if the rebellion of the bloc-lieutenants continues, and if the United States-USSR experience with limited agreements continues to be positive. Even under these favorable circumstances, certain safeguards will be required.

Such safeguards might include *remote deterrence forces* against armed intervention in the third area. As both sides withdrew their forces, as they did from Austria in 1955, they could be expected to hold these forces in high readiness outside the area to deter or counter any violation by the other side. Furthermore, some *machinery* would be necessary to investigate alleged violations of the embargo. The Communist bloc has often provided indigenous troops with arms, as was the case in Greece in 1946–1947 and in Indochina in 1953–1954, without initially arousing much public attention. On the other hand the Western press has often accused indigenous forces, such as the Moslem rebels in Lebanon in 1958, of receiving armed help from the Communist bloc when this was not the case. All this is hardly avoidable in the Cold War context but it could be highly detrimental to the "arms-out" agreement.

The task of validating the embargo rules might well turn out to be less forbidding than is generally expected. While it is almost impossible to prevent the actual flow of arms across borders, practically all secret shipments of arms in significant quantities have become known within weeks after they occurred, whether it was to Egypt, Cuba, Guatemala, or Palestine.

The presence of a *United Nations observer force* on the boundaries of the third area, ready to move to places where violations are reported or anticipated, could also assist in validating the embargo. Such a force would be equipped, not with weapons, but with inspection tools such as searchlights, infrared instruments, helicopters, and jeeps. The embargo agreement should entitle each side to ask for the deployment of this force without any right of veto. A refusal to admit the United Nations observer force to take positions on a border—say, between the USSR and Afghanistan —would in itself constitute sufficient evidence that the embargo had been violated, and would leave the other side free to take counter-measures. It is not implied that such an observer force would be completely reliable, but it would serve as an important addition to the remote deterrence forces and partisan sources of information (for example, intelligence reports).[22] All together—under the favorable conditions of our "optimistic scenario"—these measures might suffice.

UNARMED CAPACITIES

The willingness of the sides to limit their confrontation to an unarmed contest is determined only in part by their fears of an armed one; in part it is determined by their confidence in their nonmilitary capacities. From this view, by far the most encouraging sign for the disarmer is the secular trend, in both camps, to build up these capacities. The Soviets increased their foreign aid from $13 million in 1955 to $403 million in 1959; their number of technical assistants from 4500 in 1958 to 8400 by 1962;[23] their propaganda effort was also greatly expanded. At the same time, they reduced the ratio of foreign aid devoted to military assistance by two thirds and increased accordingly that devoted to economic aid. In a long struggle within the Communist parties of Malaya, Indonesia, India, Japan, the Philippines, and scores of other countries, the new Soviet line that favors progress through nonviolent means over those of terror and insurrection has won, according to Western observers.[24] Some observers are quick to add that this is merely a change of tactics, and that the Soviets believe that such constitutional means will serve their expansionist goals better than the violent ones. This is quite true, and for those who seek a full pacification of the interbloc conflict, such a change of tactics might seem of little value. But for encapsulation it is of much interest, since here the continuation of Soviet ambitions is fully expected and accepted, and the question of means used to forward these goals is all-important. No extinction of Soviet goals is hoped for, demanded, or necessary for this form of accommodation. If the

[22] A discussion of some of the problems facing such an observation force is included in Lincoln P. Bloomfield, *International Military Forces* (Boston: Little, Brown & Company, 1964).

[23] H. J. P. Arnold, *Aid for Developing Countries* (Chester Springs, Pa.: Dufo Editions, 1962), pp. 94–114.

[24] Bernard S. Morris, "Recent Shifts in Communist Strategy: India and Southeast Asia," in John H. Kautsky (ed.), *Political Change in Underdeveloped Countries* (New York: John Wiley and Sons, 1962).

Soviets are willing to limit their campaign to peaceful means, this satisfies the conditions under which encapsulation can progress. The Western stand in the limited conflict will then depend on its unarmed capacities.

The West seems increasingly ready to engage fully in such a contest; it has built up unarmed capacities over recent years. The ratio of economic over military foreign aid was greatly increased, the Peace Corps was added, technical assistance was extended, efficacy of information services was improved, association with anticolonial causes increased, and the Alliance for Progress was initiated. While there are many imperfections in most of these efforts, it must also be pointed out that the claims made about the efficacy of the opponent's efforts are often grossly exaggerated. There is little doubt that if the Western concern and effort in this area were intensified, it could fully compete in the unarmed area.

It is here that the mistaken zero-sum notion often comes to haunt the strategist.[25] Either East or West is likely to have the upper hand in the development race, it is said, and the loser will be under much pressure to broaden the means of conflict employed in an effort to restore his position. Thus it is felt that any limitation of the conflict will be temporary. This view overlooks the important consequence of the vagueness of the measuring rods of the development race. For the last fifteen years, each side claims to be doing better in developing countries in its sphere of influence; in Asia, for instance, both China and India have been watched for more than a decade as test cases for the Communist and the democratic ways of modernization, but no evidence of a "victory" is in sight. Who is doing better, India or China? [26]

Second, the nonaligned countries tend more and more to receive aid from both sides. They trade with both sides, invite their tech-

---

[25] A brief description of zero-sum strategies and their misapplication can be found in Anatol Rapoport, *Strategy and Conscience* (New York: Harper & Row, Publishers, 1964), pp. 40–47 and 105–124.

[26] For an exploration of some of the problems of comparing economic developments, see Bert F. Hoselitz, "Some Problems in the Quantitative Study of Industrialization," *Economic Development and Cultural Change*, vol. 9 (1961), pp. 537–549. The April 1961 issue of EDCC is devoted to the quantitative study of economic growth.

nical assistance, visit their capitals, without joining either bloc. Gains in the "sympathies" of these countries are transient, with Pakistan one day more inclined to the West, the next day flirting with Communist China; Egypt, Iraq, Guinea, and many other nonaligned countries "move" somewhat to the East and somewhat to the West, but the total stock of floating votes, which both blocs court, is not depleted. Gradually the two blocs may realize that neither will be victorious in this race, but both will benefit as the "have-not" countries' standard of living rises, as their prospects brighten, and as their stakes in world order are enhanced.

MACHINERY

The need for a more potent international machinery has often been spelled out. Its value in providing peaceful channels for settlement of differences of interest and viewpoint has often been indicated; its neutralizing role in conflict, its arbitrator function, its service as a neutral meeting ground, have all been told. Much less often discussed are the conditions under which this machinery is likely to evolve. This is a major subject in itself, but in the present context the following points stand out:

The international machinery—be it the UN, the International Court, or a new world disarmament agency—is most likely to evolve significantly if the major powers see it as enhancing their interests. The rebellion of the bloc-lieutenants and the threat of nuclear anarchy seem to involve such interests. In 1964, for the first time, the Soviets recognized a need for a supranational government as an element in disarmament, and the U.S. State Department initiated motions aimed at strengthening the UN.

The need to service the encapsulation process, for instance with an observer force, is another factor that makes the expansion of international machinery more determined by than determining interbloc relations.

In the short run, no major strengthening of international institutions can be expected; the veto in the Security Council is likely to continue and no effective UN police force is likely to be charged with global security. Yet such developments are not necessary for a significant extension of the encapsulation process, for a considerable broadening of interbloc accommodation. If events do follow our "optimistic scenario" of arms reductions, increased reliance on unarmed capacities, and some extension of the power and use of international institutions, a whole vista of new modes of accommodation and world order will open up—modes which can hardly be realistically assessed at this initial stage.

CHAPTER 6

Consensus Formation in Heterogeneous Systems

CONSENSUS AS A PROCESS

The political process is one in which groups of citizens who differ in belief and interest work out a shared policy. The larger the number of participants in a unit, the greater the differences of belief and interest among them, the more difficult such a consensus becomes, to form or keep.[1] This holds for students in social relations laboratories, for executives in industrial conferences, and for politicians in national government. Increasing the number of participants in a group may cause it to become so heterogeneous that one of two things will happen: either the ability of the group to form consensus breaks down or a new structure for the formation of consensus is built. In this structure, consensus is formed on two (or more) levels. On the first, participants are separated into subgroups according to the relative affinity of their beliefs and interests. Each of these subgroups forms consensus among its members and sends a representative to the second level. The second level, composed of representatives only, establishes consensus for the whole unit. This differentiation can be extended to more than two levels.

[1] Theoretically, one can increase the number of participants without increasing heterogeneity by adding new participants who are just like the old ones; this is the common justification for immigration policies, for example, that discriminate in favor of readily assimilable applicants for entry. In practice, I assume for the purpose of this discussion that heterogeneity increases with size. Note, though, that no one-to-one relationship is assumed. Actually, the marginal heterogeneity produced by increases in size probably declines.

Political systems differ in the way consensus formation is institutionalized. In some, the lower level is strictly informal, having no legal or organizational status, like the blocs in the United Nations. The well-known Russian proposal which is referred to as the "troika" system can be viewed as a suggestion to institutionalize a two-level structure in the UN. Three blocs would be recognized—a Communist, a Western, and a Neutral one. This would require each of the blocs to form consensus internally first, on a "lower" level.[2] In other systems, two or more levels are formally recognized. In the United States, for example, the state primaries serve as one level, national party conventions as another, and interaction between the parties and between the President and Congress (see below) as still another level.

In some systems, policies formulated on the top level, the most encompassing level, are brought before all the participants for final approval (for example, the initial nomination of Burma's U Thant to be acting Secretary General of the UN was approved, but hardly worked out, by the plenum of the General Assembly). In other systems, approval by the representatives of the subgroups is deemed satisfactory, as is the case in practically all bureaucratic structures.

ON THE NATIONAL LEVEL

All heterogeneous polities that effectively attain consensus have a multilevel consensus-formation structure. The major national political systems differ greatly, however, in their specific structures. In multiparty systems, as long as they work—a problem to which we will return—consensus is first formed in each faction; then the factions contained by each party reach a compromise (which all consensus formation involves). Interparty consensus is then worked out among representatives of the parties, *not* the factions. The general outline of the consensus is worked out during the negotiations over the formation of a coalition, which follows the elections; more specific consensus is worked out daily in the

[2] The obvious disadvantages of this system for the UN are irrelevant to the present analysis.

parliament, expressed in legislation and motions supported by votes of confidence.

In some instances, the minority party or parties (the opposition) may be left out of the process; quite often, though, they affect the policies formed, by reason of the fact that the coalition parties take their positions into account, in bipartisan policy (especially foreign policy), as well as through participation in other "governments." Often parties that are in opposition in the national government nevertheless participate in the national consensus-formation process by joining a coalition with government parties on the city or municipal level.[3] The effective operation of the multiparty system of consensus formation requires that the number of parties be limited, otherwise communication difficulties arise and the top level may become too heterogeneous for effective negotiations; it also requires that the parties be stable, at least to the degree that a consensus reached on the lower level will be maintained on higher levels. If members of parliament maintain only a limited loyalty to their party once the parliament is elected, party representatives cannot negotiate in the name of its factions, and we are back to the state of many participants on one level. The French parliaments of the Third and Fourth Republics were at various times confronted with this type of stalemate.[4]

In two-party countries, more consensus formation takes place on the lower levels than in multiparty countries, because only two positions can compete on the top level. So, for instance, there are only two presidential candidates for national elections, but often more than two for one party's nomination.

Totalitarian societies are not exempted from the need to form consensus, though they can rely to a greater degree on coercion and downward-produced consensus through the manipulation of the mass media, rituals, and so forth. The major upward consensus formation takes place within extra-political structures—first, in

[3] In Israel, many opposition parties share the leadership with the government leader, *Mapai* (Labor party), by joining the executive board of the Jewish Agency and the *Histadrut*, often referred to as the two other governments of Israel. On their functions and their effect on Israeli politics see my "Kulturkampf or Coalition: The Case of Israel," *Revue Française de Science Politique*, vol. 8 (1958), pp. 311–331.

[4] See Constantin Melnik and Nathan Leites, *The House Without Windows* (New York: Harper and Row, Publishers, 1958).

each major bureaucracy (for example, the military, the economic planning agency, the party) and then among the bureaucracies. One might even speak, with caution, about coalitions of some bureaucracies against others (for example, army and party against the secret police). In sum, while political systems differ in their consensus-formation structure, it is multilevel wherever it is effective.

IN INTERNATIONAL SYSTEMS

An examination of the international scene from this viewpoint shows, first, that the hypothesis that the formation of consensus within and among heterogeneous units requires differentiation, holds here too, though several additional variables have to be taken into account.

The United Nations is probably best characterized by lack of consensus because of the deep cleavages in interests and beliefs among many of its members. But when we review those infrequent decisions—limited in importance, to be sure—where an overall consensus was reached we see the same multilevel structure in operation. Representatives of various groups of nations "caucus" to work out their shared position; then, their unofficial spokesmen negotiate with those of the other caucuses or blocs, to work out a general compromise which in turn is brought, for discussion or approval by voting, to the UN floor.[5] Bloc decisions themselves are frequently reached in a two-level process of a similar sort. In this light one may wonder whether we did not exaggerate the monolithic nature of the Communist bloc. China seems to have "caucused" with Albanian, and evidently North Vietnamese and North Korean representatives also, before the Congress of Communist countries in Moscow, in October 1961.[6] Khrushchev is reported to have conferred with representatives of several, but not all, Communist countries during his boat trip to New York

[5] Private communication with UN officials, and participant-observation in a UNESCO Conference in Montreal, in 1959.

[6] Zbigniew K. Brzezinski, *Ideology and Power in Soviet Politics* (New York: Frederick A. Praeger, Inc., 1962), pp. 150ff.

in 1959. The 1961 conference of twenty-five unaligned nations in Belgrade is reported to have comprised three factions: neutral-neutrals, pro-Western neutrals, and pro-Communist neutrals. The African "bloc" seems to have at least two groupings, though their degree of cohesion is as yet hard to assess: that of the Casablanca group and that of the Brazzaville group.[7] Although the latter is reported to have taken a more moderate, pro-Western line on the Congo issue, the two groups frequently vote *en bloc* in the UN.[8]

While blocs in international organizations such as the UN, and in particular conferences such as the Belgrade Conference, are highly fluid, subgroupings of potential supranational communities seem to have a somewhat higher degree of permanency. Thus, the Benelux countries constitute such a subgrouping in the EEC, though by no means with regard to all or even most issues. Australia and New Zealand seem to constitute such a subgroup in the British Commonwealth of Nations. The EEC and the EFTA play such a part in the General Agreement on Tariffs and Trade (GATT).[9]

So far, the process of forming consensus in international systems seems to be quite similar to the national one. Moreover, further examination of international consensus formation suggests that, there too, a multilevel structure is more effective than direct representation of all participants on the same level, and points to the process by which such a multilevel structure tends to emerge. First, the lower level of consensus is attained by grouping a few states at a time; once the union of such groups solidifies, a more encompassing union—and a higher level of consensus—is produced. In the initial stages of the formation of this multilevel structure, there are seldom harmonious relations between two groups of nations (or unions). In fact, intense rivalry among them is more frequent. Such rivalry seems to help the integration

[7] Immanuel Wallerstein, "Background to Paga, I," *West Africa*, July 29, 1961, p. 819.

[8] See Thomas Hovet, Jr., *Bloc Politics in the United Nations* (Cambridge, Mass.: Center for International Studies, Harvard, 1960).

[9] The EEC is represented in certain GATT negotiations by the Economic Commission as one polity rather than six national polities. See U. W. Kitzinger, *The Challenge of the Common Market*, 3d ed. (Oxford: Basil Blackwell, 1962), p. 27.

of each group, preparing it for the next step, that is, the formation of higher level, more encompassing unions. Finally, to push an analogy further, if one group is seen as the thesis, the other as the anti-thesis, the emerging synthesis tends to include both unions. The original units are now *permanent* elements (though changed in character) of the union, acting as lower-level consensus-formation units; the new union is not built on the atomization of the groups, but on their inclusion as "individual" members. The development of several unions will illustrate this hypothesis about the dialectics of unification.

The history of Benelux is enlightening from this viewpoint. Any historical development is affected by many factors; the degree to which a multilevel consensus-formation structure is erected is, of course, just one of them. Still, it is noteworthy that after centuries of shared rule under dukes of Burgundy and kings of Spain, the Low Countries—integrated into two groups, the northern and the southern provinces—were not ready when they tried to form one republic (1795–1814), or a *United* Kingdom (1814–1830). The effort failed, among other reasons, because all provinces were thrown together. The two unions of provinces were not recognized in the new structure; efforts were made to form all consensus on one level. In 1830, the southern provinces rebelled, and formed Belgium. The ensuing war between the north (the Netherlands) and the south (Belgium) helped the integration of each, but did *not* hinder the eventual union of the two, in a structure that does recognize the distinctiveness of the two regions, that is, in Benelux. This analysis suggests that if Benelux should ever attain complete supranational integration, it would be functional to maintain some degree of local governmental structure in units that are the present Belgium and the Netherlands. The inclusion of small Luxembourg was also not simply a matter of adding a nation to an existing union; the way was prepared, as far back as 1921, by a customs union (BELU) with Belgium, which is maintained as a subunion of the present, larger union, just as Benelux itself is a viable part of the EEC.[10]

[10] See F. Gunther Eyck, *The Benelux Countries* (New York: D. Van Nostrand Company, Inc., 1959), part I. Martin O. Heisler, "Political Community and Its Formation in the Low Countries," unpublished Ph.D. dissertation, University of California at Los Angeles.

The thirteen colonies that formed the United States were more or less autonomous societal units, with internal consensus-formation mechanisms. These societal units were not abolished with the federation, but found expression in the states' governments. They still have an important influence on the federal government, both by carrying out some functions on the state level and through representation in the Senate. Moreover, groups of states—the South, East, Midwest, and West (sometimes smaller groupings like the New England States or the Southwest)———are still an important middle level of consensus formation informally recognized in Congress and in party conventions. The union here, as in Benelux, was advanced only after a war between the South and the North, which did *not* eliminate either the South or the North or the states as meaningful intermediary units in American politics. A similar analysis could be applied to the various Swiss cantons, and possibly even to their German and French-Italian groupings. Here too, civil wars, one as late as the suppression of rebellion of a Roman Catholic canton in 1847, preceded but did not prevent federation in 1848.[11] To return to the contemporary scene, the Organization of American States, which now has twenty members, may well be too large for effective, one-level unification; recent efforts to form common markets have been made between five Central American countries and seven South American ones. The possibility of forming a more encompassing union later is explicitly recognized.

It would be hasty, however, to conclude from the preceding discussion that the only or the best way to form a European community is to integrate the EEC and the EFTA—as they are—in some supersystem.[12] Before the validity of other approaches can be assessed, some additional factors that affect supranational unification need to be examined. First, there is the question of the degree of integration a union aims at and the scope desired.

[11] Charlotte Muret, "The Swiss Pattern for a Federal Europe," in E. M. Earle, ed., *Nationalism and Internationalism* (New York: Columbia University Press, 1950), pp. 261ff.

[12] Cf. Walter Lippmann, *Western Unity and the Common Market* (Boston: Little, Brown & Company, 1962), chap. 2.

DEGREE OF INTEGRATION, AND SCOPE

Political communities of nations differ from other international systems—such as alliances, blocs, international organizations—in having a "supranational" structure and not just an intergovernmental one. By definition they have one center of government that legitimately decrees and enforces decisions within its jurisdiction on matters that affect the member-nations and their citizens; this requires a higher degree of consensus than the intergovernmental structure of other international systems. Since the decisions of intergovernmental bodies are not binding, and collective international actions are under national control, consensus can often be worked out in an *ad hoc* manner, and on specific issues, even when general consensus is lacking. In short, supranationalism is a politically more integrated structure which requires correspondingly more consensus formation than typical intergovernmental organizations. This is, though, a question of degree, not a "yes" or "no" proposition. NATO, for instance, has a supranational SHAPE, the European Coal and Steel Community (ECSC) its High Authority, and the European Economic Community, the Economic Commission; but all of them also have superior intergovernmental bodies, the various Councils of Ministers. They are, thus, part supranational, part intergovernmental.[13] Since the Council of Ministers has both formal and realistic superiority, these European bodies should be regarded as predominantly intergovernmental.

We would expect that the smaller a union is, all other things equal, the more homogeneous it could be, and the more integrated and "supranational."[14] This is, in fact, the case since, while many international organizations include almost all the states there are, from five continents and from all blocs (for example, 117 members of the UN), most supranational communities have less than ten members and are comparatively homogeneous in their cultural, educational, economic, and political backgrounds. Hence, the

[13] This point is elaborated in my *Political Unification* (Holt, Rinehart and Winston, Inc., 1965), pp. 282 ff.
[14] See fn. 1, on the relationship between size and heterogeneity.

question as to whether the EEC and the EFTA should be merged, and if merged, whether they should be preserved as subunits, is in part dependent upon the degree of integration sought. A highly integrated union—a United States of Europe—is least likely to be formed by a large expansion of the membership of the EEC,[15] while a customs union—directed by an intergovernmental body—can readily accommodate a membership larger than that of the EEC and the EFTA combined. This conclusion, reached on the basis of studying the relationship between integration, heterogeneity and size, is reinforced by an examination of the relationship between integration and scope.

International systems differ in the number of societal sectors they pervade. Some, especially international organizations, are strictly monosectorial; they deal only with labor issues, or health issues, or postal services, or aviation; and as a rule only with some activities in these sectors, and not necessarily the most central ones. Other international organizations penetrate into two or more sectors (as, for instance, the Nordic Council which serves political, economic, educational, and cultural needs of the member-nations). The larger the sectorial scope of a union, the more consensus is required; and hence the fewer the number of nations (or more precisely, the smaller the degree of heterogeneity) it can tolerate, and the more it will need two (or more) structural levels of consensus formation. Thus, it is not surprising that the typical monosectorial unions have many members, while typical multisectorial unions have only from three to eight members: for instance, the Nordic Council has five members; the Eastern European Community (with two major organizations as tools, the Warsaw Treaty Organization and the Council for Mutual Economic Aid) has eight members; the *Conseil de l'Entente* has four and Benelux has three.

---

[15] The union of the United States, well "prepared" by 1789, took a hundred years and a civil war before it solidified, and yet was one of a highly homogeneous group: ". . . Providence has been pleased to give this one connected country to one united people—a people descended from the same ancestors, speaking the same language, professing the same religion, attached to the same principles of government, very similar in their manners and customs." John Jay, *The Federalist*, no. 2, cited by Gerard J. Mangone, *The Idea and Practice of World Government* (New York: Columbia University Press, 1951), p. 26, fn. 10.

Even more important than the number of sectors encompassed is the nature of any particular sector to be integrated, in terms of its articulation with other sectors of the same society. Several authorities in the study of supranationalism have pointed out that integration in one sector tends to spill over into other sectors, that is, tends to trigger integration in them as well. Haas's study of the ECSC, for instance, shows how it spilled over into Euratom and the EEC.[16] He has also suggested that various societal sectors differ in their spill-over function.[17] On the basis of various sociological considerations that need not be elaborated here, I would order international organizations in various sectors with respect to their spill-over tendencies—from low to high—as follows: (a) organizations that deal with services, such as postal services, allocation of radio frequencies, police cooperation, and so forth; (b) organizations dealing with labor, health, and cultural exchange, that is, services to which "human values" are attached; (c) tariff agreements and military organizations; (d) economic unions or common markets.

The spill-over phenomenon points to the fact that societal sectors differ in the degree to which they are interrelated. Integrating some of them triggers unification tendencies in many other sectors, while integrating some other sectors has comparatively small repercussions. The military sector, for instance, is highly segregated and autonomous, unless industrial mobilization is involved. Military units of two nations can be integrated, their war plans coordinated, their navies can participate in combined maneuvers, military information can be extensively exchanged, and so forth, without this having much effect on other societal sectors. Only when integration reaches the higher level of policy-making is there a considerable spill-over into the political sector, and this because integration here requires some governmental integration, for example, of defense departments. Similarly, standardization of weapons and other equipment often has some repercussion on the economic sector. Economic integration, on the other hand, affects all societal groups—consumers, producers,

[16] Ernst B. Haas, *The Uniting of Europe* (Stanford, Cal.: Stanford University Press, 1958).

[17] Ernst B. Haas, "International Integration," in *International Organization*, vol. 15 (1961), pp. 366–392.

management, labor, farmers, small business—and therefore tends to have extensive political repercussions. In contrast, tariff agreements, especially to the degree that they cover only some goods and concern only reduction but not abolition of tariffs, affect only some exporters and importers and a limited number of related industries. It is only as such unions become so broadly encompassing as to tend to affect the flow of capital, monetary policy, levels of employment, and so forth, in the countries involved, that they spill over into economic unions; that is, that they trigger integration of many other spheres.

In cases where the unification of a high spill-over sector has occurred and unification of other related sectors is blocked, an unbalanced state is created which generates pressures to "solve" the imbalance, either by removing the blocks or by reducing the degree of unification in the sector in which it was initiated. For instance, if furnishing nuclear weapons to NATO would require NATO to create a joint political authority to command their use (there would hardly be time to consult fifteen governments if NATO is attacked nuclearly, and contingent decisions are unsatisfactory), and if for some reason the fifteen nations are not "ready" for the required political integration, these would be two factors working against the acceptance of such weapons by NATO. The prospect that spill-over from the military into the political sector is blocked would work against military integration. (Integration, so to speak, proceeds in steps. There are several plateaus on which one can rest, but one cannot stand on two steps simultaneously; one has either to progress to more encompassing unification or retreat to a narrower one.)

Last, but not least, is the question of hegemony in the EEC. International communities seem to function best when one nation has clear hegemony;[18] sometimes, two countries can share the

[18] Cf., for instance, the period of hegemony in the British, Hapsburg, and German empires to the periods of dual or multi-leadership. Compare the Communist bloc in the days when the Soviet Union had a clear hegemony to the later period of the Soviet-Chinese rift. See T. M. Mills, "Power Relations in Three Person Groups," *American Sociological Review,* vol. 18 (1953), pp. 351–357; Georg Simmel, "The Number of Members as Determining the Sociological Form of the Group," *American Journal of Sociology*, vol. 8 (1902), pp. 45–46.

leadership, especially when there is a third outside force against which they unite. This was the situation in the EEC as long as France and West Germany shared the leadership. Systems with three leaders hardly ever stabilize.[19] There are too many latent and tempting benefits to be derived from the collusion or coalition of two against the third partner. On all these counts, Britain's entry into the EEC would make completion of the spill-over from the economic to the political area unlikely. And this may mean that the EEC will not even remain an economic union, but instead will more likely regress to the level of a tariff agreement. This point requires some elaboration.

International unions of this type seem to have two stable stages: *low* integration with little or no spill-over, and *high* integration, where unification initiated in one sector spills over to many others, especially the political. Unions that try to maintain a medium-level integration—for example, economic only, or economic with a minimum of political integration—are unstable, not because they are likely to disintegrate but because their capacity to form consensus is out of balance with the need for it: they are likely to become more integrated or regress to a lower level of integration. The chances, in case Britain joins the EEC, favor regression rather than progression.

If Britain and other EFTA members were to join the EEC as individual countries, not *en bloc*, it would make high integration of the EEC less, not more, likely, for it produces a merger rather than a synthesis on a higher level. One might therefore be inclined to favor the formation of a supersystem, to include both the EFTA and the EEC as subunits. But this will not do because the units of an effective union, one that can maintain an adequate level of consensus, have to be fairly cohesive, stable units. One cannot build a second floor structure of consensus formation unless the first one has a firm foundation. While the EEC is already quite cohesive, and becoming more so, the EFTA is not. EFTA was formed, not out of any genuine commitment to a union, but to countervail the EEC; it was viewed as a temporary

---

[19] See Miriam Camps, *Division in Europe,* Policy Memorandum no. 21, Center of International Studies (Princeton, N.J.: Princeton University Press, 1960).

union, to be used to bargain with the EEC, hardly a morale-building feature. Austria and Switzerland, for example, trade more with EEC countries than with EFTA countries. In addition, the EFTA membership is highly heterogeneous: it includes NATO and non-NATO members; democracies and Portugal; Protestant countries and Austria.

The preceding discussion suggests that western Europe includes too many countries, is too heterogeneous, to form one union. It follows that two or more unions are needed to form the units of a larger system. But it does not follow that the unification of any specific group of countries would be more conducive to European integration than any other. One unification course is the expansion of the EEC to include a few more countries (though not all the members of the EFTA), such as some that are contiguous to the EEC and less competitive for its leadership than Britain. Austria and Switzerland are natural candidates. The fact that they are not NATO countries, and in the past have taken a neutral position in the interbloc strife, is not necessarily a barrier to their inclusion, probably first as associate members and later as full members, to be included also in the political union. The neutrality of these nations is quite pro-Western, and both France (since De Gaulle) and West Germany move in the direction of a somewhat more "independent" foreign policy. (It is hard to see how the USSR could stop a gradual integration of Austria into the EEC.)

Another European union, the Scandinavian community, forms a core for a larger union. It has already grown from three to five members, adding Iceland and Finland to Sweden, Norway, and Denmark. Once European trade problems are solved in a large framework, as discussed below, Britain might find this union— which is democratic, Protestant and welfare-oriented—more appealing for political unification than the continental one. Portugal and Spain have been reported to have considered an Iberian union of their own.[20] Once the major requirements of small size and cohesion are satisfied, other possible combinations might emerge; the major question that remains is the type of supersystem to which these unions can belong.

---

[20] *Christian Science Monitor*, October 28, 1957, p. 6.

KINDS OF SUPERSYSTEMS

How encompassing could such a supersystem be, in terms of the number of unions to be included? What could be the functions of the supersystem, above and beyond those of the member unions? The major alternatives discussed seem to be a European supersystem or an Atlantic one, the latter to include the United States and Canada in addition to the European countries (including either all Western Europe or only NATO members).[21]

The following analysis suggests that a European supersystem[22] will be more integrated and stable than an Atlantic one, as long as it will itself be a part of a third-level organization. The main reason for this is that the United States, as the leading Western power, has many commitments and functions in other international communities besides the European ones, especially in Latin America, but also in the Far East, Southeast Asia, the Middle East, and to an increasing degree in Africa. Strong integration of the United States in a European union would impose sharp strains on these other American ties.

The optimal participation for the United States is on the third level of consensus formation, a structural level where supersystems —of several European unions, of several African ones, and of several Latin American ones, and so forth—are integrated in a single super-supersystem, already vaguely recognized as the "Free World." A three-level structure may perhaps seem too complicated to be attained; or if attained, to function effectively. It should therefore be pointed out that three-level structures are quite common. Most national governments and practically all large corporate enterprises have at least a three-level structure, and many of them are quite effective. Actually, the evolution of

[21] Such a union has been advocated by Henry A. Kissinger, *The Necessity for Choice* (New York: Doubleday & Company, Inc., 1960), pp. 165–168. See also Joseph Kraft, *The Grand Design* (New York: Harper & Row, Publishers, 1962). Some of the problems involved in its formation have been pointed out by Karl W. Deutsch *et al.*, *Political Community and the North Atlantic Area* (Princeton, N.J.: Princeton University Press, 1957).

[22] Not to be confused with a merger of nations as "individuals" in a European union, such as "revised" OEEC.

a third-level structure would not preclude active participation in the development of a fourth level, that of the United Nations.

The main problem is not the number of levels but the distribution of functions, powers, and political loyalties among the various levels. The formal, legal, and institutional difference between unions whose members are nations is that representation in supersystems is in the hands of those who speak in the name of the unions (for example, the EEC), either in addition to or instead of national representatives. For the division of functions, we can consider two major possibilities: one is that the supersystems will be a replica of member-unions on a more encompassing level. Such a supersystem is approximated (in limited spheres to be sure) in the relations between the EEC and the EFTA in the OEEC and in GATT (General Agreement on Tariffs and Trade). Each group, for instance, introduced some internal reductions of tariffs, then met in the wider arena of GATT to consider mutual tariff cuts—as well as small cuts for "third" countries, not members of either union. According to this plan the control of one specific function, in this case setting tariff rates, is divided between two levels beyond the national one: that of the unions and that of the supersystem.

The second way to integrate unions into supersystems is to introduce a functional division of labor among the levels instead of a differentiation of authority. One such arrangement might take the form of leaving to the small, cohesive unions the economic and political functions; to the supersystems, the role of military integration; and to the third-level system (or bloc), the coordination of foreign policy, monetary policy (through a revised International Monetary Fund, for example), and tariff agreements.[23] This might also be the best level on which to coordinate aid to underdeveloped countries.

This specific division only illustrates the nature of interlevel division of functions; of course other arrangements can be worked out. It should, though, be emphasized that the division outlined above takes into account the need to reserve to smaller, lower-level units those functions that require a high degree of consensus

[23] See Robert Triffon, *Gold and the Dollar Crisis* (New Haven, Conn.: Yale University Press, 1961), chap. 4, and Alastair Buchan, *NATO in the 1960's* (London: Wiedenfeld & Nicolson, 1959), chap. 4.

formation and hence of relatively strong supranationalism. The actual structure of the West approaches such a division with the smaller economic-political EEC and Nordic Council, the larger NATO, and the still more encompassing GATT, IMF (International Monetary Fund), and OECD. The third-level system is still highly informal, and centered around trips of premiers to Washington, foreign tours of American representatives, and regional meetings—but no Free World ministerial conferences.

Which of the two types of interlevel division is optimal has yet to be determined. It seems that they differ in effectiveness with regard to different goals: functional division of labor seems better for short-run stability, and an interlevel division of control over each function seems better for long-run integration of second- and third-level supersystems. This latter seems to be the case because here high spill-over functions are in part carried out by supersystems, and because the units which carry out high spill-over functions command more political loyalty than those which do not.

The long-run trend toward integration seems to be for functions, authority, and loyalties to be transferred from smaller units to larger ones; from states to federations; from federations to supranational unions; and from these to supersystems.[24] This transfer may progress without major upsets because a variety of processes tend to reduce the heterogeneity of the member-units— through industrialization, the spread of education, democratization, and the unification process—in lower-level units. Hence the transfer of additional powers of decision to higher levels—those encompassing more members—need not undermine stabilization as long as the pace of upgrading function or authority does not overtake that of decreasing heterogeneity. We close with the speculative, though not unimaginable, possibility that eventually, in this way, the highest supersystem, that of a global society, might develop.

[24] Harold Guetzkow, *Multiple Loyalties* (Princeton, N.J.: Center for Research on World Political Institutions, Princeton University, 1955).

Part Four

CASE STUDIES OF SOCIAL CHANGE

When studying social change, both changes in the system and changes of it are to be taken into consideration. The first of the three case studies included in this part deals with change in the system. Government coalitions in Israel are analyzed, and it is shown that one party, *Mapai,* was preeminent and highly institutionalized. Changes in public opinion, to the extent that they expressed themselves politically, were responded to by commensurate changes in the partners with which Mapai chose to form a coalition, but not by changes in the pivotal position of Mapai itself.

This study was first published in 1958; however, in the eight years that followed, the validity of the analysis was not weakened but strengthened. Subsequent elections* were followed by changes in coalition partners, but Mapai continued to hold the key ministries and provide the same central power position. Thus, although changes have occurred within the system, the system itself might appear to be relatively static.

The second study, however, shows that at the same time the system was changing to alter some of the very bases on which Mapai's unique position rests. As political life becomes less ideological, a coalition of the left and the right against Mapai in the center becomes more feasible; as party hold and influence upon its members decline, the institutionalized roots of Mapai's power weaken.

Relating the findings of the two studies suggests that there may well be a point at which changes *of* the system might enable change

* See table 7.1, chap. 7. The first three elections took place before the study was originally published; the fourth and fifth, since then. The results of the sixth Knesset elections, which took place November 2, 1965, further support our thesis. Following are the number of seats won by each party: Marach (Mapai and Ahdut Ha'avoda), 45 seats; Gahal (Herut and General Zionists), 26; National Religious, 11; Agudat Israel, 4; Agudat Israel Workers, 2; Rafi, 10; Mapam, 8; Independent Liberal, 5; Arabs, 4; New Communists, 3; Israel Communists, 1; Haolam Hazeh, 1.

within it; for example, as the Israeli social structure continues to alter, Mapai might be voted out of office. These two studies thus illustrate the value of projecting the two kinds of change on each other and the danger of conducting studies of changes in the system without some exploration of the stability and change of the system itself.

While our treatment of changes in Israel focuses on the sociopolitical system, concomitant changes in value-systems are also charted. The decline of pioneering values with the rise of interest in consumption and the decrease in the intensity of ideological commitments are two examples. The important consequences of these value-changes on sociopolitical development are apparent; the closing chapter of this volume focuses directly on this subject. The three leading American Jewish "congregations"—Orthodox, Conservative, and Reform—differ both in their value-systems and in their organizational structures. Moreover, both have changed within all three groups over the years. This provides an opportunity for an exploratory comparative study of the dynamic relationship between values and structures. No assumption of value primacy or organizational primacy seems justified, for both sets of factors affect each other.

CHAPTER 7

Change in the System:
Alternative Ways to Democracy—
The Example of Israel

Each generation seems to work out its own definition of democracy. Since the totalitarian states have imitated many of the more external signs of democracy such as elections and party systems, an effort has been made to establish a definition which will clearly distinguish totalitarian from democratic regimes. There is a strong tendency to call a state democratic if the governmental power can be transferred from one party to another in a regularized way; that is, peacefully and in accordance with the rules of the constitution.[1] The party in office must not use its power to block the return of the other party or parties. Any attempt to do so is a violation of the rules of the game and is in itself an argument for a change of administration. In short, it is to the system and not to a leader or a party that the supreme loyalty of the voters is directed.

The frequent alternation of parties, it is further argued, keeps the government in harmony with the shifting distribution of power in society. Social changes quickly have their influence on the politi-

[1] For some relevant discussions, see Joseph A. Schumpeter, *Capitalism, Socialism and Democracy* (New York: Harper & Row, Publ., 1950); S. M. Lipset, M. A. Trow and J. S. Coleman, *Union Democracy* (New York: The Free Press of Glencoe, 1956); Carl J. Friedrich, *Constitutional Government and Democracy* (New York: Blaisdell Publishing Company, 1950); H. H. Gerth and C. Wright Mills, *From Max Weber: Essays in Sociology* (New York: Oxford University Press, 1946), pp. 225–226, 242.

cal situation and on the policies that are pursued. The equilibrium of the political system is maintained.[2]

It is obvious that this understanding of democracy draws heavily on Anglo-Saxon experience with a two-party system and the rule of law. But is the Anglo-Saxon form the only possible form of democracy? A priori this would hardly seem likely. It is the purpose of this article to describe what may be regarded as an alternative form, and to try to explain some of the political, economic, and social conditions in which it appears and is maintained.

We shall use the government of Israel as our example of a political system which is democratic and yet different from the Anglo-Saxon model.[3] Among the basic features of the Israeli government are a multiple party system and coalition ministries in which one center party (Mapai) is always present and always stronger than the other parties. To leave this party out of the government is simply not a part of the accepted procedures of the system. The party is one of the political institutions of the country and is identified with the state in the minds of many voters. In fact, too, because of its long term of office it has permeated the political, administrative, economic, and other institutions of Israel. Yet that country is democratic, for shifts in public opinion and in the distribution of social power lead to changes in governmental policy, and a congruence between the direction of the state and the structure of society is maintained.

Having analyzed the Israeli system in the main body of this chapter, we devote some concluding paragraphs to a comparative note. Its purpose is to relate this analysis to that of some other political systems that are also democratic but different from the Anglo-Saxon model.

[2] See Talcott Parsons, " 'Voting' and the Equilibrium of the American Political System," in Eugene Burdick and Arthur J. Brodbeck (eds.), *American Voting Behavior* (New York: The Free Press of Glencoe, 1959), pp. 80–120.

[3] For a general discussion of the Israeli political system, see Oscar Kraines, *Government and Politics in Israel* (Boston: Houghton Mifflin Company, 1961); on the Israeli parliament, see Benjamin Akzin, "The Knesset," *International Social Science Journal*, vol. 13 (1961), pp. 567–582.

MAPAI: A CASE OF AN INSTITUTIONALIZED PARTY

MAPAI—A DOMINANT CENTER PARTY

An analysis of Mapai (Labor party) is the key to an understanding of the Israeli political system. Mapai gained more votes in all three elections to the *Knesset* (parliament) than any other party. Actually it obtained more seats than the next three parties combined. (See Table 7.1.)

Mapai has been the major party in all eight Israeli governments during the ten-year period following the establishment of the state of Israel. Usually it has held nine out of sixteen portfolios in the various coalitions, always including the key ones of prime minister, defense, foreign affairs, police, treasury, and education, leaving to other parties the post office, welfare, justice, agriculture, interior[4] and other secondary ministries. Thus Mapai has been the dominating political force in the Israeli government.[5]

Mapai's control over the political life of the country goes far beyond a strong control of the government. Israel differs from other societies by having three major national political organizations, each with a "government" of its own. In addition to the regular government the Jewish Agency and the General Federation of Labor (*Histadrut*) have important political functions. The former is a major agency which recruits financial aid for Israel from Jews in the Diaspora and organizes migration to, and settlement in, Israel. The scope of its activities is well illustrated by the size of its budget, which was 211.5 million Israeli *lirot* (about $122 million) for 1958–1959, compared with the budget of the Israeli government, which amounted to 969 million Israeli *lirot* in 1957–1958.

The political significance of the Jewish Agency will be clarified

[4] The Interior Ministry has limited political significance in Israel because it has no control over the police force (which is under the control of a separate ministry), because its budget—like the budget of all ministries—is under scrutiny of the Treasury, and because the local municipalities have a strong tradition of political independence.

[5] B. Akzin, "The Role of Parties in Israeli Democracy," *Journal of Politics,* vol. 17 (1955), pp. 507–545.

Table 7.1 KNESSET ELECTION RESULTS

Party	First Jan. 21, 1949 — Seats	%	Second July 30, 1951 — Seats	%	Third Aug. 26, 1955 — Seats	%	Fourth* Nov. 3, 1959 — Seats	%	Fifth* Aug. 15, 1961 — Seats	%
Mapai	46	35.7	45	37.3	40	32.2	47	38.2	42	34.7
Herut	14	11.5	8	6.6	15	12.6	17	13.6	17	13.7
Liberals[1]	7 5	5.2 4.1	23 4	18.9 3.2	13 5	10.2 4.4	8 6	6.1 4.6	17	13.6
National Religious	} 16	12.2[2]	4	3.2	5	4.4	6	4.6	12	9.8
Agudat Israel	} (16)		} 5	3.6[3]	} 6	4.7[3]	} 6	4.7[3]	4	3.7
Poalei Agudat Israel	} (16)		}		}		}		2	1.9
Mapam	} 19	14.7[4]	} 15	12.5[4]	9	7.3	9	7.2	9	7.6
Achdut Ha'avoda	} (19)		} (15)		10	8.2	7	6.0	8	6.5
Communists	4	3.5	5	4.0	6	4.5	3	2.8	5	4.1
Arabs (associated with Mapai)	2	3.0	5	4.7	5	4.9	5	3.5	4	3.5
Others	7[5]	10.1		0.7		1.9		3.4		0.7

* See page 154.

[1] Figures given for the first four Knessets refer respectively to the General Zionists and the Progressives, who merged in 1961 to form the Liberal Party.

[2] In 1949 these three parties submitted a joint list, the United Religious Front.

[3] In 1951, 1955 and 1959, these two parties submitted a joint list, the Torah Religious Front.

[4] In 1949 and 1951 Mapam included Achdut Ha'avoda.

[5] These included 4 Sephardim, one Yemenite, one WIZO, and one "Fighters' List."

by examinations of the political significance of immigration. According to Israeli law, new immigrants become citizens upon arrival in the country and immediately obtain the right to vote. Since the Israeli political parties have cognate parties in the Jewish communities abroad, regulation of immigration has direct political consequences.

The Jewish Agency is governed by a coalition of all the major Israeli parties except the Communists. As in the government of the state of Israel, Mapai has more representatives on the executive board of the Jewish Agency than any other party.[6] More than that, its members hold important positions, as, for instance, chairman of the board in Jerusalem, heads of the departments of settlement, of absorption of new immigrants, of education and youth.

The third national political organization of extraordinary importance is the General Federation of Labor. Its special position in Israeli society has often been discussed.[7] The *Histadrut* is governed by an executive board elected by a national convention. The elections are organized according to the proportional system, and representation is by political parties. The board is a coalition government in which all the major Histadrut parties except the Communist participate. Mapai has an absolute majority in the Histadrut (see Table 7.2). In 1957, eight out of thirteen members of the executive board of this organization belonged to Mapai. Thus Mapai is not just the major partner in the government of the state; it is also the strongest political force in the Jewish Agency and the ruling party in the Histadrut.

Mapai domination in the political realm antedates the establishment of the Israeli state. The Jewish community in Palestine had a semiautonomous political status under the British mandate. A political organization was established in 1920 and later was formally recognized by the British government. While the organization officially had only education and welfare functions, attempts were

[6] The Zionist Congress elects two branches of the executive board, one seated in Jerusalem and one in New York. The Jerusalem branch is believed to have more political significance. *Mapai* had five out of eleven members, including the chairman, on the board elected by the 23rd Zionist Congress in August 1951. In New York, *Mapai* had two members out of eight.

[7] See Margaret L. Plunkett, "The *Histadrut:* The General Federation of Jewish Labor in Israel," *Industrial and Labor Relations Review*, vol. 11, no. 2, pp. 155–182.

Table 7.2 POLITICAL COMPOSITION OF HISTADRUT CONVENTIONS, V–IX, 1942–1959

Party	V April 1942 %	VI Jan. 1945 %
Mapai	69.3	53.7
Hashomer Hatzair	19.2	20.7
Left Poale Zion	5.8	17.7
Unity of Labor Party		3.0
Haoved Hatzioni		3.0
Aliya Hadasha		0.2
Revisionists		1.0
Religious Workers		0.5
Yemenites		0.2
Unattached		
General Zionists Workers	3.5	
Proletarian Group	2.2	
Total	100.0	100.0
Valid Votes	81,198	106,420

Party	VII May 1949 %	VIII Feb. 1955 %	IX May 1959 %
Mapai	57.1	57.5	56.0
Ahdut Ha'avoda	34.4	14.6	16.9
Mapam		12.5	13.0
Progressives	3.8	5.2	6.3
Religious Workers	2.0	2.0	1.5
General Zionists		3.0	3.8
Communists*	2.6	4.1	2.0
Total	99.9	98.9	99.5
Valid Votes	130,670	410,435	667,718

* Varying composition between 1949 and 1955.

made by the Jewish community, in its struggle for full political independence, to increase the functions and the significance of this organization. Its semiofficial parliament was called Assembly of the Elected,[8] and the "government" elected by it was named the National Committee.[9] (See Table 7.3.)

Mapai originated in 1930 from a merger of two smaller parties. Since then it has become a major political party in the Histadrut (see Table 7.2) and an important political factor in the Zionist Congress. Mapai showed its power for the first time in the 1931 elections to the Assembly in which it obtained 43.7 percent of the vote and gained control of the National Committee. From this election till the day a premiership was created in the first Israeli government, a Mapai member was the head of the National Committee. Thus it can be said that Mapai has been in office ever since; it has never been replaced.

MAPAI—AN INSTITUTIONALIZED PARTY

Does this mean that Mapai cannot be replaced? There are countries in which one party remained in office for similar periods (Democrats in the United States for twenty years; Liberals in Canada for twenty-two years, in one province—Manitoba—for forty-three years) and was ousted by legitimate procedures. Can Mapai be ousted in a similar way? While there is no unqualified answer to this question, a number of factors make such a change quite unlikely in the near future, short of a major economic crisis or an international rupture.

The multiparty system and the coalition structure of the government are important factors. We suggest *that if parties elicit strong ideological commitments and the center party is relatively large, no stable government can be formed without the center party.* Mapai is such a center party, with a "hard core" of more than 30 percent of the votes. Thus Israel has a "right" coalition—Mapai with General Zionists and other parties (December 23, 1952– January 26, 1954); a "left" coalition—Mapai with *Ahdut Ha-Avoda,* Mapam and other parties (November 3, 1955); and a center coalition—Mapai with the Progressive party and some reli-

[8] *Aesfhat HaNivharim.*
[9] *HaVaad HaLeumi.*

Table 7.3 CONSTITUTION OF THE FOUR ASSEMBLIES OF THE ELECTED

Party	I April 19, 1920		II Dec. 6, 1925		III Jan. 15, 1931		IV Aug. 1, 1944[a]	
	Seats	%	Seats	%	Seats	%	Seats	%
Ahdut Ha'avoda (Mapai)	70	22.3	54	24.4	31	43.7	63	52.9
Hapoel Hatzair (Poalei Zion)	41	13.1	30	13.6	1	1.4	21	17.6
Communists			6	2.7	2	2.8		
Yemenites	12	3.8	20	9.0	3	4.2		
Other Oriental Lists	60[a]	19.1	20	9.0	c			
Religious Parties	64	20.4	19	8.6	5	7.0	17[e]	14.3
Revisionists			15	6.8	15	21.1		
Various Middle Class Lists	67[b]	21.3	44[b]	19.9	14	19.7		
Aliah Hadasha							18	15.1
League for Women's Rights			13	5.9				
	314	100.0	221	99.9	71	99.9	119	99.9
Registered Voters	28,755		64,714		89,656		303,000	
Valid Votes	22,257		36,737		50,436		202,448	
Valid Votes, Percent of Registration	77.0		56.7		56.2		67.0	

[a] Includes: Sephardim, 54; Bucharim, 5; Gurgim, 1.
[b] 10 lists in 1920, 13 in 1925, 3 in 1931.
[c] Sephardim votes included 6 Middle Class, 5 Revisionists, 4 Mapai.
[d] Sephardim, General Zionists and Revisionists boycotted the elections.
[e] Only Hapoel Hamizrahi participated.

gious parties (March 10, 1949–November 1, 1950), but never a government without Mapai. *There seems to be no basis for a coalition without Mapai.* The only way to create a government without Mapai which would have the confidence of the absolute majority of the Knesset is by a coalition which would include parties of the left *and* of the right. In a country like Israel where ideological commitments to parties play an important role, such a coalition is not a realistic alternative.

The fact that parties other than Mapai have no realistic chance to become coalition leaders and must, in effect, choose between permanent opposition and more or less minor coalition partnerships seems to generate in them "irresponsible" tendencies. The term "irresponsible political behavior" is usually applied to extreme parties that have little or no chance of coming into office and therefore make promises to the voters and claims upon the government that they would not be able to fulfill if they were to get into office. The Communists and *Herut* (extreme right) come close to this type of total opposition party. But there is another type of irresponsibility which develops when one party seems to be a constant and dominant partner of coalitions. Other parties tend then to become irresponsible in the sense that they are ready to bargain about many issues of public interest in order to be included in the coalition or as a price for staying in it. As they have to choose between being an insignificant opposition or a minor member of the coalition, they often choose the latter. The religious parties in Israel have often followed such a pattern.[10] Irresponsible politics in turn causes some voters to shift to the major party which "does the job" and manifests responsible leadership. This, in turn, validates the claim of the Mapai that there is no alternative to the party in office. Thus a vicious circle is created: one party remains in office for a long time; this creates irresponsibility in other parties; and this in turn strengthens the position of the party in office.

What are the social conditions on which this political structure is based? How permanent are those conditions? Would it be conceivable that in the next elections to the Knesset (in 1959) about 10 percent of those who voted for Mapai in previous elections would vote for another party, thus undermining the basis of the

[10] Amitai Etzioni, "Kulturkampf ou Coalition: Le Cas d'Israel," *La Revue Française de Science Politique*, vol. 8 (1958), pp. 311–331.

present coalition system? Most well-informed political observers would agree that such a change can hardly be expected. The major reason rests on the assumption that, like many parties in office for a long period, Mapai has become so strongly institutionalized that it has a strong grip on a "hard core" of voters needed to maintain its superior position.

On the one hand, a party which remains in office for a long time often loses some public support because of the necessity of occasionally introducing a measure that alienates one group or another. For example, a responsible government frequently has to introduce legislation which alienates large contingents of the voters, creating only little support from any special group (new taxes, for instance). Even if a party tries to avoid taking action on controversial issues, as Mapai does with the Israeli constitution and some religious issues, it alienates those groups which expect the party to take action. Thus, on one hand, being in office leads to the accumulation of enemies. On the other hand, holding office may have a beneficial effect, as far as the party is concerned, for future elections. The leadership of the state and that of the major party are often fused; people who identify with the state tend also to favor the leading party. The party tends to receive credit for any progress which is achieved during its regime. The opposition is labeled as a group of people who "only talk."

Party patronage is another factor. The amount of patronage available depends to some degree on the moral atmosphere and on the institutionalization of a civil service. But not less important is the amount of control which the political organizations have over economic activities. In Israel, as well as in many other newly developed countries, conditions encourage a widespread political influence on the allocation of manpower, capital, land, and power positions. The sources of foreign currency are of major significance in a small, expanding economy. The scope of government control over these sources is well reflected in the following figures. Compared to 28.4 percent of income from exports and 4.3 percent of income from private investment, which are only regulated by the government, about 65 percent of the foreign currency income is allocated and controlled by the government or by the Jewish Agency.[11] It is almost inevitable that partisan considerations have

[11] These figures represent the period from 1949 to 1956.

some influence when political organizations control the economy, and when this control is extensive, these considerations are weighty. In such political allocations and controls, largely channeled through the state, parties in power have an advantage over those in opposition.

Probably the most important economic control which the Israeli parties exert on their members concerns place of employment. In an economy where the closed shop is the rule, parties control trade unions and labor exchanges. Parties also organize services for their members including health plans, housing projects, vacations, and recreation.[12] Thus all parties, especially the stronger ones, can expect to hold the allegiance of a large proportion of their members.

But in a society where ideology plays an important political role, economic control is not sufficient. The parties attempt to secure ideological control by maintaining their own media of communication and by curbing the access of their supporters to communication media of other parties. All Israeli parties publish their own newspapers and most exert some pressure on their members to subscribe to these newspapers. The larger parties have publishing houses of their own. Until recently, parties were quite influential in the school system. The separate party housing projects, vacation centers and social clubs serve also to increase intraparty communication and to decrease interparty communication. The members' *Weltanschauung* is constantly reinforced so that they will be ready to resist any "hostile" communication.

In this sphere also the parties in office seem to have some limited advantages over other parties. Israel has no television; the single radio station is controlled by the government. The government has an elaborate information service headed by a Mapai member. This service usually does not communicate political ideology, but it functions to increase the loyalty of new and old citizens to the state by emphasizing its achievements and its bright future. This inevitably has some political repercussions.

While the Israeli parties in general and Mapai in particular have considerable economic and ideological control over a good many

---

[12] See Gerda Luft, "The Party That Shapes Policy," *The Jerusalem Post*, July 11, 1955, quoted by M. H. Bernstein, *The Politics of Israel* (Princeton, N.J.: Princeton University Press, 1957), p. 71.

of their members and supporters, this hold is far from being strong enough to make shifts of voters' loyalties impossible. Less than a third of all the voters are party members, and in every election thus far at least 15 percent of the voters have changed their party allegiances.[13] On the other hand, this very control gives each party a stable core and gives Mapai a hard core of 30 percent of the electorate, which is sufficient to maintain its dominant role in the coalition system unless some serious crisis should occur.

About half of the voters who will participate in the next (1959) parliamentary elections have emigrated to Israel between 1948 and 1958. Could this group cause a considerable change in the outcome of the election? Judging by past elections the answer is clearly in the negative. All attempts to establish new immigrant parties have failed.[14] New immigrants are known to distribute their votes roughly in the same way as the old citizens.

The politics of many other new nations illustrate the problem of a third form of institutionalization, namely the investment of the parties in office in the armed forces, police, and other security agencies. These "instruments of violence" can be neutral in the political game and thus serve equally all parties which may come into power. If this is the case, they support the institutionalization of the democratic system. If, on the other hand, they support parties in office, they increase the institutionalization of these parties and undermine the system. If they support moderate or, more likely, extreme opposition parties, they endanger the parties in office and the democratic system at the same time.

Mapai's position from this point of view has undergone a considerable change. In the pre-state period its control over the various underground forces was relatively weak, compared to its control over other national political organizations. This difference between the power distribution in the civic political bodies and that in the underground forces sometimes caused "lack of subordination" of these armed forces to the civil authorities.[15] When the State of Israel was established, action was taken to change this situation.

---

[13] But note that most changes are among parties with similar ideologies. Thus while more than 15 percent shift, only about 6 percent or less shift from parties left of Mapai to parties right of Mapai or vice versa. Thus Mapai's superior and center position is maintained. See Table 7.1.

[14] No such parties were successfully formed by 1965.

[15] On this point see chap. 8, pp. 187–188.

First of all, the armed forces have been depoliticized. Units which had political loyalties have been disbanded. Soldiers and officers are not allowed to be politically active. There has not been a case of "lack of subordination" since the establishment of the Israeli defense forces. In 1956 this came to a significant test when these forces were ordered to withdraw from Sinai amid strong public protest.

Depoliticizing of the defense forces has been considered an insufficient safeguard for the regime in a country where such forces are so powerful. This may explain why today many of the top positions in the defense forces are in the hands of Mapai members or neutrals. Out of the five chiefs of staff of the Israeli defense forces during 1948–1958, two have been active Mapai members before and after their service, two are known to be supporters of Mapai in their private life, and the fifth has never shown any special political inclinations. The names of generals and colonels are usually not published in Israel, but the government year book gives a list of twelve of the top commanders of the defense forces.[16] Most of them are known as members or close adherents of Mapai. The Israeli police commander-in-chief and his deputy are Mapai members; so are many of the higher officers. There is little information on other security agencies, but they seem to be staffed similarly. It is of interest to note that when, in January 1952, a political demonstration by Herut (extreme right) members broke through the police lines in front of the Knesset, an army unit was called to help.[17] This shows that the government, and first of all Mapai, can rely on the loyalty of the army.

DEMOCRACY AND AN INSTITUTIONALIZED CENTER PARTY

The party in office has never been replaced in Israel and it is unlikely to be replaced in the near future. Still the changing power distribution in society corresponds to the changing policy of the

[16] *The Government Year Book* (Jerusalem, 1958–1959), p. 84.
[17] *Ha'aretz*, Hebrew daily, Tel Aviv, Jan. 8, 1952.

government. What are the mechanisms which enable a democracy to function without replacing the party in power?

CHANGES IN THE COMPOSITION OF THE COALITION GOVERNMENT

Mapai, like other parties in democratic countries, is quite sensitive to public opinion. Although its control over some of its supporters is quite extensive, Mapai can never be secure in its control over its followers. While it never lost its core support, its leaders feel that this was achieved only by the party steering a cautious course, based on a combination of responsible leadership with enough "flexibility" (opponents say "opportunism") not to lose the support of its voters.

Mapai has some difficulty in determining what the public wants. There are no by-elections to the Israeli parliament. If a member dies or resigns, his party appoints a new representative. Since local elections usually take place on the same day as parliamentary elections, they cannot indicate public attitudes between elections. Experience has shown that other elections, as for instance to the Histadrut conventions, do not reflect clearly the outcome of forthcoming national elections, and therefore they are not considered as reliable political indicators.[18] There is no Israeli Gallup Institute or any close equivalent which could serve as a means for assessing the public. Therefore, the main test for the policies of each government coalition comes with the general elections to the Knesset. If the electorate then shows dissatisfaction with the government line, Mapai tends to change its policy and its partners in the coalition. Thus, while Mapai stays in office, the government policy may change considerably and in relation to changes in public opinion and pressures.

The first regular Israeli government (March 10, 1949 to November 1, 1950) consisted of a coalition of Mapai, Religious United Front, the Progressive party (later, Liberals) and Sephardim. The government was under criticism from three major opposition parties: from Mapam (left-wing party) in regard to the Israeli

[18] For instance, Mapam lost 7.25 percent of its seats in the Histadrut convention between 1949 and 1955 (in 1955 both splinters are counted together) but in elections to the Knesset in the same years it received about the same percent of the seats.

stand between East and West; from Herut (extreme right) with respect to the defense policy; and from the General Zionists (right wing; later, Liberals) in the matter of economic policy.

As this was a time of mass immigration and rapid economic expansion, a strong inflation developed.[19] The government introduced a far-reaching system of control which included licensing of imports and exports, complete control over foreign currency, and government allocation of raw materials and of consumer goods. Nearly a thousand different products were rationed. Luxury items were highly taxed. Credit allocation was regulated by the government.

The General Zionists, a party of big business, exporters, importers, citrus plantation owners, and to some degree supported by small businessmen and artisans, objected to all this. The party advocated a liberalization of economic policy—that is, the curtailment or abolition of governmental regulations and of various allocations. The ration system, which many loathed, was made the symbolic target in the election campaign.

In the elections to the second Knesset which followed, the public shifted its support to the General Zionists. While the General Zionists were a small party with 5.8 percent of the seats in the first Knesset (1949), they obtained almost three times as many seats in 1951 (16.7 percent), to become the second largest party. The other two opposition parties lost considerably (Herut fell from 11.7 percent to 6.7 percent and Mapam from 15.8 percent to 12.4 percent). Mapai lost only 0.8 percent of its seats, but the lesson was obvious. Large groups of the public were not satisfied with Mapai's economic policy, and it adjusted to this situation in several ways. First, the party abolished some of the more disagreeable measures of control. Then, in December 1952, the General Zionists were included in the government. Finally, a "New Economic Policy" was introduced which was a compromise between Mapai's policy and the General Zionists' line. Mapai economists argued that the changes in economic policy were

[19] The amount of money in circulation tripled in three years (end of 1948 to end of 1951). Credit expanded in the same period from 80 million to about 150 million Israeli *lirot*. The consumer's price index jumped from 100 (September 1951) to 178 (December 1952). On the effects of mass immigration, see Judah Matras, *Social Change in Israel* (Chicago: Aldine Publishing Co., 1965).

possible now because the economic situation had improved, mainly by the 1952 reparation agreement with Germany. But it is clear that the election played its role. Although the General Zionists left the government at a later time and the economic situation changed again, Mapai never tried to return to the 1949–1951 system of rationing.

A similar change took place after the elections to the third Knesset. The primary cause of conflict and adjustment this time was defense policy. During the days of the second Knesset (1951–1955), the pressure from the Arab countries increased by means of economic boycott, border incidents, and infiltration activities inside Israel. Israel reacted by retaliatory operations which were focused on the centers from which the Arab activities were launched. The frequency and scope of these activities varied in relation to the pressure exerted by other nations on the Arabs and on Israel. Public opinion in Israel was split on these retaliatory activities. Herut and Ahdut HaAvoda (left wing) demanded a more militant line and questioned the military and political expediency of limited retaliatory activities. All the other parties were for continuation of the more moderate line.

The election to the third Knesset showed that the public now was more concerned with the defense issue than with economic problems and that it protested against the continuous lack of security. The public supported the "hawks" (or activists, as they are called in Israel); Herut almost doubled its seats (from 6.7 percent to 12.5 percent) and became the second largest party in the Knesset. The other party which supported the activists' line also improved its position. Mapai lost a considerable number of seats (4.2 percent), and so did other parties.

Mapai's reaction was as quick and determined as in the earlier case. Ben Gurion reassumed the Prime Ministership and the Defense Ministry; Sharet—who supported the moderate line—resigned from the government. Since a coalition with Herut is inconceivable for Mapai, for ideological reasons, a left-wing coalition was formed on November 3, 1955 which included the left-wing activists. When Nasser arranged a weapons deal with the Soviet Union and nationalized the Suez Canal only one year later, the Israeli government switched from limited retaliatory activity to broader military activity. In October 1956 the government ordered the Israeli armed forces into the Sinai peninsula. Thus again the government acted in accord with a new public trend. A new policy was introduced and a new coalition was formed.

Of course a change in public opinion was not the only cause of the change in government policy, but the election results had considerable influence. The objective situation was interpreted differently by moderates and activists. If moderate parties had gained in the elections and the activists had lost, Sharet might have remained in the cabinet as prime minister and/or foreign minister, and the policy as well as the composition of the cabinet might have been quite different. It is not accidental that public support turned to the activists; the international situation generated pressure in this direction. Thus one can see the elections as one mechanism through which the policy of the government is adjusted to the situation and to the electorate's view of it without a change of the party in office.

CHANGES IN THE INNER BALANCE OF MAPAI

The study of factions and pressure groups within a party is of special interest from several viewpoints. First, these groups determine to a considerable degree the party's policy and the composition of party representation in the various political institutions. Secondly, the larger the party and the more interests and groups represented in it, the more some functions of the parliament, such as policy-making and consensus formation, are taken over by party organs. The party's higher bodies have to reach a working consensus among the various groups before party policy can be determined.[20] Mapai itself comes close to being a federation of groups.[21] The major groups are: an organization of collective settlements, or kibbutzim (about 97 percent of the eligible popula-

[20] In cases where there is only one party, as in totalitarian states, the factional struggle is an uninstitutionalized substitute for rivalry among parties. In some states in the United States where there is only one active party, the factional struggle is the most important form of political expression. Unlike the totalitarian countries, it is here institutionalized in party conventions and primaries. See V. O. Key, *Southern Politics in State and Nation* (New York: Alfred A. Knopf, Inc., 1949).

[21] Factions have not been tolerated since 1944 when a faction split Mapai and created its own party.

tion votes Mapai); an organization of cooperative villages, or *Moshavej Ovdim* (about the same ratio of support); the Histadrut group, professionals and intelligentsia, Mapai members in government administration, and representatives of new immigrants. All these groups are represented in the Mapai Center (196 members) and many of them in the Mapai secretariat (fifteen members, in March 1958).

How does this pluralistic structure influence the democratic process? Through it, those who support Mapai have a voice in the decision-making process in nonelection years and without changing their party alliance. Thus, before Mapai changed its defense policy, the fight between moderates and activists was taken up in the Mapai Center, with Ben Gurion heading the activists section and Sharet the moderate one. Only after it was decided here by a majority vote that Ben Gurion's policies should be promoted did Sharet resign and Mapai offer the new policy to the whole government.

Although the functions, prestige, and voting power of collective settlements are declining (while those of the cooperative villages are increasing), collective settlements still have considerable privileges and power.[22] But in the last years the cooperative villages have struggled for increased representation of their group. To some degree their demands have been met, but the collective settlements are still over-represented. This is likely to diminish in the near future. Thus, changes in the social significance of groups are reflected in changes in their political power through change in their representation in Mapai's policy-making bodies.

Another group struggle which aroused much public interest was that between Histadrut (trade union) leaders and Mapai economic experts concentrated in the Treasury. The economists press for enlarged investments in order to achieve an increasing degree of economic independence and strength. The trade-union leaders insist that this should be done without a considerable decrease in the standard of living of the workers. Till now the trade-union leaders have had the upper hand. One of the reasons why they are so influential is that they represent a much larger and better-

[22] See Amitai Etzioni, "Agrarianism in Israel's Party System," *The Canadian Journal of Economics and Political Science,* vol. 23 (1957), pp. 363–375.

organized group of voters than the economists, and the segments of the intelligentsia who support them.

Is group representation really democratic? First of all, it should be noted that it is part of the democratic process in all democratic countries, especially in those where there is a two-party system, because fewer interests are directly represented on the party level, and more are represented on the faction level. It is more important to examine the way in which faction representation is determined. Even where there are officially controlled and supervised primaries, nomination is still open to much abuse. Oligarchic procedures in units which participate in the democratic mechanisms seem to be almost an "iron law." While there are no primaries in Israel, two thirds of the members of Mapai Center are elected by Mapai locals and one third suggested by the Mapai secretariat and approved by the convention. The latter are in most cases group representatives, often elected leaders of their groups or organizations. New immigrants, intelligentsia, and youth representatives are frequently selected in less formal ways. Thus group representation in Mapai is quite democratic. It is an important mechanism through which powerful groups and Mapai's policy are maintained in balance.

STRUCTURAL WEAKNESS OF MAPAI

Mapai has a major weakness which is important because it increases the party's sensitivity to group pressures and public opinion. Mapai is often seen as an omnipotent party, a strong monolithic political body with branches in all the major power centers. This description is misleading in one important respect: it does not take into account the pluralistic nature of Mapai, in which the main power rests in each group and little in Mapai as a party. There are powerful groups of Mapai members in the trade unions, in the cooperative movement, in the three major cities, in the Treasury, and so on, but their relations to other Mapai groups vary all the way from close cooperation to open hostility. In most cases the relationships are highly voluntary because each group is quite independent. The weakest group is the party bureaucracy which supposedly ties them all together. The party personnel is small in number, low paid, has little prestige, and consists mainly of party representatives who failed to maintain a position in other organizations. Many Mapai branch secretaries are merely clerks for party activities and mediators among the various local centers of power. The Mapai Center itself is a place where the various groups determine their relative power and work out common policies, rather than a center of a powerful party machine which has strong control over its representatives in various political organizations. This is an important reason why Mapai, with all its weight and power (when it comes to coordinated action on the national scene), is internally weak and highly sensitive to pressures of various groups.[23]

A COMPARATIVE NOTE

Is Israel an exception to the "normal" democratic model, or are there other countries which come close to her form of democracy?

The Swedish government in the last twenty-six years (since 1932) has seen a coalition government in which the Social Democratic party is the basic political partner. Since 1949, Germany has been run by a coalition government in which one party, the Christian Democrats, plays the role of the decisive partner. The situation formally resembles a two-party system because two parties, the Christian Democrats and the Social Democrats, obtain the majority of the votes, but many commentators agree that this is misleading since the class and religious structure of Germany does not give the Social Democrats a real chance to obtain much more than 35 percent of the vote—which means that there is no alternative party to the CDU at the moment.[24] The special importance Adenauer held for the maintenance of the system can be compared to the position which Ben Gurion held in the Israeli system. While Ben Gurion had the charismatic role of the state founder, Adenauer played a similar role as the one who restored the new German Republic to a respectable place among the nations. The

[23] That unorganized voters or weaker groups lose out in this process is obvious, but this is a problem of democracy in general.

[24] Since these lines were written, the Social Democrats gained 39.5% of the vote in 1965 but continued to be unable to gain enough support to become an alternative party to the CDU.

coalition partners of the CDU are weaker than the partners of Mapai, especially since the CDU gained an absolute majority of the seats in the Bonn parliament (1957). On the other hand, nine years in office have been enough for the CDU to become considerably institutionalized. Group struggles within the CDU (Catholic labor, big business, Catholic and Protestant clergy, liberals and others) are an important mechanism of German democracy as well.

Another illustration is the French Fourth Republic which in some respects functioned similarly to the Israeli system. The MRP, like Mapai, participated in a large number and variety of coalitions. The decisive difference between Israel and France is that the MRP was much weaker than Mapai and therefore the coalition system never achieved the stability of the Israeli system. No central party became institutionalized, and the extreme parties on left and right were considerably stronger. The final blow was given to the system by power organizations which had political orientations different from those of the elected government of France.

Thus if coalition governments are formed on a continuum according to the strength of the center party, the Israeli and Swedish governments would be in the middle, Germany on one side, and the Fourth Republic on the other. There are other types of coalition governments without one center party, but a discussion of those and of their democratic quality would take us far beyond the scope of this study.

Mapai is often compared to the British Labour party and the Social Democrats in the Weimar Republic. These comparisons have certain merits when one attempts to point out the ideological position of Mapai in an *abstract* continuum of political ideologies. Mapai subscribes to a left-wing noncommunist ideology. But beyond that, the comparison is of little help. The British Labour party is one in a two-party system; it entered and left office several times in the last three decades, while Mapai's dominance remained high.

The comparison to the Weimar Social Democrats is even less meaningful. The Social Democrats were not able to continue in office because among other reasons rightist forces were highly entrenched in the army, the bureaucracies, and the judicial system.

This is almost the opposite of the situation in Israel. The center of the Israeli political spectrum is not liberal, as in so many Western societies, but social-democratic with an approximately even distribution of the more leftist forces on one side and conservative and liberal groups on the other side. More than that, for historical reasons the left-of-center ideologies and groups have stronger political, economic, and prestige positions than the right and liberal forces. While socialist parties in Western societies are often parties of reform and change, Mapai is more representative of the Israeli values and social structure than any other party. To be a Social Democrat in Israel—and the same holds for many of the newly developed countries—means to be in conformity with the majority of the politically conscious members of society. It is like being a moderate liberal in the present Congress of the United States. Thus in conducting a comparative analysis we have to take into account not only the substance of political values but also the place of such values in the political spectrum of the society. What is quite revolutionary in one society may be rather on the conformist side in another society. The different place in the political spectrum is of great significance, in view of the different political conditions with which revolutionary and reform parties are confronted as compared to those in which conforming and status quo parties are placed, disregarding the actual content of their ideologies.[25]

Mapai can be compared to other state founding parties which have become highly institutionalized in young nations, as, for instance, the Congress party in India, the Neo-Destour in Tunisia, the Convention People's party in Ghana, and the AFPFL in Burma. Of course, there are considerable differences among these countries, and between these countries and Israel, but they all seem to have in common a leader and a party with the charismatic role of gaining independence and establishing the state; left-of-center ideologies; state-regulated economies; a high degree of economic dependence on external sources (with perhaps the exception of Ghana); and control over the labor organizations, excluding the Communists.[26]

---

[25] On this, see more in chap. 8, p. 181.
[26] See S. M. Lipset, "Socialism—Left and Right—East and West," *Confluence*, vol. 7 (1958), pp. 172–192. See also Richard Rose, "Parties,

A comparative study of democratic societies cannot be carried out here. The main purpose of this study has been to describe a democratic polity that functions and changes through mechanisms other than the frequent alternation of the party in office. The concluding paragraphs are meant to suggest that such mechanisms can be found also in countries other than Israel and that a comparative study of these countries might throw light on the nature and organs of modern democracy.

Factions, and Tendencies in Britain," *Political Studies*, vol. 12 (1964), pp. 33–46. See also E. A. Bague, *Four Ways of Politics: State and Nation in Italy, Somalia, Israel and Iran* (New York: American University Field Staff, 1965); also, David Apter, "Some Reflections on the Role of a Political Opposition in New Nations," *Journal of Comparative Studies in Society and History*, vol. 4 (1962), pp. 154–168.

CHAPTER 8

Change of the System: The Decline of Neo-Feudalism in Israel

━━━━◆•◆•◆━━━━

The struggle for national independence is often led by a charismatic movement. Once independence has been gained, such movements tend, to use Max Weber's terminology, to become "routinized" by developing either "traditional" or "bureaucratic" structures. The outcome of the conflict between these two tendencies determines to a large extent the degree of political stability, the measure of civil rights, and the economic viability of the young nations. In the case of Israel, the bureaucratic elements are rapidly gaining over the charismatic ones. Traditional elements are clearly secondary as compared to the bureaucratic ones. An examination of this process as it is occurring casts some light on the process of bureaucratization in other newly independent nations.

The pre-independence nationalist movements manifest the elements typical of charismatic movements. First, they are led by potent leaders such as Gandhi, Nkrumah, and Ben-Gurion. Secondly, their mass membership is drawn from the disintegrating traditional structures, whether they be villages in India, tribes in Ghana, or traditional Jewish communities in the Diaspora. The traditional bonds are usually broken at least in part by some ecological dislocation. This often takes the form of migration from the country to the emerging cities, or, in Israel, emigration from the cities in the Diaspora to the countryside of Palestine. Thirdly, like other charismatic movements, movements for national independence command intense ideological commitments.

180

They are anticolonial, nationalist, and subscribe to some kind of reform or revolutionary doctrine of a socialist character. Finally, there is little interest in economic, administrative, or scientific activities; neither are there available to the movement the social instruments which these activities require. Rarely do the independence movements have elaborate administrative apparatuses or stable economic resources and income of their own (for example, their activities tend to be financed by contribution rather than by taxation).

Routinization begins either with the gaining of independence or shortly before it.[1] With independence—when the movement's charismatic leader becomes the first premier or president and the members become citizens—the movement has to take charge of whatever economic and administrative machinery already exists, and thus the process of routinization begins or is greatly accelerated. The degree to which routinization is begun before the gaining of political independence depends on the length of the struggle preceding it, the degree to which the colonial power allowed the independence movement gradually to assume responsibilities, and the degree to which the movement developed autonomous administrative and economic organizations. In the case of the Jewish community in Palestine, all of the foregoing conditions were met to a relatively high degree: hence, preindependence routinization was comparatively advanced and the transition to statehood smooth.

As previously indicated, routinization may take one of two courses: the charismatic movement may give birth either to a highly bureaucratic or to a traditional social structure. In the first case, the powers of the charismatic leadership are transferred to the state's elite. The old leader becomes the recognized head of the young state; other leaders gain positions as members of cabinets or parliament, heads of administrative agencies, and so forth. The followers transfer their commitments from the movement to the state, from rebellion to loyalty, from support of the particular norms of a subgroup (the movement) to the universal norms of the legal system of the state.

[1] See pp. 15–18 for the importance of the shift from expressive specialization to full autonomy of control of instrumental activities. Routinization discussed here is obviously an aspect of epigenesis, not differentiation.

In the second case, a particularistic "fixation" occurs. The central power continues to reside outside the government in the person of tribal chiefs, village heads, union or party leaders. The followers' loyalty remains primarily committed to the traditional units (for example, tribes) or to those created by the independence movement but are not transferred to the state. The situation in the Congo in 1961 provides an extreme illustration.

Here it may be well to provide a brief conceptual note. Weber referred to the two products of the routinization of charisma as "bureaucratic" and "traditional." The latter is a particularly inadequate concept for our purposes since we must be concerned not only with such local traditional units as tribes and villages but also with recently created foci of loyalty such as the independence movement itself and various political units (such as parties or labor unions) which might withhold loyalty and power from the state after independence. Following Parsons, we will designate as universalistic those units which uphold norms that apply without discrimination to all citizens (this being both the essence and the prerequisite of a true bureaucratic structure) and as particularistic those units, either traditional or new, which are committed to norms limited only to certain subsocieties.

Highly particularistic political systems have been referred to as neo-feudal. The various political organizations which, unlike the state agencies, encompass only parts of a society, are reminiscent of barons; as in a feudal state, there are no true citizens but vassals and subvassals. These provide the "baron" of the neo-feudal state with political support (votes), in exchange for which he supplies services which may range from employment opportunities (or patronage) to a rich variety of welfare services. The political machines of some American cities approached a neo-feudal structure, since each ethnic group (or ward) had its own "boss" or overlord to whom it was bound by reciprocal obligations and loyalty and showed little normative commitment or political loyalty either to the city government itself or to its laws.

It is important to stress that the universalism-particularism distinction is not a sharp dichotomy but rather a continuum. For no political system, or any society, is either completely universalistic or wholly particularistic; each contains some of both elements, though they differ greatly in the proportions and the ways in which they are combined.

Extreme universalism is characteristic of totalitarian states in which the particularistic units have been disintegrated or subordinated to a single overriding political unit. In such systems the autonomous intermediary bodies between the citizen and the state (or the party) are very few and weak. On the other hand, in confederations particularism is predominant, intermediary bodies are strong, and universalistic governmental agencies are limited and weak.

It is crucial to realize that the optimal structure for the implementation of many social values is not—as numerous students of bureaucracy assumed in the past—a highly universalistic one. Minority rights, and to a considerable degree civil liberties, often depend upon the existence of relatively strong particularistic units and sentiments. These are also the basis for the emotional stability of the average citizen which is, in turn, the foundation of his ability to accept universalistic norms and to engage in politically responsible behavior.[2] A viable democracy, for example, requires not only identification with the constitution, the president, and the supreme court—all universalistic institutions—but also with some particularistic political party. Public administration, economies, and professionalism, however, can tolerate and even benefit from higher degrees of universalism.

We shall now examine the development of particularism, or feudalism, in Israel. During the period of British rule and before the establishment of the State of Israel, neo-feudalism was powerful. Since independence, however, political particularism has been constantly declining while bureaucratization, and with it increased stress on universalistic norms, has been progressing rapidly.

THE EMERGENCE OF NEO-FEUDALISM

The "barons" of the Jewish community in Palestine were not village heads, tribal chiefs or landlords, but political parties.[3] The

---

[2] For a fine discussion of the general sociological issues involved see Robert A. Nisbet, *Community and Power* (New York: Oxford University Press, 1962).

[3] It should be noted that the Jewish community at this time was definitely a "dependent" collectivity in the terms used above.

Palestinian Jewish community was established mainly by the process of immigration, and as a result the traditional units were left behind and new social bonds were formed.[4] These new bonds took the form of numerous small, highly solidary political bodies which organized immigration to Palestine and subsequent settlement there. Joining a political party often even before emigrating to Palestine (for party emissaries traveled through the Diaspora to recruit members) provided the potential immigrant quite frequently with the financial backing for his trip, the assurance of a reception in the new country, training for his new way of life, and —as the parties increased in size, power, and financial resources —with all the major services, including health, welfare, housing, schooling, and employment.

In exchange, the immigrant owed the party "baron" his allegiance. Like the ethnic bond which often tied the political machine and the immigrant in some American cities, in the case of the Jewish community in Palestine there was a close social relationship between the immigrant and the political leader. This provided the typical paternalistic element of "feudal" relations. Also, an intense ideological commitment to the party made political allegiance natural and easily enforced. The "vassal" had to give much more than his vote; he had to be willing to serve the emerging political collectivity in ways specified by the party, from drying the swamps ("pioneering") to serving as a soldier of the underground units. Lacking a framework of a Jewish state and rejecting the colonial one, the parties and some interparty organizations carried out the various political functions usually carried out by the nation-state.

As is common in feudal structures a second layer of "lords" developed over and above the political parties. In 1920, the Histadrut, or the General Federation of Labor, was established. It was founded by a number of parties of the left and by several labor unions. Gradually it took over some of the financial and administrative activities of its component parts, and the Histadrut eventually developed a large number of activities of its own. But, as in a genuine feudal structure, the ultimate loyalty of each vassal was

[4] For a recent discussion of immigrant groups, see Judith T. Shuval, *Immigrants on the Threshold* (New York: Atherton Press, 1963); see also E. Katz and A. Zloczower, "Ethnic Continuity in an Israeli Town," *Human Relations*, vol. 14 (1961), pp. 293–327.

to his immediate lord rather than to this overlord. The parties remained the focus of identification and the predominant centers of power.

Not all parties were equal in power. As in many developing countries, in the Jewish community of Palestine the political bodies on the left were considerably more powerful than those of the right and of the center.[5] The existence of the Histadrut as the "roof"-organization of the left without an equivalent in the other political wings was an indication of its power and further contributed to its strength. Other factors leading to more powerful parties of the left were their larger membership and greater degree of legitimation compared with parties of the right and of the center.

The latter point is of much importance. Most observers of developing countries are accustomed to think in terms of the Western model of industrialization in which the bourgeois, free-enterprise, liberal middle class emerged first and gained both power and legitimation, and in which the working class, labor parties and unions came later. The left had to fight for recognition in a society dominated by middle-class values and powers. On the other hand, in practically all newly independent nations the process is reversed. Because of the close association of the middle classes (merchants, white-collar employees) with the colonial power, and the tendency of the independence movement to be led by left-wing groups, the newly independent nations tend to have parties in office which are left of center and to grant more legitimacy to left-wing ideologies than to right-wing ones. Here middle class representatives and ideas have to struggle for position and recognition rather than those of the working class. This will be of relevance when we come to analyze the role of the left-wing parties and Histadrut in the process of routinization in Israel.

THE DECLINE OF NEO-FEUDALISM

With the establishment of the State of Israel, the role and power of the political parties and other political associations declined; many of their functions were transferred to the state, as was a

[5] See various case studies in Morton A. Kaplan (ed.), *The Revolution in World Politics* (New York: John Wiley & Sons, 1962).

good measure of the loyalties of their followers. Party members acquired a new role, that of citizen. The parallel growth of universalism is of much interest to the student of bureaucratization and hence deserves some detailed reporting. For that purpose it may be well to focus upon its progress in a number of different institutional spheres. Such an examination reveals that the process develops unevenly. Thus, in the case of Israel, the process is completely successful in one sphere, almost completely successful in another, highly successful in a third, moderately successful in a fourth, and has hardly begun in the last. The process is still continuing, markedly in the bureaucratic direction.

COMPLETELY SUCCESSFUL: THE JUDICIAL SYSTEM

During the Palestinian, or mandate, period, the courts of what is now Israel were run under what was mostly British law with an admixture of some Ottoman legal traditions from the earlier rulers of Palestine (prior to 1917). The Jewish community, in its efforts to develop its own political institutions, put considerable pressure on its members to refrain from using the British courts and to use instead informal courts provided by various Jewish organizations. Nevertheless, in most criminal and many civil matters Jews did turn to British courts, though there was an effort to minimize litigation. Some segments of the law—such as those which restricted the use of weapons by Jews, their immigration to Palestine, and their purchase of land there—were strictly particularistic, explicitly oriented against one group, the Jews, and by this very token favoring the Palestinian Arab.

With the establishment of the State of Israel on May 15, 1948, a new court system was instituted. The law upon which it is based is a mixture of traditional Jewish law, British and Ottoman legal traditions, and a large and growing amount of new legislation. The system utilizes appointed judges; there are no juries. It is extremely universalistic. Particularistic laws, of the earlier period, were rescinded. The same laws, with the exception of those which are based on religious preference of the citizens (10 percent of Israel's citizens are Arabs, the majority of whom are Moslems), apply to all groups of the population. The impartiality of the judges and of the courts is accorded the highest respect. Throughout the state's existence, the courts have been the only institutions against which the charge of political favoritism was never seriously raised. Judges are appointed by the President (who, unlike that of the United States, is a nonpolitical figure) on the recommendation of a nominating committee which includes members of the Knesset, a Supreme Court judge, the Minister of Justice, and members of the Bar Association. Their appointments are based upon merit and they enjoy permanent tenure. The impartiality of the Supreme Court is especially respected. That the majority of its judges are members either of the Mapai (Labor party) or the Progressives (Liberals) is hardly known and seems to have no effect upon the discharge of their duties.

ALMOST COMPLETELY SUCCESSFUL: THE MILITARY

The anti-British underground of the Jews in Palestine, like the various undergrounds in France and other European countries during World War II, had strong political affiliations. The largest underground organization, the *Haganah*, was long split into two groups or factions, known simply as *A* (left wing) and *B* (right wing). Moreover, the Commando units of Haganah, known as the *Pal-Mach*, which were established in 1941, drew about 80 percent of their members and practically all of their officers from one left-wing political party (Achdut Ha'Avoda). Similarly, the *Irgun*, a dissenting underground force, recruited many of its officers and obtained much of its financial support from the Revisionists (today Herut, of the right). At least in one instance, the Pal-Mach came to the aid of strikers at a factory, while the Irgun helped the strikebreakers.

Before 1948, Haganah A and B merged to form a more universalistic organization, directly under the control of the Jewish National Committee, a weak super-political organization representing the political parties of the Palestinian Jewish community. The Pal-Mach or the Commando units were subordinated to the united Haganah, while the Irgun continued throughout most of this period in its independent dissenting course.

When the State of Israel was established, an Israeli defense army, basically grafted onto the Haganah, was officially proclaimed. At this point came one of the most crucial tests of universalism of the new nation-state, the same faced by any emerging from a feudal state: would the various politically bound particu-

laristic armies join the united defense force created by the state
or would they insist on maintaining their "private" force? In
July, 1948, the Irgun and Pal-Mach still maintained their own
military organizations and fought on separate fronts in the War of
Independence. In the same month, a thirty-day armistice was
signed under the supervision of the United Nations. It included a
provision forbidding arms to be imported by either Israel or the
Arabs. When the Irgun landed a ship carrying weapons close to
United Nations headquarters on the Tel Aviv beach, thus violating, in a highly visible manner, the commitment of the Israeli
government, the government ordered the ship halted and disbanded the Irgun. A half year later, the Pal-Mach was also disbanded.

At present, Israeli military units are strictly apolitical. None is
known to have any political affiliations or commitments. Officers
and enlisted men are forbidden to be active politically either in
the army or in the civilian society though all have the right to
vote.

With the continuing sensitivity to security matters and the resi-
due of the conflicts which accompanied the disbanding of the
Irgun and the Pal-Mach, it would seem that the Israeli government still must pay considerable attention to the political backgrounds of the higher-echelon officers. All six Israeli chiefs of
staff either have had no political affiliation or were members of
Mapai (Labor party). None of the senior officers is known to
be a member of opposition parties of the extreme left or the extreme right. The loyalty of the military to the state and conformity
to its orders seems to be highly assured not only because of the
neutral universalistic character of the army as a whole, but also
because its key leaders favor the particular party in power. That
some elements of particularism are maintained is, therefore, at
least functional for the stability of the political structure.

HIGHLY SUCCESSFUL:
THE DEPOLITICIZATION OF SCHOOLS

Since the British government in Palestine neither financed nor
organized a school system for the Jewish population, and since
the municipal governments were financially weak, various Jewish

political associations assumed the task of developing the schools. In the pre-state period, each major political body financed its own school system, trained its teachers, supervised the quality of education, printed textbooks, and so forth. Although there were only three major school systems—labor, religious, and "general" (right-wing)—considerable subdivisions existed to allow for the expression of more subtle political differences. (The extreme left-wing *Hashomer Hatzaier*, for instance, had its own subsystem, tied to its Kibbutz movement.)

Shortly after the establishment of the state, considerable attention was given to the depoliticization of the schools. In 1950, appropriate laws were passed in the Israeli parliament despite strong objection from some religious groups and from much of the left, which had by far the strongest educational system. The law leaves place for the needs of particularistic groups. While it decrees that 75 percent of all studies be uniform in all schools, to be determined by the Ministry of Education and to be taught by textbooks approved and often issued by it and by teachers trained under its supervision, the remaining 25 percent of the curriculum is to be determined by the local school in accordance with the parents' preferences. The law recognizes only two types of schools—state education (the standard 75 percent plus various other secular studies, like handicrafts, for the other 25 percent) and state-religious education (the standard 75 percent plus religious studies for the other 25 percent). The various leftist Kibbutz movements *de facto* use the 25 percent clause to introduce their Socialist education. Teachers for the "twenty-five percent" are often trained in separate teaching institutions of the various particularistic groups though their standards are under state supervision.

In 1950 it was widely believed that the law nationalizing the schools would, to a large degree, remain a piece of paper with teachers and parents combining to assure the kind of ideological education they preferred. But within a few years the old system all but disappeared. The particularistic preferences of parents and teachers find adequate expression in the 25 percent clause. The issuing of new textbooks, the transfer of teachers and principals which reduced the political homogeneity of a school's staff, the reorganization of the teacher colleges by the Ministry of Education, and above all, the opening of many new schools to absorb the mass of immigrant children, all made for surprisingly rapid and far-reaching rise in the universalism of schools.

MODERATELY SUCCESSFUL: WELFARE AND THE CIVIL SERVICE

Universalization has been more limited in its success in the diverse areas of labor exchanges, housing, welfare, and in the development of the civil service.

"Labor Exchanges," or employment agencies, serve to supply workers with jobs and employers with workers. In the period before independence, these exchanges were to a very large degree controlled by the Histadrut, the Federation of Jewish Labor. Considerably smaller and less powerful exchanges were run by the right-wing Revisionist parties and by a religious-labor party, *HaPoel HaMizrachi.*

The exchanges were a source of much political power; it was widely known that a "note" from the local secretary of a party could go a long way in getting a job. The system operated more or less smoothly on what was known as the "key system" by which various parties obtained a number of representatives on the exchange staff and a number of jobs roughly proportional to their national and local power as reflected in election results. Obviously, the parties were very reluctant to give up this important source of power.

It was ten years after the nationalization of the army and of the schools that the major law was passed regulating the Labor Exchanges. The law nationalized the Labor Exchanges so that they are now agencies of the Ministry of Labor. According to the law their clerks are appointed and salaried by the state, and promotions are based upon merit and upon examinations. The state determines the regulations according to which work is allocated. In actuality, the state has been only gradually gaining control over the exchanges, primarily because the old staff, which carries over much of the earlier traditions, still remains. Nonetheless, the direction of the change is unmistakably universalistic.

Welfare, which was previously supplied by the parties and various "roof"-organizations, is now to an increasing degree administered by a host of nonpolitical voluntary associations, by the Ministry of Welfare, and through various municipal programs. While there is some overlapping, with the various agencies penetrating each other's spheres, a division of labor of sorts has developed. The state focuses on relief and social security, which in Israel includes old age pensions, survivors' insurance, industrial accident insurance, and maternity benefits. The voluntary associations tend to focus on specific problems such as rehabilitation or homes for the aged. The parties and especially the Histadrut, while conducting some of each of these activities, often augmenting the sums allotted by the state, concentrate on needs which are not met by the government, such as nursery schools and retraining programs. In those allocations particularistic criteria prevail. That is, services are restricted to members.

The situation in housing is rather similar. While a great deal—and an ever-increasing amount—of construction in the development areas (for example, the Negev desert) is conducted by the state and in the development areas such as Tel Aviv by private construction firms, the parties still continue to build projects for their members as they did in the period prior to independence. Typically the allocation of housing constructed by the state is governed by a host of highly universalistic principles which rigidly allocate apartments according to age, size of family, length of stay in the country, etc., while parties allocate houses built under their auspices—with clear preference to their adherents, functionaries, and so forth.

The development of universalism in the civil service is of much interest. Some of the employees were on the staff of the preindependence British civil service, and some on the staffs of various Jewish institutions, in particular the Jewish Agency. But both contributed together only 13 percent of the present civil service. The large majority of employees joined the service after the state was established.

Over the years, many kinds of regulations were developed which are typical of modern civil services in other countries, particularly the British. Regulations require that workers for the lower unskilled positions be recruited through the state-controlled Labor Exchange (that is, according to its universalistic rules which attempt to assure an even distribution of work among the unemployed, taking into account differences in the size of family, and other factors). All other positions, with the exception of a few top ones, are recruited on the basis of examinations after public announcement of open positions. Promotions are based on merit; there is a certain minimum length of service required for advancement; and seniority is given consideration. Many ranks require specific training and degrees. Salaries are standardized by ranks, training, and other considerations. With the exception of standardization of salaries, which is generally enforced, all other regulations are quite frequently circumvented or violated. The extent of such particularism is hard to establish, but informed observers seem to agree that it is declining.

Particularism still exists on all levels of the civil service. The State is run chiefly by sixteen ministries (their number changes). The ministers in charge are political appointees and constitute the Cabinet. But since the Israeli government is a multiparty coalition, the Cabinet is composed of representatives of various parties. This means that with a change in the composition of the coalition, the parties in charge of various ministries change, but the change is far from random. As pointed out in some detail in the preceding chapter, the nine central ministries have always been in the hands of the Mapai (Labor party). Other ministries have traditionally, though not always, drawn their heads from one party or another; for instance, development was often the province of a left party, welfare of a religious party, and justice of the liberal Progressive party. Hence a good way of testing the degree to which the civil service is universalistic is by checking the party affiliations of the employees of the various ministries. There are no direct data to support the following contention, but those familiar with the situation seem to agree that while members of most parties will be found in most ministries, there is considerable over-representation within a ministry of the party in charge which increases the longer the party is in control and the higher the level of rank examined.[6]

Universalization occurs through the expansion of the examination system as the basis for recruitment and promotion. This limits the degree to which particularism can prevail; that is, each party has to recruit from among those of its members who can pass the

[6] This becomes especially apparent in the case of the Post Office which was for long periods in the hands of the religious parties, and hence the percentage of its staff which follows the orthodox Jewish custom of covering the head with a skullcap is visibly higher than, let us say, in the Mapai-dominated Treasury.

various tests. Moreover, since many employees are hired when fairly young and unions make dismissal practically impossible. even with a change in the party holding office, a certain amount of mixture of party affiliates occurs in many ministries. This is true especially in those ministries in which the party in charge tends to change with changes in the composition of the coalition government. In addition, training develops a certain amount of civil service *esprit de corps* which itself builds up resistance to particularism. Still, *in toto*, the civil service is only moderately universalistic.

HIGHLY PARTICULARISTIC: THE HEALTH SERVICES

Health services, such as welfare, housing, schools, and so forth, were not sufficiently supplied to the Jewish population by the British government; therefore, various Jewish political bodies organized their own health plans. The Histadrut health service serves the left and most independents; there is a much smaller right-wing medical service, and another one organized by the religious-labor party. Thus doctors, nurses, and patients were divided by their political affiliations.

The *Histadrut* health service (the Sick Fund), whose budget in 1960 was almost twice that of the state's service, is especially successful. It includes a vast network of hospitals, clinics, medical training institutions, and so forth, serving about 70 percent of the population. The service is paid for out of union dues; as a rule one cannot enjoy its benefits without being a union member, nor can one be a union member without paying for the service. This health plan is widely believed to be a most powerful hold the Histadrut has over its members.[7]

Since the establishment of the state, the government has developed some health services, primarily by taking over the few hospitals left by the British. In addition, it supervises medical standards in the clinics and hospitals run by the various political units. Compared to universalization and nationalization in other areas, however, little has been done here.

[7] See Judith T. Shuval, "Ethnic Stereotyping in Israeli Medical Bureaucracies," *Sociology and Social Research*, vol. 46 (July 1962), pp. 455–465.

There are several reasons for this. First, health happened to remain the last major item on the list of services rendered particularistically, and thus the Histadrut used all of its great political power to protect this hold it had over its members. Secondly, the health operation is much more extensive than the others. It is estimated that were the government to nationalize the health service and compensate the Histadrut for the property involved, it would have to divert all of its development budget for ten years to this purpose alone. (Nationalization without due compensation was never a practice in Israel.) Finally, the government does not relish the large increases in both taxes and number of civil servants that would be required to maintain these services.

In sum, of the eight institutional areas examined (which include all the important ones affected by political organizations), universalization has progressed to a high degree in three, in four it has been fairly successful, and only in one has it just begun.[8]

SOME GENERAL COMMENTS ON UNIVERSALIZATION

First of all, it is crucial to realize that the transfer of functions, responsibilities, and budgets from particularistic units (the political parties; the Histadrut) to the state involves a *reallocation of power*. The state, which had little, is gaining power while the various political units are losing it. This, in turn, is surely one factor accounting for the increase in the floating vote in Israel; as the power of the parties declines, more people "dare" to change sides. This further decreases the power of each single party. Hence, the parties, especially those successful in providing services to their members, are naturally, at best, ambivalent about turning these functions over to the state. Since the left has been more powerful in the neo-feudal period, naturally it is more resistant to the universalization process, though without its consent—however reluctant and ambivalent it may be—the process could not be carried out. The fact that Mapai (Labor party) heads the gov-

[8] For a treatment of another institutional area, see Haim Halperin, *Agrindus: Integration of Agriculture and Industries* (New York: Frederick A. Praeger, Inc., 1963).

ernment as well as the Histadrut, is, of course, helpful to the process.

Nationalization of functions does not necessarily mean universalization. For instance, transferring the management of the Labor Exchanges from the Histadrut, whose executive committee has a majority of Mapai members, to the Ministry of Labor, which now runs the exchanges and which is in the hands of a Mapai minister, involves some universalization but less than one would expect from the sheer fact of nationalization. Thus, as long as the particularistic elements are still powerful in the civil service, nationalization will bring about only a decline in particularism but will not eliminate it.

Not only does nationalization not spell automatic universalization, but not every lessening of particularism is achieved by transferring functions and powers to the state: (a) To a small degree universalism is attained by the development of the apolitical, nongovernmental sector (for example, voluntary associations such as *Hadassah* which set up and ran TB hospitals). (b) More important, *the rapid growth of population* requires constant *development of new units* of all services. These can be rather freely developed along the more universalistic lines even when the old units are left relatively intact. (c) Once the universalism of the new units is well established, mobility between them and the older ones allow the extension of the new orientation, although they may sometimes provide an opening for the old one to reassert itself. (d) Much progress is attained by imposing new *universalistic standards of supervision* on old units.

Finally, as we have pointed out above, completely universalistic systems are by no means the most effective or desirable ones. Thus, for example, the fact that none of the Israeli generals and chiefs of staff is of the extreme left or right introduces an element of particularism, but one which is not necessarily dysfunctional for the Israeli democracy. That only 75 percent of the school program is universalistic allows various subgroups to fulfill their own educational needs, while still assuring that all children will acquire a large set of universally shared values and knowledge. The failure to nationalize the health services may be detrimental to universalization in other areas because it leaves important power in the hands of the political bodies, especially the Histadrut; but in a state in which the population is very highly taxed, allowing one major service to be financed by voluntary payments may be functional, at least from the economic viewpoint. The fact that no one is forced to use any particular service (there are at least three health services, while the state cares for relief cases, and, of course, there is private health care) reduces possible undesirable side-effects of any one particularistic health plan. State supervision of the standards of the health services provided by the political units for their members is another way in which the universalistic and particularistic structures penetrate each other.

FUTURE TRENDS[9]

Further universalization is almost unavoidable. First, past universalization breeds that of the future. As the number of individuals who were educated in state schools, served in the unified national army, obtained their jobs through the state-controlled Labor Exchanges, and so forth, continues to grow, the number of young voters who are considerably less party-oriented than their elders also will continue to increase. As the power of the parties continues to decline and that of the state to increase, even the party allegiances of the older generation will diminish.[10]

The increasing role of apolitical voluntary associations, especially charitable and professional ones, creates a nongovernmental universalistic sector, competing with the particularistic units and further reducing their impact. The same is true of the increasing size of the private enterprise sector.[11]

[9] In this section a "future-system" is employed, as suggested on pp. 5–6.

[10] Evidence in support of this proposition was published since the above was written. See Lester G. Seligman, *Leadership in a New Nation* (New York: Atherton Press, 1964), pp. 42ff. See also Emanuel Gutmann, "Some Observations on Politics and Parties in Israel," *India Quarterly*, vol. 18 (1961), pp. 12–13.

[11] Several of the factors effecting this transformation are reviewed by George Grassmuck, "Polity, Bureaucracy, and Interest Groups in the Near East and North," paper presented to the Comparative Administration Group Research Seminar, University of Michigan, 1964, esp. p. 20; and Azvid Brodersen, Introduction to "Cultural Assimilation and Tensions in Israel," *International Social Science Bulletin*, vol. 8 (1956), pp. 7–12. For a decline in the importance of the kibbutz movement, see David Patterson, "The First Fifty Years of Collective Settlement in Israel," *Jewish Journal of Sociology*, vol. 2 (1960), pp. 42–55.

The assimilation and education of immigrants, especially of the less educated types, as occurred in the United States, will surely reduce their propensity for accepting particularistic bonds.

The intellectual assaults on neo-feudalism, common in the last decade, will also continue to aid in building up an ideology of antiparticularism and pro-universalism.

Thus, while particularism or neo-feudalism is far from dead in Israel, it has declined very markedly and will in all likelihood continue to decline in the near future. Its complete elimination, we suggest, is undesirable from the viewpoint of the values to which most citizens, parties, and the state are all committed.

CHAPTER 9

The Dynamic Relations between Values and Structure: National Religious Organizations of American Jewry[1]

————— •••• —————

The American Jewish community is often analyzed by distinguishing the theological or social or economic differences of the groups that make it up. The religious organizations of this community have been examined much less frequently. Investigators have usually assumed that Jewish religious life is more or less "congregational" and that control of it rests in the hands of local leaders. Over the last eighty years, however, each of the three religious branches of Judaism has developed—as have the Baptists and even the Congregationalists—a rather extensive national organizational structure.[2] It is a commonplace to note that strongly hierarchic religions can widely affect the religious life of their members; and though Jewish organizations are very far indeed from being neatly ordered parts of one hierarchic structure, the organizational structure does exist, and it does affect the religious life of the community.

Superficially, the organizational makeup of the Reform, Conservative, and Orthodox movements are quite similar. Each has a so-called lay organization of congregations; each has a profes-

[1] Statements of facts not otherwise referenced refer to interviews with leaders and members of the three movements conducted by the author.
[2] For a case study of this question on the local level, see J. Porter, "Differentiating Features of Orthodox, Conservative, and Reform Jewish Groups in Metropolitan Philadelphia," *Jewish Social Studies*, vol. 25 (1963), pp. 186–194.

sional association of rabbis; and each has a rabbinical school which serves as a spiritual and, to some degree, administrative center of the movement. But the influence exerted by these organizations varies quite considerably within each of the three groups.

In examining the influence of these organizations on Jewish religious life, an inquiry which deserves many volumes, we choose to focus on one central issue: the degree to which the national structure supports more traditional as against more innovative forms of religious expression and ritual. Following the Jewish tradition, we see in the continuous observance of the various Jewish rites a central indicator of the degree to which each movement is "traditional," whatever its theology may be.

Rabbis and laity often use the term "right" to refer to what we call here traditional, and "left" to what we refer to as innovative. But since "left" and "right" are used also to designate differences in theology, and since a person who is, let us say, "left" in ritual might be "right" in theology, these terms seem to add more confusion than clarity and hence will be avoided. We will characterize groups as more or less traditional, or innovating, keeping "traditionalistic" to refer to the most traditional groups. Of course, there are in all three movements individuals whose religious behavior varies a great deal; our concern here is with the effects that national organizational structure has on general trends toward traditionalism or religious innovation. Hence we will necessarily have to make generalizations, not doing full justice to the special position of Rabbi X in movement Y, or even to this or that subgroup which follows a course different from the rest of their movement.

THE CONSERVATIVES

Of the three national religious Jewish congregations, the Conservative organizations are the most elaborate and most centralized; their effect is somewhat similar to the effect that is often attributed to a hierarchical religion: the organizations support the traditional elements of the religious movement, countering the secular pressures of the laity; they generate a traditional "party line"; they tend to support the rabbi in conflicts with the congregations when the issue is one of tradition versus change. Conservative organizations are succeeding increasingly in their endeavor to make the rabbi the movement's representative; he is encouraged if he successfully supports its traditions and is himself supported if—while serving the cause prudently and wisely—he clashes with the laity. Of course even religious organizations are not composed of saints: personal loyalties, sympathies, and cliques play a role. But since, as we shall see, the "higher ups" tend to be more traditional in their position toward religious behavior than those lower down the organizational scale, and since they have a personal commitment to the success of their view, these personal ties and cliques often lend support to the traditional policy.

The Conservative framework has three tiers: at the top is a charismatic leader who also serves as the organizational head, Rabbi Louis Finkelstein, the chancellor of the Jewish Theological Seminary; the second level consists of the faculty of the seminary; and the third, of two national organizations, the professional association of Conservative rabbis (the Rabbinical Assembly) and the lay organization of the congregations (the United Synagogue of America). Formally, these three organizations—the seminary, the assembly, and the United Synagogue of America—are autonomous, equal in standing and rights. But formal relationships have a way of adjusting themselves to the needs of particular situations. In practice, it is clear that the seminary is the dominant organization of the Conservative movement.

Rabbis, board members, and worshippers in Conservative synagogues are quick to point out, with an admiration that is mixed with a trace of annoyance, that the seminary is actually Orthodox. Members of the Rabbinical Assembly point out that to all intents and purposes the service in the seminary is Orthodox (while there is no *mechizah*, men and women are not seated together); that the seminary chapel uses an Orthodox and not the Conservative prayerbook; and that the rabbi of the chapel and the pattern of his service are both Orthodox. Finally, while there are "all kinds" of faculty in the seminary (even the head of the "innovative" Reconstructionists), the majority, and in controlling authority, are quite Orthodox in their personal religious life. This generally

traditional orientation of the seminary affects the outlook and activities of the other two organizations and so affects the orientation of the entire Conservative movement.

One channel is the personal influence of the leader, which goes
much beyond the boundaries of the seminary. Secondly, the seminary has a monopoly on the training of Conservative rabbis; as a
highly effective educational institution, it often succeeds in in-
stilling its orientation into its graduates. Moreover, the leaders of
both the Rabbinical Assembly and the United Synagogue are also
seminary graduates and hence have the usual indebtedness and
respect students feel for their masters. But not less important than
these factors and more frequently overlooked is the administrative
hold the seminary has over the other Conservative organizations.
The fact that the headquarters of both the assembly and the
United Synagogue are in the buildings of the seminary (which is
not the case with either the Reform or the Orthodox movements)
illustrates this informal subordination.

This is not to imply that the Rabbinical Assembly is without
influence in "higher circles" or never "talks back to authority."
There is, though, constant grumbling among the assembly's membership, the rabbis, about what some of them consider excessive
control from above. A young rabbi, who examined the minutes of
the national meetings of the assembly, found that at every single
meeting of the assembly this complaint was expressed in one
covert way or another, frequently in the argument over some
"verdict" laid down by the seminary authorities in matters of
Jewish rites. But never did the grumbling amount to more than a
decision to appoint a committee to study the relationships between
the assembly and the seminary. Rabbis are even reluctant to mention, much less to use, the big club they hold over the seminary:
the fact that they head the local drive for funds by which the
activities of the whole movement are financed. The money is
turned over to the seminary, which then grants a small part of it
to the assembly. Thus, the informal subordination of the Rabbinical Assembly is even better illustrated in its subdued grumbling
than in its overt acceptance of the seminary leadership and
guidance.

Of the Rabbinical Assembly and the United Synagogue the
former is the more powerful. It is, in fact, the most powerful pro-

fessional association of rabbis in America; many of its members fondly refer to it as "our labor union," for in addition to enforcing an ethical code, the association maintains a welfare program for its members and, to some degree, also controls the allocation of pulpits among them. Congregations are free to choose any rabbi who fulfills their special needs, but they are expected to do so through a placement commission. The commission is composed of representatives from the seminary, the assembly, and the United Synagogue, and is situated in the seminary. If the slate of available rabbis it provides is rejected, another one is supplied; but each slate is accompanied by efforts to convince the congregational representatives of the necessity of retaining rabbis the commission believes are both suitable for the congregation and within the movement's tradition. These efforts often result in sending the congregation a somewhat more traditional rabbi than the congregation would have itself selected. The single most powerful member of the commission is the executive director of the Rabbinical Assembly—currently Rabbi Wolfe Kelman, a graduate of the seminary who works in close cooperation with it.

The assembly's influence lies in the control it can exert over its own members, the rabbis: the majority of Conservative rabbis will not accept invitations from congregations without the approval of the placement commission.[3] For rabbis who are in great demand, getting approval is mainly a matter of good form; they know it is very likely to be granted. Asking for it is in conformity with the rules and habits of their association. For young or less popular rabbis the gaining of approval is more significant. To move from one congregation to another without such approval—and many rabbis often move from five to eight times in the course of their careers—means that a rabbi might well lose the commission's support for his next move.

It is true, of course, that at present there is a general scarcity of rabbis, among the Conservatives in particular (this is documented in a fine study of the "rabbinical labor force" by Eli Ginzberg).[4] Thus, practically every rabbi, with or without the assembly's or the commission's support, can find a pulpit, even a small pulpit

---

[3] For a discussion of a similar organizational device in the Catholic Church, see the author's *A Comparative Analysis of Complex Organizations* (New York: The Free Press of Glencoe, 1961), pp. 244ff.

[4] Unpublished report.

in the South, or become a chaplain in the armed forces, in a prison, or in county hospitals. But rabbis, like ministers and other professionals, prefer to serve large congregations in big cities close to centers of Jewish and cultural life. Appointments to these pulpits, to the degree that the assembly controls them, provide informal sanctions and rewards which help the assembly to enforce its "line." This is not to imply that all the "plum" pulpits are controlled by the commission. The older, larger, richer congregations of the bigger cities tend to be independent in spirit and to carry considerable weight in the movement. Hence, when they want to retain a specific rabbi, let us say a rabbi who would build some national reputation for himself by writing articles in Jewish magazines and delivering speeches at national conventions, they are likely to get him. Moreover, the rabbi who builds up such a reputation gains considerable independence from the various sanctions and controls. Still, the majority of the rabbis, and it seems an ever-increasing number, "play it safe" by getting at least the approval—if not the assignment—of the assembly; and many congregations, it seems in growing numbers, use the placement commission, hence the seminary and the assembly, in their search for a rabbi.

Like many associations which control attractive positions, the Rabbinical Assembly is a rather exclusive organization. Only graduates of the seminary, advocates of the proper mixture of tradition and innovation, are assured automatic membership. Though quite a few graduates of the rabbinical school of Yeshiva University (Orthodox) serve Conservative congregations, only a limited number of them have been accepted by the assembly. Those who are not graduates of the seminary are now requested to take some courses in the seminary before applying for membership, and when they are interviewed about their religious positions they cannot appear too Orthodox (it is not considered "wise" to wear a headcover during the interview), nor too un-Orthodox (recently a rabbi was rejected because he said that his wife shopped on Saturday). In general, to be accepted they must hew closer to the line of the seminary than the average Conservative rabbi.

The assembly has a code which its members are required to follow, a code supported by such formal sanctions as suspension of placement privilege and even expulsion. Two items of the code read as follows: "Members of the Rabbinical Assembly may negotiate only through the offices of the placement commission."

"At no time will a member of the Rabbinical Assembly submit his name, or even indirectly cause his name to be submitted, as a candidate without the prior approval of the commission." Some ten additional items spell out the other "don'ts" which are intended to strengthen the assembly's influence over the rabbis, the pulpits, and, through both, over the religious tendencies of the movement.

The United Synagogue of America is the weaker sister of the assembly, and the second arm of the seminary. It is, presumably, an organization of the congregations. More accurately, however, it is an organization *for* the congregations that was founded by the seminary and is run by a rabbi according to rules and standards formulated under the active leadership of the seminary faculty. In part its function is to increase lay cooperation in maintaining the proper religious orientation. (A congregation was recently suspended for not following the ruling against Bingo in the synagogue; and another was not accepted as a member because its members' children write in its school on Saturday.)[5]

The relatively weak position of the congregational organization is reflected in its "Standards for Synagogue Practice," a code for lay leaders. Considerably influenced by the "employees," the rabbis, and their representatives in the seminary court, these "standards" explicitly recognize the superior authority of the rabbis in all "spiritual" matters—and there seem to be no others.[6] The first article of the "Standards," which were adopted in 1957, reads: "The United Synagogue of America recognizes the Committee of Jewish Law and Standards of the Rabbinical Assembly of America as its authority on Jewish Law." (As we shall see, the parallel article in the constitution of the Reform congregations stresses the autonomy of these congregations.) The second reads: "Each congregation shall look to its rabbi, by virtue of his election as spiritual leader of the congregation, as its authority on all matters of Jewish law and practice . . ." One function of this item, it has been suggested to the author by a leading authority in the field, is to assure the rabbi that whatever he decides to do about Halachah in his

---

[5] For a general study of this group, see Marshall Sklare, *Conservative Judaism* (New York: The Free Press of Glencoe, 1955). There are few published studies on our subject. One of the best unpublished reports is Paul Ritterband, "Some Aspects of Authority and Leadership in Conservative Judaism," 1961.

[6] This implies a superiority of the normative elite over other, especially instrumental ones.

own congregation shall not be questioned by the Rabbinical Assembly or the seminary. In other words, it assures each rabbi that he will not be censured for siding with the laity in such matters as organs, mixed seating, and driving to the synagogue on the Sabbath. At the same time this item, strongly supported by the assembly and actually formulated by one of its leaders when the standards were drawn up, defends the rabbi who wishes to adhere to the line he internalized while a student at the seminary, within the limits that local circumstances and prudence allow, against undue pressure of the lay congregation. Whatever power and impact the laity might have in real life, it is one indicator of the power of the movement that the standards do not contain a single word about the authority of the laity or its representatives.

In short, then, of the three Conservative organizations, the most powerful is the seminary. Through its head, its former students, and its control of certain key positions in the Rabbinical Assembly and the United Synagogue of America, it manages to exert a rather constant "traditional" pressure upon the Conservative movement.

THE REFORM MOVEMENT

The Conservative pattern is not typical of Jewish religious organizations in America. In the Reform movement the administration of rabbis, laity, and school are less centralized; and the movement in general concerns itself somewhat less with the struggle of tradition and innovation and considerably more with a commitment to "social action" and a struggle over Zionism.

Unlike the Conservative movement, one building does not house all three Reform organizations: the Hebrew Union College–Jewish Institute of Religion (its rabbinical school, widely referred to as the College); the Central Conference of American Rabbis (known as the Conference); and the Union of American Hebrew Congregations (its organization of congregations, often called simply "the Union"). Moreover, the Reform movement not only does not consider its rabbinical school its central authority but operates under the dual authority of the rabbinical and the lay associations. The stronger of these two, again unlike the Conservative movement, is the lay one.

Historically, the Conservative Seminary developed long before the Conservative movement. It served as the basis of the Conservative expansion that came with the Americanizing of the East European Jews at the turn of the century, and it has always been the single source of Conservative rabbis. But the Reform College is the result of a recent merger of two schools (the Hebrew Union College of Cincinnati and the Jewish Institute of Religion in New York), and until this merger rabbis could receive their training in either school. Reform lacks, in other words, the centralizing strength of a common training place of all its spiritual leaders. (It remains to be seen whether the recent merger will change this.)

Because of this lack, because the college is not led by as strong a personality as the head of the seminary, and because the organization of congregations (the Union) has separate headquarters, the staff members of the Union—though many of them are rabbis— are more inclined to give their allegiance to the Union's "line" and to its leader, Rabbi Maurice Eisendrath, than to the rabbinical association or to the college. The fact that the president of the Union, many heads of its divisions, and many members of its commissions and committees are rabbis does not mean that the Union is strongly affected by the Conference (the Reform rabbinical association), the way the Conservative United Synagogue is affected by the Rabbinical Assembly, or that the Union is not predominantly "lay" in outlook and line. Because of the rapid turnover of the leadership in the Conference and the continued leadership and stability of career in the Union, and because of the considerable lay interests of the Reform rabbis in general (more in humanist than narrowly religious matters), the Union—staffed with rabbis as it may be—is an organization of the laity, responsive to its positions and needs, not an organization *for* the congregations by rabbis. Yet the Union's influence in itself is comparatively small, in part because of its constitution, whose preamble reads:

Nothing contained in this Constitution or the By-Laws shall be construed so as to interfere in any manner whatsoever with the mode of worship, the school, the freedom of expression and opinion, or any of the other congregational activities of the constituent congregations of the Union.

This clearly limits the Union's ability to control the congregations.

Article VIII of the constitution is now under criticism by the Union leadership precisely because it obstructs the development of a guide for the congregations. Without taking any position regarding an innovation-tradition issue, Rabbi Eisendrath, speaking for the Union, has made a strong appeal for the guide:

> Hats on, hats off: rabbis robed, rabbis unrobed; *avec* Atorah, *sans* Atorah; one day Rosh Ha-Shana and two days likewise; Ashkenazic pronunciation and Sephardi likewise; kosher kitchens in Reform social halls—all this and ham and bacon too . . . some may call this the "free development of the religious idea" and bless it with the sacrosanct shibboleth of "autonomy, autonomy, autonomy"—but with a candor borrowed from a courage inspired by [Isaac Mayer] Wise, I too call it "anarchy, and utter chaos."

Any such guide would require a change in Article VIII so as to increase the role of the national organization in the local congregational life.

Despite the absence of one central authority in the Reform movement, there is an influential source of traditional or neo-traditional tendencies among some local congregations and their leaders. There is, in fact, a long tradition in some Reform congregations to be more "traditional" than the Reform national organizations.[7] This tendency is reflected in demands of rabbis to reintroduce such "rituals" as Bar Mitzvah and the observance of the second day of Rosh Ha-Shana (in some cases under the explicit threat "to go Conservative," otherwise) and their attempt to return to more traditional American Jewish patterns, such as having the main service on Friday, using Hebrew instead of English, and so on.

The Reform movement has about 600 congregations, of which half have been established since World War II. Since these newer congregations are in many cases more "traditional" than the older ones, strictly speaking there are only fifty to one hundred that can properly be called classical Reform, high "innovators," compared to the new Reform, or neo-traditionals. (That the new laity seems to be "on the side of history," that is, the general trend to more traditional orientation, may be one of the deeper reasons why the Union, the lay organization of congregations, has gained in influence since World War II, that is, since the beginning of a general religious revival).

[7] Nathan Glazer suggested that the development of the Conservative movement can be traced to a protest of "rightist" Reform members against the "leftist" leadership concentrated around the College in the 1880s. See also Melvin M. Tumin, "Conservative Trends in American Jewish Life," *Judaism*, vol. 13 (1964), pp. 131–142.

All the Reform *national organizations*, however, present a middle-of-the-road religious position; moreover, in matters of tradition *versus* innovation they play a less active role than the Conservative Seminary does. The Reform structure exerts its greatest influence and leadership on questions of social action and Zionism.

Social action has continued to be one of the most important issues of Reform from its very first days. ("The heart of religion concerns itself with man's relation to man," Rabbi Eisendrath has said.) The Reform national leadership has opened a bureau in Washington from which it supports legislation concerning desegregation, anti-discrimination, and fair employment. Some of the more powerful older congregations objected violently. They argued that a Jew who joins a synagogue does not give it a mandate to represent him politically; that action should be taken by individuals or single congregations but not by the movement as such. (Others suggest that these congregations, which include many of America's richest Jews, are politically conservative and their real objection is to the strong liberal bent of some of the Reform rabbis and national leaders.) Despite such objections, Union leadership wields its influence and guidance on questions of social action with the strong support of the rabbinical association, and the national leadership will probably continue to sponsor a strong social action program. In the other two movements, social action stirs relatively little interest, partly because it is felt to be "Reform business."

Zionism is another major issue in the Reform movement. Rabbis, board members, and other leaders all talk with considerable pride of Reform's internal struggles concerning the American Council for Judaism, an anti-Zionist organization that draws most of its members from the Reform movement. "They cannot get any more anti-Zionist rabbis," a major Reform leader said. "All they can do is check that the rabbi we send them is not an adherent Zionist who will talk about Israel all the time." To Conservatives and to the Modern Orthodox, on the other hand, Zionism is not such a central issue; both movements take a practically unanimous (and basically positive) position.[8] Thus, in summary, the Reform leadership is

[8] Herbert Parzen, "Conservative Judaism and Zionism (1896–1922)," *Jewish Social Studies,* vol. 23 (1961), pp. 235–264, is an account of the conservative movement's views on the growth of Zionism. Ben Halpern, "The Import of Israel on American Jewish Ideologies," *Jewish Social Studies,* vol. 21 (1959), pp. 62–81, attempts to separate the religious from the

less centralized than the Conservative leadership and somewhat less active in regard to the religious issues of tradition *versus* innovation, exerting its influences more clearly on the secular issues of social action and Zionism.

THE ORTHODOXY

The Orthodox movement is quite different from the other two.[9] Most importantly, it is no longer growing. Both the Conservative and the Reform membership tripled between 1945 and 1960, and each is hard pressed to find enough rabbis to staff its congregations, the number of which have doubled during that time. But the Orthodox have difficulty holding both congregations and rabbis: less than a third of the rabbinical graduates of Yeshiva University hold pulpits; many of those who do not, become businessmen or scientists (there is an association of Orthodox scientists, many of whom have graduated from the Yeshiva *rabbinical* school); and some become teachers or take other non-pulpit, though "Jewish," positions.[10] Even a number of those who become rabbis, however,

Zionistic elements of American Jewry, and tries to link each with a specific religious group. Abraham G. Duker, "Some Aspects of Israel's Impact on Identification and Cultural Patterns," *Jewish Social Studies,* vol. 21 (1959), pp. 25–45, treats the effect of the creation of the State of Israel, and the attendant growth of Zionism, on American Jewry. Aside from interest in the article itself, its footnotes provide a good bibliography on many aspects of this complex relationship. For a discussion of the uses of tradition by Reform groups, see Jakob J. Petuchowski, "The Grip of the Past—A Study in the Dynamics of Religion," *Judaism,* vol. 8 (1959), pp. 132–141. See also Bernard J. Bamberger, "The Developing Philosophy of Reform Judaism," *The Central Conference of American Rabbis Yearbook,* vol. 68 (1958), pp. 260–271. See Herbert Parzen, "The Passing of Jewish Secularism in the United States," *Judaism,* vol. 8 (1959), pp. 195–205, for a discussion of Zionistic aims and their effect upon American Jewish secularism.

[9] For some characteristics of Modern Orthodoxy, see Howard W. Polsky, "A Study of Orthodoxy in Milwaukee: Social Characteristics, Beliefs, and Observances," in Marshall Sklare (ed.), *The Jews* (New York: The Free Press of Glencoe, 1958).

[10] It should be noted that many of the students at the rabbinical school of Yeshiva University never intended to become practicing rabbis in the first place, like their predecessors in European Yeshivot.

eventually end up serving Conservative congregations, out of conviction or because of economic pressures.

The framework of the Orthodox organization is also quite different. In the first place, it offers almost no centralization. There are four main rabbinical associations and many Orthodox rabbis are "free-lancers"; there are many Yeshivot, all of which train rabbis; and there is no one central organization of congregations. Finally, there is no central authority that regulates these organizations and associations.

Modern Orthodoxy (which represents the more innovating part of Orthodox Jewry) includes the most centralized elements of the Orthodox movement and somewhat resembles the Conservative movement in its structure. Yeshiva University serves as its spiritual and organizational center. The majority of the members of its rabbinical association (the Rabbinical Council) and most of the association's leaders are graduates of Yeshiva and work in close contact with its masters. The Union of Jewish Congregations of America, however, Modern Orthodoxy's parallel to the United Synagogue, is less tied to this spiritual center than its Conservative counterpart and draws rabbis and leadership from sources other than Yeshiva. The most striking difference between this segment of the Orthodox movement and the Conservative movement lies in the degree of control their respective rabbinical associations can impose. A Modern Orthodox rabbi can readily attain a gratifying pulpit without the support or consent of his rabbinical association or the Yeshivot. Because of the strong tendency to leave the pulpit for non-rabbinical positions, few sanctions can be applied. Hence, whatever "line" the Yeshiva supports, it brings to that "line" much less influence than do its counterparts in Conservative or even in Reform Judaism.[11]

To what effect, then, is the limited institutional power of the Modern Orthodox movement used? Yeshiva University, like the seminary, is more traditional than the rabbis, and the rabbis that it produces are more traditional than their congregations. It is a commonplace among the Modern Orthodox rabbis that most of

---

[11] To some degree, Modern Orthodoxy, again unlike the Conservative movement, also contains a separation of spiritual and administrative leadership under the respective guidance of Rabbi J. B. Soloveitchik, a professor at Yeshiva University, and Dr. Samuel Belkin, its president.

them cannot eat in the homes of the presidents of their congregations, or even of the more devoted members, because the latter do not observe *Kashruth* to a degree their rabbis consider satisfactory.

While the Yeshiva, like the seminary, serves to counter lay pressures, there is a crucial difference in that, while the seminary is instrumental in moving the Conservatives to the more traditional side, the Yeshiva—because of its limited power—cannot block the innovative trend of Modern Orthodoxy; it can only slow it down.

The emphasis which the leaders of Modern Orthodoxy, the Yeshiva heads and faculty, place upon day schools reflects both the weaknesses of the movement and the tenor of its efforts.[12] To an increasing extent, Hebrew day schools have become the core of the "conservation" and restoration activities of Modern Orthodoxy. Parents are often thought of as lost, a desert generation, but with the day school Modern Orthodoxy attempts to save the children. The Orthodox movement has learned that children who go to the day schools not only tend to accept and maintain the Orthodox tradition but sometimes bring their parents back to that tradition as well. (The parents first participate in the children's services, then develop their own Orthodox *shul*.) The head of a central Yeshiva pointed out that he assesses his graduates first of all according to their ability to run day schools. This emphasis upon the younger generation is a common reaction of a movement doing less well than its counterparts.

[12] Rena Shapira, "Patterns of Attitudes Towards Israel Among Jewish Adolescents in New York City Jewish Schools." Ph.D. dissertation, Department of Sociology, Teachers College, Columbia University, 1965. Also, Arnold Jacob Wolf, "Adult Education in the American Synagogue," *Judaism*, vol. 10 (1961), pp. 353–359. One indication of the current interest concerning day schools is Boris M. Levinson's article, "The Intelligence of Applicants for Admission to Jewish Day Schools," *Jewish Social Studies*, vol. 19 (1957), pp. 129–140, which concludes, after systematic sociological study, that these students are of above average intelligence. Arnold J. Baud, "Trends in the Jewish School System—Boston: A Case Study," *Jewish Social Studies*, vol. 21 (1959), pp. 7–14, gives figures which indicate the large increase in enrollment in Jewish schools in Boston between 1945 and 1951. Judah Pilch, "Changing Patterns in Jewish Education," *Jewish Social Studies*, vol. 21 (1959), pp. 91–117, attempts to describe the pattern of and support for the growth of various kinds of educational groups. For general background see Joshua A. Fishman, "Childhood Indoctrination for Minority-Group Membership," *Daedalus*, vol. 90 (1961), pp. 329–349.

RABBIS IN A COMPARATIVE PERSPECTIVE

One measure of the difference in organizational structure is the different role of the local religious leadership in each of the movements. Rabbis constitute, so to speak, the middle range of the contemporary Jewish religious community, standing somewhere between the national superstructure and the congregations and their members. J. Carlin and S. Medlovitz have shown, in their outstanding study, "The American Rabbi: A Religious Specialist Responds to Loss of Authority," [13] that the trend among all these movements is toward the "Protestantization" of the rabbi. Sometimes deliberately, sometimes unwittingly, contemporary rabbis tend to emulate the Protestant minister. The traditional Jewish conception of the rabbi is in decline; the stress today is not upon the roles of judge, scholar, or teacher of one's "generation," but those of preacher, congregational organizer, and administrator. This much can be said in common for all American rabbis (short of those belonging to the highly Orthodox); even so, there are enormous differences among the three movements in the degree to which the traditional elements have been lost.

The Modern Orthodox rabbi "by definition" is the least affected; yet because of the movement's "innovative" trend, he too is under pressure to "adjust." Moreover, since the movement has few sanctions over its rabbis, since many leave the rabbinate, and some choose to serve Conservative congregations, it can hardly offset such adjustment under pressure from below.

The modern rabbi tends the sick, counsels the mentally ill, directs those who need relief, and above all, he preaches.[14] The quality of the sermon has become a major criterion by which

[13] Sklare, *The Jews.*

[14] The general lack of acceptance of the rabbi's need for special training as a counselor in family and marriage affairs—seen by many psychologists as a prime rabbinical role—is documented by Jeshaia Schnitzer, "Rabbis and Counseling: Report on a Project," *Jewish Social Studies,* vol. 20 (1958), pp. 131–152. This study compares the responses of the three religious groups, interviewed during the annual meeting of the rabbinical association of each. See also Seymour Martin Lipset, "The Study of Jewish Communities in a Comparative Context," *The Jewish Journal of Sociology,* vol. 5 (1963), pp. 157–166.

congregations elect rabbis and by which promotion is gained to more important pulpits and to national reputation. (This is less true of the Conservative but more true of the Reform rabbi; Reform rabbis report that they spend, on the average, about two days a week working on their sermons, considering this their major single duty.)

Because of the different institutional arrangements, both Reform and Conservative rabbis are under different kinds of pressures. Each of them must be a super-administrator in order to run efficiently the various activities, institutions, and associations which make up most modern congregations; in addition, each must direct, or at least participate in, a large number of "social" activities that have little or no religious meaning. The strains that these requirements impose on the rabbis are sometimes exaggerated; the new generation of rabbis in particular is much more able to deal with them. Nevertheless, most of the graduates of the college, the seminary, and the Yeshiva tend to identify with their teachers and masters. Many, at least for a few years, hope to be religious scholars, or "intellectuals." Rabbinical education as often as not rather deliberately prepares its students for the pulpit as it was or ought to be and so increases the crisis that ensues upon graduating and getting out into the congregational world.

One should not be too hasty in pointing out the dysfunctional nature of such training. Congregations pressure the rabbi in the direction of social (solidaric) administration; the educational institutions train him in the direction of scholarship and spiritual aspirations (normative)—with the result that between these opposed approaches a rabbi often has to compromise. Of course, if the gap is too large, a compromise is often difficult to reach; if the resulting role-conflict or role-strain is too great, the rabbi might leave the rabbinate. Training that is too far removed from "reality" is one reason why about two thirds of the graduates of Yeshiva University's rabbinical school do not hold pulpits.

Yet once the rabbi is "out there," in the local congregation, despite the official policy of the Conservative and the Reform bodies that he is the final authority on Jewish law, the national structure is more inclined to help him reach a "proper" compromise with the congregations, that is, in line with the movement's policy as interpreted by its national leadership and organizations; the need to reduce conflicts between the rabbi and the congregation is also taken into account. But even in the centralized Conservative movement, the support—which concerns not only questions of tradition versus innovation but those of "intellectual" interpretation of the role of the rabbi versus administrative and "social" ones—seems to be far weaker than that given by any churchlike religion.

An analysis of the role of the rabbi suggests the same general conclusion which emerges from the analysis of the interplay among the national framework of the three movements and their normative orientations: the general trend is toward a *more* traditional (or neo-traditional) pattern of Jewish religious life, but *not* toward a traditionalistic one. The Reform movement, with the exception of a hard core of "Classical Reform" congregations, seems to be moving in a relatively more traditional direction; the Conservatives *in toto* are becoming still more traditional. Modern Orthodoxy, on the other hand, tends to accept some of the innovative patterns introduced by the other two movements, with only a small segment sticking to a militant, traditionalistic line.

The role played by the national structures of the three movements in this trend toward a more traditional Jewish life varies from movement to movement. In the Reform the major driving force seems to be at the moment a grass root movement, led by the young new Reform congregations. Among the Orthodox, where the organizational structure is the weakest, the grass root movement is in the less traditionalistic direction. The structure is playing a limited anchorage role, attempting to reduce the drift in the innovation direction. It is among the Conservatives that the organizational framework exerts itself most, in leading the movement, despite some congregational resistance, in the more traditional direction.

The comparative analysis suggests that the central question for the study of the interaction between organization and values, administrative structures and normative orientations, has to be broken up into several specific questions, such as the number of organizations in each movement, their relative power, the degree to which control of these organizations is centralized, and so forth. And, that the interaction between organizations and values has to be studied in the context of general trends in the sociological environment,[15] such as the general religious revival, changes in the Protestant movements, the rise of the civil rights movement (as background for understanding the Social Action of the Reform, for instance), the decline of Zionism after the establishment of the State of Israel, and so on.

[15] For a view of these changes by an active participant, see Saul L. Goodman, "Jewish Secularism in America—Permanence and Change," *Judaism*, vol. 9 (1960), pp. 319–330. For a viewpoint of an observer, see Herbert J. Gans, "American Jewry, Present and Future," *Commentary*, vol. 21 (1956), pp. 422–430.

AUTHOR INDEX

217

SUBJECT INDEX

———————◆●◆———————